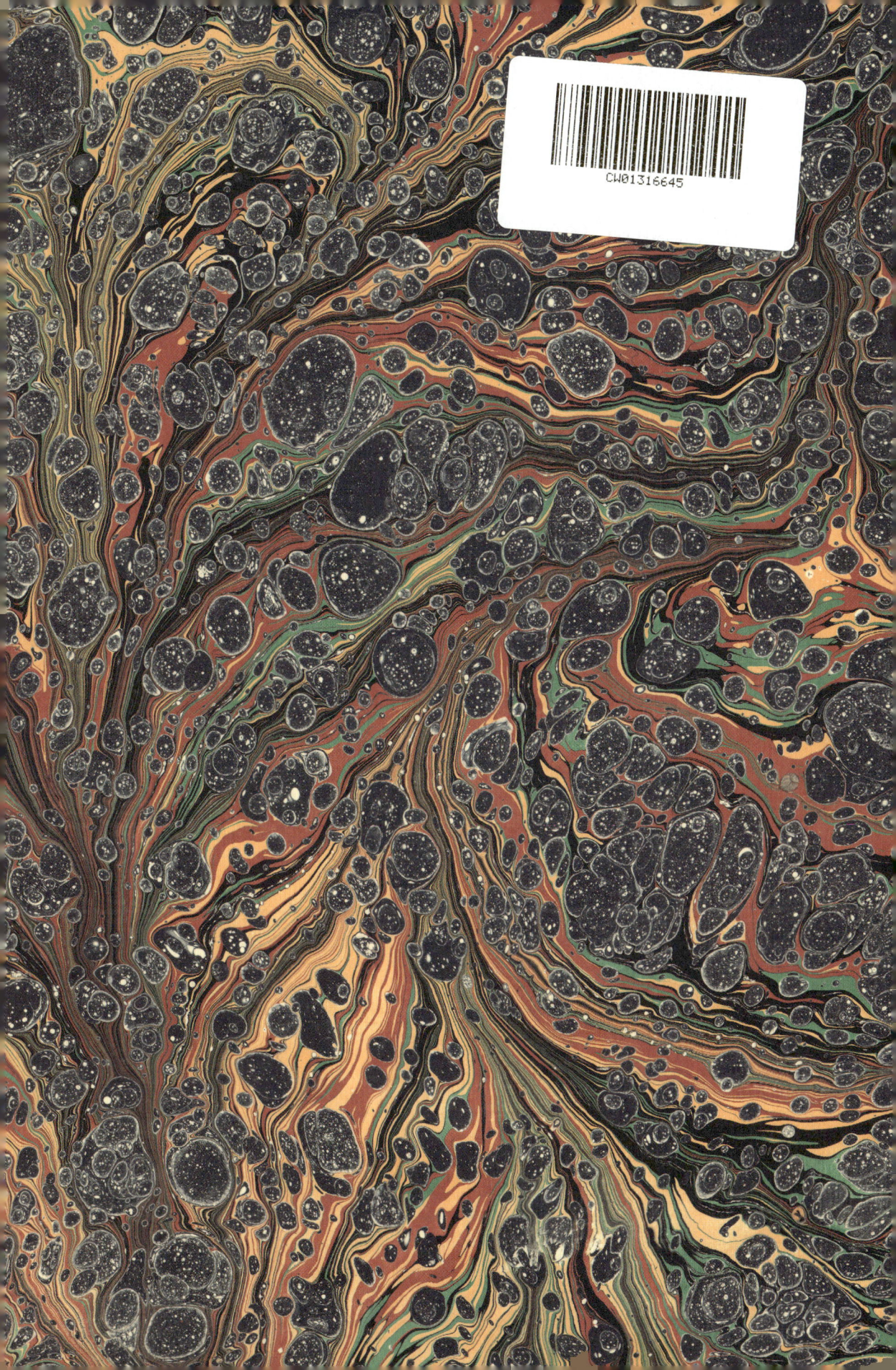

THE "EASY" BOYS

Also by Martyn R. Ford-Jones
Desert Flyer: The Log and Journal of Flying Officer William Marsh
Oxford's Own: The Men and Machines of No.15/XV RFC/RAF

THE "EASY" BOYS

THE STORY OF A BOMBER COMMAND AIRCREW IN WORLD WAR II

Based on the Wartime Diaries
of Flying Officer Reg Heffron, RAAF

Martyn R. Ford-Jones

4880 Lower Valley Road • Atglen, PA 19310

Dedication
This book is dedicated to: Reg, Max, Arthur, Bill,
Roger, Tom, Paul, Beatrice Gebhardt and Ann Hill.

Copyright © 2014 by Martyn R. Ford-Jones.

Library of Congress Control Number: 2014945470

All rights reserved. No part of this work may be reproduced or used in any form or by any means—graphic, electronic, or mechanical, including photocopying or information storage and retrieval systems—without written permission from the publisher.

The scanning, uploading, and distribution of this book or any part thereof via the Internet or via any other means without the permission of the publisher is illegal and punishable by law. Please purchase only authorized editions and do not participate in or encourage the electronic piracy of copyrighted materials.
"Schiffer," "Schiffer Publishing, Ltd. & Design," and the "Design of pen and inkwell" are registered trademarks of Schiffer Publishing, Ltd.

Designed by Robert Biondi
Type set in Times New Roman/Helvetica Neue

ISBN: 978-0-7643-4789-4
Printed in China

Published by Schiffer Publishing, Ltd.
4880 Lower Valley Road
Atglen, PA 19310
Phone: (610) 593-1777; Fax: (610) 593-2002
E-mail: Info@schifferbooks.com

For our complete selection of fine books on this and related subjects, please visit our website at www.schifferbooks.com. You may also write for a free catalog.

This book may be purchased from the publisher. Please try your bookstore first.

We are always looking for people to write books on new and related subjects. If you have an idea for a book, please contact us at proposals@schifferbooks.com.

Schiffer Publishing's titles are available at special discounts for bulk purchases for sales promotions or premiums. Special editions, including personalized covers, corporate imprints, and excerpts can be created in large quantities for special needs. For more information, contact the publisher.

Contents

Preface 6
Acknowledgments 8
Introduction 11

Chapter 1	The Birth of a Crew 12
Chapter 2	Operational Training Unit 29
Chapter 3	Heavy Conversion Unit 47
Chapter 4	No.3 Lancaster Finishing School 56
Chapter 5	No.622 Squadron 60
Chapter 6	Return to Operational Flying 81
Chapter 7	Fifteen Down, with Fifteen to Go 94
Chapter 8	The Sheffield Incident 103
Chapter 9	The Loss of a Friend 121
Chapter 10	The Move to Church Broughton 148
Chapter 11	Applying for a Commission 154
Chapter 12	Victory in Europe 164
Chapter 13	Two Marriages, Two Commissions and Masses of Leave 172
Chapter 14	Japan Surrenders 186
Chapter 15	The Voyage Home 193
Chapter 16	Back in Australia 206

Appendices

Appendix 1: Reg Heffron Family Tree from Thomas Dawson and Martha Sinclair 218
Appendix 2: Operational Sorties Undertaken by Flying Officer Reg Heffron 219
Appendix 3: Aircraft Flown On by Flying Officer Reg Heffron 220

Bibliography 221
Index 222

Preface

No.622 Squadron, RAF, was formed from 'C' Flight, No.XV Squadron, on Tuesday, 10th August 1943, at RAF Mildenhall. No.XV Squadron had been resident at the Suffolk airfield since 14th April that same year, when it relocated there from RAF Bourn, in the neighboring county of Cambridgeshire.

No.622 was to be a two-flight squadron, with an establishment of sixteen available Short S.29 Stirling bombers with four more in reserve, although initially only seven aircraft were on strength. The new unit was granted a squadron badge, which took the form of a long-eared owl volant affrontee, carrying a flash of lightning in its talons. It adopted the motto, *'Bellamus Noctu'* ('We Wage War by Night').

Squadron Leader John Martin was installed as acting Officer Commanding, with Flight Lieutenant H.M. Goode as Adjutant. However, ten days later, Wing Commander George H.N. Gibson, DFC, arrived at RAF Mildenhall to assume command of No.622 Squadron. Having handed over command to Gibson, Squadron Leader Martin remained with the squadron with whom he completed a tour of operations. His courage and leadership skills were recognized with the award a Distinguished Flying Cross, which was gazetted on 16th November 1943.

Due to the fact the crews who formed the personnel of the new squadron were battle experienced, no settling in period was granted and they undertook operational duties that same night. The only clue to any change of squadron for the crews, apart from operating from the other side of the airfield, was that over a short period of time, the No.XV Squadron code 'LS,' which adorned the rear fuselage sides of their Stirling bombers, was replaced with the letters 'GI,' the code which was to identify No.622 Squadron.

The target designated for the first mission was an attack against Nuremberg. Although all seven designated Stirling bombers took off, two returned early due to mechanical problems, but the remaining five aircraft and crews were to set the standard for future attacks undertaken by the new squadron. Indeed, on 23rd August 1943, only thirteen days after its inception, following an attack against Berlin, Sergeant Jack Bailey, RCAF, piloted a Stirling on which he was the bomb aimer, home to a safe landing after his pilot had been critically wounded. For this action Jack Bailey was granted the award of an immediate Conspicuous Gallantry Medal and commissioned to the rank of Pilot Officer.

On the 20th December 1943, No.622 Squadron flew its last operational mission using Short Stirling bombers, when three aircraft undertook mine-laying (Gardening) operations in the Frisian Islands. During the period December 1943/January 1944, the squadron re-equipped with Avro Lancaster bombers, with which it was to see out the remainder of the war.

Preface

On 1st February 1944, Wing Commander I.C.K. Swales assumed command of No.622 Squadron. Ian or '*Blondie*' Swales as he was known to some, was a very experienced officer with numerous operations recorded in his logbook. Not only had he seen action piloting Bristol Blenheim aircraft in 1940, as a sergeant pilot with No.XV Squadron, he had also flown operationally on Stirling bombers with the same unit. He relinquished command of No.622 on 19th October 1944, and later retired from the Royal Air Force as Group Captain Ian Swales, DSO, DFC, DFM.

Wing Commander G.K. Buckingham took over as Officer Commanding, No.622 Squadron and remained as such until the unit's disbandment.

Having undertaken a number of 'Manna' operations (dropping food parcels to the starving Dutch people), 'Exodus' operations (returning Allied prisoners of war in Germany to the U.K., and 'Dodge' operations (returning PoWs home from Italy), at the end of hostilities, the squadron disbanded on 15th August 1945.

During its relatively short period as a Lancaster bomber squadron (it reformed as a Royal Auxiliary Air Force transport squadron in 1950), No.622 dropped a total of nearly 10,500 tons of bombs and laid a large quantity of mines in 'enemy' waters.

It has been stated that during the second half of 1944, just over half the pilots based at RAF Mildenhall and just under half of the aircrew based there, were Australians. Many of them, like Reg Heffron, Arthur 'Max' Bourne, Roger Humphrys and Paul Taylor served with No.622 Squadron.

Acknowledgments

I first met Ann Hill during one of the Mildenhall Register reunion weekends when we began talking about her father, Bill Vincent, who was a flight engineer with No.622 Squadron. Ann showed me some photographs of her father and his crew and talked about them with much affection. Later that same morning, Ann showed me copies of a diary and other notes she had, which were compiled by Reg Heffron, RAAF, the mid-upper gunner who flew with the same crew as her father. The more we talked, and the more I saw of the diary, the more I thought Reg's story, and that of his pilot and crew, should be put into print.

Having shown me the document, Ann undertook to approach Reg for his permission for me to edit the diary. Needless to say, I am indebted to Reg Heffron for not only giving his consent for me to use his diary, but also for producing a wealth of other information and photographs all relating to the same period.

Another Australian who went to great lengths to assist me was Max Bourne the pilot. Ann undertook the initial approach to Max, who had also written a lengthy screed appertaining to his own life story; a copy of which he had supplied to Ann. Although his logbook was in a very delicate state, Max very kindly managed to produce a very readable and helpful document that, together with the above mentioned family screed, helped enormously. Sadly, Max Bourne passed away shortly after the manuscript was completed. However, both Deborah McGrade, Max's daughter and Philip Bourne, his son have confirmed their assent for me to use their late father's work as Max wanted.

I also extend my grateful thanks to the navigator Arthur Bourne, no relation to Max who, like Ann, very kindly entertained me at his home on a number of occasions, where he related many of the stories of his, and the crew's experiences, not all necessarily for publication. Again, like his former crewmembers, Arthur was able to produce a number of interesting documents and facts.

Although Tom Brown the bomb aimer passed away a few years ago, Ann Hill very kindly paved the way for me to meet and chat with Daphne Brown, Tom's widow, at her home where I also met Daphne's and Tom's daughter, Carol. These charming ladies not only gave me an insight to Tom's service life, but also some details of his private life, all of which has been very useful material. They also very kindly allowed me to peruse family photographs; a number of which have been selected for publication in this book.

My membership of the Mildenhall Register, which spans over thirty years, enabled me to make a number of friends and acquaintances who flew or served with No.622 Squadron. Many of those friends provided photographs, stories, anecdotes or items of memorabilia for inclusion in my collection. John and Elisabeth Cox, stalwarts of the Mildenhall Register, have been amongst those friends for many years, and have always responded to pleas of help for information when approached. Unfortunately, many of those I had the pleasure of knowing or calling a friend, who merit my thanks, have sadly passed on, they include Don Clarke, MBE, former President of the Mildenhall Register, Group Captain Ian 'Blondie' Swales, Bill Anderton, Peter Atkinson and Bob Kerr. Sadly, John Cox's name must also be added to this list of esteemed gentlemen.

I would also like to thank Gary Wenko and Mark Howell, 100th Air Refuelling Wing Historian, both based at RAF Mildenhall, who have not only been valuable sources of information, but also friends who have assisted me without hesitation.

Although Reg Heffron kept a meticulously recorded diary, the checking of records at the National Archive is always a necessity if only to fill in some of the gaps. Therefore, as always, thanks must be extended to the staff at the National Archive, Kew for their help and assistance during various stages of the research.

I would like to express thanks to the staff of the Lygon Arms Hotel, Broadway, and the staff of the Broadway Tower whose assistance during my visits to their respective establishments is very much appreciated. Likewise, I would like to thank Robb F.W. Jones for his input relating to the Devon resort of Ilfracombe.

I have, over the last fifteen years, enjoyed a good customer based relationship with Aces High Aviation Gallery at Wendover, Buckinghamshire, England, where I, and many other like-minded people, have had the pleasure of meeting numerous World War II veterans, from the RAF, the USAAF, the Luftwaffe and many other military forces. I am therefore particularly grateful to Colin Hudson for allowing me to reproduce the artwork entitled, '*Berlin Boar Flight*' by Anthony Saunders, on the cover of this book. I would also like to record my thanks to Colin for the generosity and kindness he and the Gallery staff have shown me over the past sixteen years, not only at Wendover, but also at their other venues in Ojai, California and the Utah Beach Museum, Normandy, France.

Another patron of Aces High Gallery to whom I owe a great debt of thanks is David Green, who attends many of the Gallery's events with his charming wife Bernadette and their two daughters Emma and Lisa. When I approached David on the subject of proofreading the *Easy Boys* manuscript, he accepted the arduous task without hesitation. I must state however that the final responsibility for any errors that do slip through, are down to me and not David.

As with my two previous books, I would like to thank Bob Biondi and the staff of Schiffer for the help, guidance and giving me the opportunity of having a third book produced by Schiffer Publishing.

I apologize if I have inadvertently omitted to acknowledge anyone who assisted, in anyway, with the production of this book.

Finally, as always, I must thank Valerie, my loving and long-suffering wife, who has supported me in all my RAF related endeavors over the last forty-nine years. Valerie's tireless help and on-going support is never taken for granted and is always very much appreciated, as is the support and encouragement given by my two daughters Emma and Alexandra.

Introduction

The title of this book comes from a term of endearment used by Ann Hill towards the crew of a No.622 Squadron Lancaster bomber, coded GI-E – 'Easy,' which included her father, who was the flight engineer.

The contents of the book are based on the diaries and log books of Reg Heffron. They were written at, or around, the time the events occurred, be they happy reminiscences, general day to day occurrences or traumatic events, at a time when Reg and his fellow crew members were under stress through either training or combat. Stress in training, knowing that if they failed their respective courses they would not make it to operational status. Then, having achieved aircrew status and being declared 'Ready for combat,' came the trauma endured flying night after night over enemy occupied territory; something which could not be experienced whilst under training. Added to this was the strain endured by anguished thoughts of not letting fellow crewmembers down, along with the silent, but shared tension of getting through a tour of thirty operational missions unscathed; something not openly discussed.

The entries in Reg Heffron's diary give the reader an insight into the way a small group of strangers came together to form an efficient crew, which lived, trained, played and fought together against a common enemy.

From the beginning, although strangers initially, the seven men who made up this crew became friends. True friends as indicated by the companionship between Reg Heffron and Roger Humphrys, the two air gunners on the crew, who were inseparable. Friendships formed in wartime, created a bond between young men which later generations may not be able to understand. They were friendships that have stood the test of time and have lasted to the present day. It was the trust reposed in each of these young men to do their best by each other that got them through some of the most harrowing experiences of their young lives.

They volunteered to join the fight to give peace and freedom back to the world. It was a fight they, and many other young men like them, accepted and won.

Sadly, since the completion of this manuscript, both Max Bourne and Arthur Bourne have lost the battle against the passing of time and have passed away.

This, however, is their story as seen and recorded through the eyes and hands of Reg Heffron, one of '*The 'Easy' Boys.*'

Martyn R. Ford-Jones
Swindon, Wiltshire

1

The Birth of a Crew

Arthur Maxwell 'Max' Bourne was born on 13th May 1924, at Cottesloe, Western Australia. He was the third son of Reginald Arthur Bourne and Ethel Mary Bourne (*nee* Davis). Apart from having brothers, namely Don and Colin, Max also had a sister by the name of Pam.

Although he was born at Cottesloe, the area from which his mother came, from his birth until the age of eleven young Max lived at Broome, the pearling port on the northwest coast of Australia, overlooking the Indian Ocean.

Broome was a great place for Max, his two older brothers and their friends, especially as they lived practically on the beach in Roebuck Bay. Max's father had built a shark-proof enclosure below the water line for their safety, and they had a dinghy in which the boys would venture out to go spear fishing. Being so close to the beach Max and his friends spent most of the time barefoot, only putting on their shoes just before reaching school or Sunday school.

School was pretty basic, there being only two teachers to cover from the infant class up to the age of fourteen; thereafter it was necessary to 'go South' (to Perth) to boarding school.

It was probably due to the lack of suitable schooling (and later employment options), during 1935, that led Max's mother to leave Broome and take her family to live in the city. They made the trip south by sea on board the '*Koolinda,*' during what the Australians call the '35 Blow.' Max's father, whose livelihood depended on seafaring contracts, including the monthly trip to re-supply the Cape Levique lighthouse with provisions, remained behind in order to tidy up matters and then sail his last remaining lugger '*Bonza*' down to Fremantle in order to sell it. As a result of which, Reginald Bourne did not join his family until 1937.

Another reason for moving was that Max's mother had been left a house in the suburb of Mosman Park, between the river and the sea. There was sufficient land on the plot for a retail store to be built next to the house, so a delicatessen was established on the site, where Max's parents worked long and hard.

Max's education continued, from March 1935 to the end of the 1936 school year, at Cottesloe primary school. Thereafter, and for the following three years, he attended the highly thought of Fremantle Boys Schools, where he enjoyed his time immensely and was always near the top of the class. He became a prefect and was vice-captain of the school rugby team.

A former pupil of the same school was Air Commodore Hughie Idwal Edwards, who joined the Royal Australian Air Force and gained his 'wings' in June 1936. Two months later, having applied for a transfer, he took a commission with the Royal Air Force and was posted to No.XV Squadron, based at Abingdon, Oxfordshire. Hughie Edwards was to become a distinguished bomber pilot who finished the war having been awarded a VC, DSO and a DFC. His post war awards, apart from a Knighthood, included a CB and OBE. In later years he became Governor of Western Australia.

Outside of school, Max and his brothers were kept busy as members of a Sea Scout troop, with sailing, camping and exploring expeditions. When leaders of the troop volunteered for the armed forces, younger able members of the troop would take over the reins of leadership. So it was that when Max's older brothers enlisted for service with the military, Max became troop leader at the tender age of sixteen.

Max was just under sixteen years of age and had recently left school when war in Europe was declared, but this did not stop him from trying to convince his parents to let him join the Royal Australian Navy. He was, after all, a member of the Sea Scouts, but needless to say, their permission was not forthcoming. Discussing the problem with his Sea Scout master, who by this time was in the Navy himself, the latter strangely enough persuaded the young Australian to apply for aircrew training.

Max obviously gave the suggestion some thought as six months later he sat an aptitude test and underwent a medical at the Royal Australian Air Force recruitment office. He was also issued with a set of twenty-one books, each containing a lesson on a number of subjects including the principles of flight, navigation and meteorology etc. Most evenings over the next twelve months saw Max attending night school at Perth Technical School, where classes had been set up for the benefit of aircrew reservists. Although he could not become a reservist until he was eighteen years of age, Max voluntarily attended the lectures. He also spent time at classes for radio operators, where he learned Morse code, and kept himself in shape by attending a gymnasium.

On top of all this, Max had managed to secure employment as a junior salesman with the largest and most prestigious jewelry store in the city. He still wonders if he only got the job because he owned a three-piece suit, which had to be worn at all times. During his two years with the store, Max learned some valuable lessons that were to stand him in good stead when he joined the RAAF. First, he learned to continue to respect his elders and secondly, to mind his P's and Q's; thus he was able to accept the discipline in the RAAF with reasonable grace.

As his eighteenth birthday loomed nearer, Max began to pester the people in the Recruitment Depot to ensure his name was on the list for the earliest possible intake. Thus, having turned eighteen in May, just five weeks later on 21st June 1942, he joined the Royal Australian Air Force. Standing in the company of approximately 100 young men, all aged between 19 and 29 years, Max felt it was one of the best things he had ever done. A sentiment he held dear all his life.

His voluntary attendance at night school was to stand him in good stead, as the following four months were crammed with class work in the afore-mentioned subjects. However, there were additional studies in the subjects of air force law, armoury and gas warfare. On top of all this there was drill, known as 'square bashing' and physical training;

the latter not proving too difficult for Max. During his time at Initial Training School, officers from the rank of corporal upward were constantly observing the young airmen. The outcome of this scrutiny being that by the end of the course, there was a comprehensive dossier on each recruit on the table at the Selection Committee. The dossiers enabled the Senior Officers to decide who was to become a pilot, who was to be a navigator and so on.

When his turn came, Max sat through and answered the many questions put to him. Finally the Senior Officer present said, *"Well Bourne, I suppose you want to be a pilot?"* to which the young candidate blurted back in Oliver Twist like fashion, *"Oh yes please sir."*

Max's dream seemed to becoming true, as a few days later he, along with about twenty-nine other hopefuls, arrived at No.9 Elementary Flying Training School at Cunderdin, approximately 100 miles east of Perth. The airfield itself was huge, but only boasted one runway, although a number of take-off points could be utilised at any one time if necessary. Furthermore, it was set in flat countryside with a number of empty salt lakes scattered across the terrain, which added dramatically to the natural thermals as soon as the sun gained height. The rough air, caused by this act of nature, induced more than one of the would-be pilots to see his breakfast again, including Max. Fortunately, Max's instructor, Flight Sergeant Mansfield, was a good type and not a 'screamer' like some at Cunderdin. One particular instructor, it is recorded, could be heard berating his pupil, whilst on the glide approach and still a couple of hundred feet up.

The fear of being 'scrubbed' was ever present, particularly in the early stages. A pupil who had not gone solo after approximately ten hours dual instruction was usually for the chop. Quite a few pupils from Max's course were 'remustered' as navigators, bomb aimers or air gunners. Yet, feeling as if he were 'Bourne' to fly, young Max sang to himself as the aircraft (D.H.82A, serial A17-134) climbed away on his first solo flight, on 5th November 1942, after eleven hours dual. As he said later, *"It was the greatest feeling I had ever experienced until that time, [but then] I had not found girls yet."*

Training continued. Half of the day was taken up with ground studies, whilst the other half was spent flying. Unfortunately, as the flying training became more intense, with loops, spins and aerobatics, regular bouts of airsickness still occurred. The course eventually came to an end. When Max read his final report it showed he had logged a total of sixty hours flying time and was rated, like everybody else, as average. However, there was another comment added, which read, *"Should become a proficient pilot if [he] can overcome airsickness."* As it turned out, Max was not airsick in any other aircraft, only the de.Havilland D.H.82A Tiger Moth.

Apart from a few who were posted for further training on single-engine aircraft, the majority of graduates on Max's course were posted to No.4 Service Flying Training School at Geraldton, a coastal town approximately 300 miles north of Perth. Here they were introduced to the Avro Anson, a twin-engine aircraft used mainly for light transport and training. They were much-loved aircraft, and respected by the pilots who flew them; hence the Service name applied to them of *'Faithful Annie.'*

The first half of the four-month course at Geraldton was given over to learning to fly the twin-engine aircraft. Although the Anson had few, if any, vices, for one reason or another some members of the course were 'scrubbed.' The second half of the course was taken up with flying cross-country navigational exercises, both as pilot and as navigator, bombing exercises, as pilot and then as bomb aimer, and low-level air to ground gunnery, again, not only as pilot but also as air gunner. This form of training not only prepared the pilot in some degree, to flying an aircraft as a war machine, but also gave him an insight as to the actual tasks undertaken by each member of his (future) crew.

The course finished during the first week of April, and Max was assessed as a 'Good Average Pilot,' presented with his pilot 'wings' brevet and promoted to the rank of sergeant. A few lucky members of the course were commissioned as pilot officers. It was also a time for 'goodbyes' as some friendships were broken up due to the various postings issued and the various further training courses specified, such as Bomber Command, Transport Command and Reconnaissance roles.

Sergeant Max Bourne was posted to No.2 General Reconnaissance Course at Bairnsdale, Victoria, with temporary attachment to 'B' Flight, No.2 Air Observers School (A.O.S.) at Mt. Gambier in South Australia. It was at the latter on 13th May (Max's 19th birthday), that an incident occurred which left him wondering for a moment whether he might reach the age of twenty, but then gave him an unexpected birthday party. He was flying as second pilot to Sergeant Wilson in Avro Anson, DJ233, on a cross-country exercise; also on board the aircraft were two trainee navigators, two pilots and a wireless operator. Soon after they had taken off cloud moved in beneath them obscuring all visual contact with the ground, which meant the 'rookie' navigators could not get fixes on their actual position. After flying around for some time, and with only ten gallons of fuel left in the tanks, Sgt. Wilson and Max were able to take advantage of a small hole in the cloud. Descending through the said hole, they found to their horror that they were flying above very hilly countryside. Immediately to the east of a range of hills they espied a small town, which they later discovered to be called Blyth, surrounded by recently harvested wheat fields. Selecting a beautifully flat field near to a hotel, they put down and radioed for fuel,

A portrait photograph of Flying Officer Arthur 'Max' Bourne, pilot, in RAAF uniform, taken in London, 1944. *Courtesy of the Late Max Bourne*

which was brought in drums, on a truck, by road. It fell to the local policeman to guard the aircraft overnight, whilst the crew took advantage of the hotel and its bar facilities. Max was left wondering whether the navigators were given a second chance at a cross-country exercise.

Max was granted a couple of weeks leave, but due to the distance involved and vagaries of transport for the general public, he decided it was not practical to attempt the journey home to Western Australia. Instead he opted to join a pilot officer friend and take a room in a very good guesthouse in Kilda St Road, Melbourne. This was his first trip to a city larger than Perth and he enjoyed many new experiences, including seeing his first live musical show, in this instance, *'White Horse Inn.'*

Towards the end of his leave, he received a telegram informing him that the General Reconnaissance Course at Bairnsdale had been postponed, and that he was to report to the Posting Depot in Melbourne. A week later he was on board a ship heading for the United Kingdom, via the United States of America. The ship docked at San Francisco, but to the surprise and disappointment of the 100 or so Australian pilots on board, they were not allowed a stopover period. They were ushered straight on to a train, on which they were to spend the next six days, as it rattled and steamed its way across the American continent, on its way to New York.

"New York, New York. What a wonderful Town" says the lines of the song, but again the 'Aussie' pilots were in for a second shock. The majority of them thought that after the lengthy sea crossing from their homeland, followed by six days on a train, they would get at least one weeks leave in the bustling town, but this was not to be. Having de-trained, they were directed to a fleet of trucks, which conveyed them to the berths where the ship *'RMS Aquitania'* was waiting. Their plight got worse due to the fact that, not only were they embarking on the ship bound for the U.K, but so were thousands of U.S. troops. For six days they endured the vagaries of the Atlantic weather, packed like the proverbial sardines in a tin, on an unescorted crossing. Bad news if you were either not a good sailor, could not swim or had a fear of U-boats.

Eventually the *'Aquitania'* docked at Greenock, approximately twenty miles to the west of Glasgow in the estuary of the River Clyde. Again, they were herded on to a train, which conveyed them overnight almost the length of the country, to Brighton on the south coast of England. The trip was a bit of an eye opener for Max and his contemporaries as they had their first experience of Double British Summertime (daylight saving) which, combined with the high latitude, enabled them to read newspapers by natural light at 10.30pm.

The contingent arrived at No.11 Personnel Depot Reception Center, Brighton on 12th August, where they were billeted in one of two hotels, four to a room. The Royal Australian Air Force had taken leases on both the Grand and Metropole Hotels, both pre-war establishments that catered for those with a taste for affluence.

Finally, after their long and exhausting journey, the Australian airmen were given, in Max's words, *"a degree of freedom."* He, and a few friends, wasted no time in taking a day trip to London where, standing in Piccadilly Circus, they felt they were standing at the 'center of the universe.'

The Birth of a Crew

No.35 Course, No.18 (Pilots) Advanced Flying Unit, Snitterfield, Warwickshire, October 1943.

Back Row: Stuart Bogle; Ken Seage; Unknown; 'Boof' Smith.
Middle Row: 'Butch' Hutchings; Roy Jennings; Unknown; Unknown; Max Bourne; Joe Lynch.
Front Row: Unknown; Arthur Holland; Unknown; 'Mate' McCurdie; 'Flip' Phillips.
Courtesy of the Late Max Bourne

Back in Brighton, Max and his closest pal Stuart Bogle took a flat, which they escaped to occasionally whenever they wanted to do whatever 19-20 year olds do when they are away from home. However, life in Brighton was not all fun and frolics, there was still the military routine. Parades, drills and route marches around the town were overseen by an officer and an NCO from the RAF Regiment (the RAF's own soldiers). Unfortunately for the officer and the NCO, at the end of each month as they undertook the route marches, they found fewer and fewer men boldly marching along behind them, as the 'Colonial Gentlemen' were dropping out of line and disappearing into the local cinemas.

During the period at Brighton, in early September, Max and a colleague were detailed to attend the Empire Central Flying School at RAF Hullavington, Wiltshire, to undergo a standard flying test. It transpired that in order to assess the standard of training given by the countries participating in the Empire Air Training Scheme, a couple of pilots were selected at random from each batch of arrivals, to be submitted to a flying test. Two forty-minute flights were scheduled utilising Airspeed Oxford aircraft, a type never seen or flown by Max before. With feelings of great apprehension, he had to undertake instrument flying, blind flying and various maneuvres. He never received any feedback relating to the tests, but he did get to fly Oxfords again and subsequently became very fond of them. Max did however receive a form of feedback about his character when, around this same time, he was promoted to the rank of flight sergeant.

The next move was to No.18 (Pilots) Advanced Flying Unit, based at Snitterfield, north of Stratford-upon-Avon, where Max renewed his acquaintance with the Oxford aircraft. He commenced flying these delightful little twin-engine aircraft on 5th October 1943. The purpose of the AFU, according to Max, was aimed at *"acclimatising us 'foreigners' to flying in English weather and becoming accustomed to the immense amount of detail on the ground when it came to map reading and navigation in general."* In Australia of course, they were used to flying over vast areas of uncultivated land, whereas in Britain there were towns, villages, rivers, canals, railway lines and roads everywhere. But, as Max also said, later in their careers, they all had navigators to worry about that side of things.

In mid-November, some of the course members from AFU, including Max, were attached to No.1513 Blind Approach Training Flight, at Bramcote, between Nuneaton and Coventry, for a period of eleven days. Max felt the location for the Blind Approach Training Flight was very apt, especially as for ten of the days he was there the place was shrouded in fog! However, being pretty keen on instrument flying, Max thoroughly enjoyed the course and was especially pleased when, at the end of it, he was rated above average. Although it was winter, Max returned to No.18 (P) AFU during the first week of December 1943, with a spring in his step, and continued his training.

Towards the end of the course, when there were only about thirty Australian pilots left, including Max, there was a glitch in the system, which meant their progress on to an Operational Training Unit was delayed by more than a month. However, this delay proved in Max's favour and that of some of his pals, when they were selected for additional flying duties outside of normal training. Their task was to carry out night flying tests, which meant they flew several aircraft each day on thirty to forty minute flights. The tests were to ensure that aircraft to be flown that night were serviceable in every respect. It was all experience for the chosen crews.

With over 365 hours flying time recorded in his logbook, Flight Sergeant Arthur Maxwell Bourne was posted to No.26 Operational Training Unit, where he met a young navigator by the name of Arthur Philip Bourne.

Arthur Philip Bourne was born on 16th July 1922, at Minworth, seven miles north east of the center of Birmingham. He was the youngest of five children born to John and Annie Rebecca Bourne (nee Norrey). The eldest was William, obviously known as 'Bill,' then came Ethel, the first of two sisters, followed by Harry, Nancy and then Arthur, who was born twenty-one years after his eldest brother. There was also a considerable age difference between Arthur's parents, his mother being ten years younger than her husband. Both John and Annie originated from Shropshire, although John spent the majority of his early life at Ilkley Moor, Yorkshire, living with an uncle, whilst Annie had spent her formative years in Worcestershire. When he was about twelve years of age, John moved to Worcestershire, where he met Annie and fate took its own course. They eventually married and moved to the Birmingham area where John took employment as a bailiff, with what is now the Severn Trent Water Company.

The Birth of a Crew

Lying crushed and crumpled on a mist-covered field are the remains of an Avro Oxford twin-engine aircraft, which crashed at Snitterfield RAF Base. The Australian pilot, 'Flip' Phillips, walked the short distance back to the airfield! *Courtesy of the Late Max Bourne*

Arthur was educated at the local school in Minworth, which he attended until he was fourteen years old, but soon realised the error of his action in leaving. To overcome this situation, he enrolled for classes at night school, where he was fortunate in being taught by Jack Lewis, B.Sc. With the help of the latter, Arthur qualified to School Certificate level in a number of subjects. He was also fortunate to have secured employment as an office junior with the local Water Company. However, sitting behind a desk soon proved to Arthur to be a boring and unsatisfactory way of making a living, he therefore volunteered to work as a plumber's mate. Unfortunately, all he seemed to do in his new occupation was dig trenches, but he did confide that it had one advantage; the work built him up physically. This proved extremely useful when, although he had not yet joined the Royal Air Force, Arthur had his first encounter with a low-flying aircraft. He was approximately twenty-five feet above ground level, working on a Dutch barn, when he looked up and saw a low-flying, twin-engine, aircraft coming towards him. As the machine got closer he realised that not only could he see the pilot, but as it flashed past, he also saw the rear gunner and the swastika painted on the tail fin. To this day, he still feels he holds the record for descending a twenty-five foot ladder! Once he had regained his senses, he realised that the Luftwaffe aircraft was not after him, but heading towards the Austin Motor Co. factory at Castle Bromwich, where fighter and bomber aircraft were built for the RAF.

Arthur's decision to join the Royal Air Force was made following the devastating attack on Coventry, which was approximately seventeen miles from his home. On the night of 14th November 1940, Arthur and his parents watched as the German bombers, using the River Tame as a turning point, headed for the cathedral city. John Bourne was very worried about the vast number of enemy aircraft flying almost overhead and wanted to go into the Anderson shelter in their garden. Unfortunately, for whatever reason, the shelter was leaking very badly and Arthur and his mother did not want to go in, preferring to stay where they were. However, seeing the increasingly agitated state his father was in, Arthur could stand it no longer and proceeded to bail the water out of the shelter. It was then, as he scooped up buckets of water, he swore revenge against the Germans for frightening his father who, at the time, was well over seventy years of age.

As Arthur's trade was listed as a 'Reserved Occupation,' he had to get consent to enlist for the services. This was eventually approved and he volunteered for service with the RAF at Dale End, Birmingham at the end of 1940. After a lengthy wait he was called to Viceroy Court, Bristol Road, Edgbaston, where he underwent aptitude tests and an interview. It was during the latter, sitting in front of three RAF squadron leaders, that he was suddenly asked what 17x18 equalled. To the utter amazement of the three officers he replied with the correct answer; the former not knowing that Arthur enjoyed mental arithmetic and had studied the subject at night school. He passed the interview and was categorised for pilot training providing that he passed the medical. Arthur found the medical to be a rather stringent affair consisting not only of a full medical check-up, but also various tests, which included being spun round in a chair and then told to walk a straight line, closing his eyes and standing on one leg and a hearing test. To test his hearing, Arthur was placed in the center of a room whilst the medical officer stood in a corner of the same room. From that position, the M.O. whispered the word "*butterflies*" and was amazed when Arthur responded with the same word. As his vision also proved excellent, Arthur was re-categorised for possible night flying.

In March 1942, the airman-under-training was sent to the Aircrew Receiving Center at St. John's Wood, London, home of Lord's Cricket Ground, where he was billeted for six weeks in a flight comprising of approximately thirty other potential flyers. He was then posted to the Personnel Reception Center at Brighton, Sussex, for a further three weeks. Although billeted in the Grand Hotel on the sea front, life was no holiday as training continued. The next move was to the University Air Squadron at Cambridge, the Initial

Arthur Philip Bourne, RAFVR, navigator, from Minworth, near Birmingham. *Courtesy of the Late Arthur Bourne.*

Training Wing where Arthur and his fellow trainees were billeted in Clare College. Here they ate alongside students, had lectures in various college buildings and undertook initial flying training at a local airfield. The course lasted between ten and twelve weeks at the end of which, those with the highest marks in navigation were sent to South Africa, whilst the others went to America or Canada.

Having completed his course, Arthur was sent home on leave before being posted to Blackpool via Bridgenorth, Shropshire and then Heaton Park, Manchester; the latter being a holding camp. Whilst stationed at Blackpool, Arthur was billeted in a guesthouse, where he teamed up with a fellow airman by the name of Pete Edwards. The landlady had issued rotas and instructions as to what the young airmen staying in her establishment could and could not do. Strict rules also applied to the closing and locking of the front door every night; ten o'clock on the dot, without exception. Unbeknown to her, Arthur and Pete infringed this latter rule on many occasions, being let in by the landlady's daughter, whom they had befriended. Unfortunately, the proprietress eventually discovered their ruse and threw them both out of the accommodation. Arthur and Pete both faced disciplinary charges but, as they were both going overseas, nothing more was heard.

Arthur's last view of a British city, for a while anyway, was taken as he boarded the *'QSMV Dominion Monarch,'* a passenger/cargo liner berthed in Liverpool docks. This ship was to take Arthur and a great many other souls, to South Africa for further training. One of those 'other souls' was a young man by the name of Kenneth (Kenny) Henry Turner who, like Arthur, was training to be a navigator. Naturally, as their respective lives followed the same course, they were destined to spend a lot of time together and, as a result, became good friends.

The trip to Durban took six weeks, due to the ship joining a convoy after receiving reports of U-boats being present in the Bay of Biscay and eastern Atlantic waters. The first port of call was Gibraltar, followed by Dakar, but in each case the troops on board were not allowed to disembark.

The six-week sea journey was followed by three days and three nights on a train, which took Arthur and some of his fellow travelers to East London, 1000km from Cape Town on the south east coast of South Africa. The final destination in South Africa, where they arrived at the beginning of June 1943, was No.48 Air Navigation School, Colindale. It was at No.48 A.N.S. that Arthur very nearly left a perfectly serviceable aircraft in flight. During this part of the training, navigators operated in tandem, with one undertaking the navigational work, whilst the other undertook various tasks including issuing parachutes to the rest of the crew in the event of an emergency. On one such occasion, when Arthur was acting as 1st navigator, the 2nd navigator misheard the captain's instruction and thought he said, *"Abandon ship."* Arthur, having been issued with his parachute, clipped it on, removed the emergency escape panel near the navigator's table and proceeded to climb through. He hesitated momentarily as he saw the hills and rock terrain below, at the same time he thought of the unusual 'non-RAF' term the pilot had used in ordering the crew to leave the aircraft. Just as he was about to push himself away from the twin-engine Anson, the 2nd navigator grabbed hold of Arthur and bellowed against the wind, *"THE CAPTAIN SAID ABANDON TRIP."*

The course, which included map reading exercises, wind and compass bearing exercises, over sea navigation exercises and many other related exercises, continued through to the middle of September. Having passed his course with a recommendation for more practical experience, Arthur was posted back to England, to No.1 (Observer) Advanced Flying Unit, based at RAF Wigtown, near the coast in Galloway, Scotland. The site of the airfield, on farmland at Baldoon, was originally selected during 1938, but it was not until the summer of 1940 that construction work actually began. Opened in 1941, the airfield was designated as part of Flying Training Command and was placed under the administration of 29 Group, Dumfries. It had three concrete runways, the usual array of RAF operational buildings, Bellman and blister hangers and accommodation which was listed as 'Temporary.'

Arthur arrived at No.1.Advanced Flying Unit during the last week of December 1943, and joined No.188 Air Navigator Course on 29th of that same month. In this case, the course consisted mainly of DR 'Dead Reckoning' and astro-navigation exercises and was completed by the middle of February 1944.

As a qualified navigator, with the rank of sergeant, 1579300 Sergeant Arthur Bourne was posted to No.26 Operational Training Unit at the beginning of March 1944, where he met an interesting Australian pilot by the name of Sergeant Arthur Maxwell Bourne.

Bill Vincent was to be the crew's flight engineer, although he was not to join the crew until they graduated to the four-engine Short Stirling bomber at Heavy Conversion Unit. Being thirty-six years of age, Bill was the 'grandfather' of the crew. He was also possibly the oldest member of aircrew to serve with No.622 Squadron. Max was never sure who was the steadying influence on who.

Bill Vincent was born in Wandsworth, South London on 25th November 1908. He was one of twelve children in a family, which comprised of six girls and six boys. The eldest boy, Harold, stood out amongst his siblings, due to the fact that, whereas they were all short in stature with dark hair, Harold stood about six feet tall and was blond!

Bill's father is reported to have come from a well-to-do family but, as with many families, was disowned and disinherited by them due to his choice of wife.

Not much is known about Bill's early life, but one comment mentioned by him to his daughter Ann, was that he survived on a diet of custard cream biscuits. What is known about Bill is that he achieved family notoriety as a persistent and dedicated school truant and, on more than one occasion, was frog-marched to school by his elder brothers. However, somewhere along the line, he gained enough knowledge to secure employment as a motor mechanic and, after a long period of unemployment during the depression, Bill managed to acquire a job as a bus driver with London Transport.

At the outbreak of war in September 1939, Bill was living in the London borough of Balham, adjacent to Wandsworth, with his wife and young daughter Ann. After the family maisonette was rendered almost uninhabitable as a result of bomb damage during the blitz, mother and daughter were evacuated to Sidmouth in Devon. Eventually, Bill found a suitable house for rent in Chessington, Surrey, where the family was re-united and took up residence. It was also fortuitous that Bill was able to transfer to the London Transport garage at Kingston-upon-Thames.

The Birth of a Crew

Derelict operational buildings on the site of the former RAF airfield at Wigtown. *Author's Collection*

Air raid shelters which were possibly never used on the former airfield at Wigtown. *Author's Collection*

A view of part of the perimeter track, on the site of the former airfield at Wigtown looking towards the Machars Hills. *Author's Collection*

On 10th May 1943, in response to a call for volunteers to serve as flight engineers on Short Stirling and Avro Lancaster bombers, Bill attempted to enlist with the Royal Air Force Volunteer Reserve. However, being that his job was listed as a reserved occupation, he needed permission to proceed with his application. Consent was granted on 30th July 1943, when he received notification from the Attestation Section, RAF, that he had been released from the Schedule of Reserved Occupations and that his enlistment had been approved. The letter went on to say that the Air Officer-in-Charge of Records, at Reading, Berkshire, would issue further instructions.

Bill attended the Flight Engineer Course at No.4 School of Technical Training at St.Athan, South Wales. It was here, during early May 1944, he passed his exams with a 67.7% result. He also attended No.1653 Heavy Conversion Unit between 20th June and 22nd July that same year.

Thomas Leonard Brown, the bomb aimer, was born in Claremont Street, Greenwich, South London, on 23rd December 1920. He was the fourth of five children, three sons and two daughters, born to Frank and Elsie Brown. The eldest child was Frank, who was born in 1910, followed by Arthur, who was in turn followed by Elsie. Thomas Leonard was the fourth child and finally ten years later, in 1930, Gwen entered the world. Frank Brown junior joined the peacetime Royal Air Force but, whilst on leave, was tragically killed along with his family, during an air raid on Bath.

Tom's father enjoyed cycling and thought nothing of cycling the ten to twelve miles every day to Dagenham, Essex, where he worked. However, after having had two bicycles stolen, Frank Brown decided to go to work by bus, a journey that also encompassed a river crossing on the Woolwich Ferry.

During his early years, Tom attended Randall Place School, Greenwich. At the age of ten his family moved to Charlton, where he is known to have attended Charlton Central School, where he remained and completed his education. Tom enjoyed all of his lessons, especially the afternoons spent in the carpentry shop. Unlike his future fellow crewmember Bill Vincent, Thomas Brown did very well at school and left at the age of sixteen to take up employment, as a junior clerk, with an old established firm of Estate Agents and Surveyors.

Young Thomas was an all round sportsman and enjoyed being a spectator as well as participating in snooker, tennis, cricket and football. He was an avid supporter of Charlton Athletic Football Club. Another sport Tom enjoyed was that of cycling and on one occasion cycled from Charlton to Land's End, although he did make the return journey by train! The reason for this marathon ride had nothing to do with the love of cycling it was in fact to overcome the heartache of a broken romance. However, he need not have despaired, for romance would come his way again via a bicycle. During 1940, aged only seventeen, Tom, together with a few friends, formed the Eagle Cycle and Social Club in Charlton. As word spread around the area about the club, many local youngsters showed an interest, including sixteen-year-old Daphne Baker. It was not long before Thomas Brown and Daphne Baker developed an interest in each other and became very good friends.

On 18th September 1941, Tom journeyed north of the River Thames to Euston, where he volunteered for service with the Royal Air Force. He had earlier been refused entry into the RAF on medical grounds as he had hammer toes, a deformity of the bones in his toes which bent them into the shape of an inverted 'V.' The wearing of badly fitting shoes

The Birth of a Crew

Left: Sergeant William "Bill" Vincent, flight engineer. *Courtesy of Ann Hill* Right: Leading Aircraftman Tom Brown photographed in Canada, in August 1943. The white 'flash' in the cap signifies an airman under training for aircrew. *Courtesy of Daphne Brown & Carol Artley*

was the usual cause of this infirmity, for which surgery was usually undertaken to correct the problem. However, still suffering from this same 'disability,' Tom passed a further medical and a selection board, was sworn in by the attestation officer, and was accepted as a candidate for aircrew training as an observer. Given the service number 1396259 and placed on Reserve with the rank of Aircraftman Second Class (ACII), he was then sent home to await call-up. The call came on 2nd March 1942, when Tom was instructed to report to No.1 Aircrew Receiving Center at St. John's Wood, London, where he found himself to be one amongst hundreds of other young like-minded candidates.

After a period of three weeks at No.1 ACRC, Tom reported to Aircrew Despatch Wing on 21st March. Almost one month later, on 18th April, he was sent to No.5 Initial Training Wing (I.T.W.), at Torquay, Devon, for basic training. The cadets were billeted in hotels, usually on the seafront. It was here, at I.T.W., where physical fitness, discipline and esprit de corp were brought to the fore through lectures, drills and marches; the latter otherwise known as 'square-bashing.'

The hard work was beginning to show signs of reward when on 12th June 1942 Tom was promoted to the rank of Leading Aircraftman (LAC), which brought with it a few pence increase in his pay.

Following completion on his course at No.5 I.T.W., Tom was posted to No.3 Elementary Flying Training School, based at Shellingford, Berkshire, a grass airfield with three runways, on 7th August. Exactly one month later, whilst still at No.3 E.F.T.S., Tom was recommended for remustering for training as a navigator. This was brought about due to the fact that as a result of the ever-increasing advances in air navigation techniques and equipment, the Air Ministry decided, in September 1942, that the trade of observer should be relinquished in favour of a new navigator status. This was promulgated by Air Ministry Order AMO1019, published that same month. Three weeks later, on 22nd September, under training navigator LAC Tom Brown was posted again, on this occasion to Heaton Park, Manchester, where it is believed he remained for approximately three months.

Following embarkation leave, Tom was posted overseas to complete his training, and left England on 13th January 1943. Ten days later he was reporting in at No.31 Personnel Depot at Moncton, New Brunswick, Canada. Having spent nearly two weeks at No.31 PD he was sent, on 5th February, to the Central Navigation School at Rivers, Manitoba, which formed part of No.3 Training Command.

For reasons unrecorded, on 12th March, Tom was recommended for re-mustering to training as a bomb aimer and was instructed to report to No.2 Manning Depot at Brandon on the same day. He remained at Brandon for one month before being transferred, on 11th June, to No.5 Bombing and Gunnery School.

A further posting occurred on 4th September, when Tom was posted back to No.1 Central Navigation School, at Rivers, Manitoba. Whilst there, on 14th October, he was, in accordance with Air Force Regulations, discharged on being granted a temporary commission in the rank of Pilot Officer. Having achieved officer status, he was issued with a new service number (153817) and "reposted" to No.1 CNS the following day, for a further two weeks.

Having returned to England, Pilot Officer Tom Brown reported to No.7 Personnel Reception Center, on 1st November. During his period of training Tom's feelings for Daphne had continued to grow and flourish and, whilst based at No.7 PRC, he sought permission to marry Daphne. Consent was granted and on the 20th day of that same month, a foggy day in southeast London, they were married at St Luke's Church, Charlton Village. Unfortunately, very few photographs were taken at the wedding. This had nothing to do with the fog, but was due to the lack of cameras and availability of rolls of film, although one photograph has survived. Initially, Tom had been granted two weeks leave but, due to errors and backlogs of posting trained personnel to various locations, Tom's leave eventually extended to nine weeks. Obviously there were no complaints from his young bride, but the honeymoon had to end and on 25th January 1944 Tom was posted to No.9 [Observer] Advanced Flying Unit, based at Penrhos, North Wales. On completion of his six-week course on 22nd February, he was posted to No.26 Operational Training Unit at Wing, where he met a newly qualified Australian pilot by the name of Max, who invited Tom to join his crew.

Paul Lambert Taylor, who was to become the wireless operator on Max Bourne's crew, was born on 22nd June 1921, at Drummoyne, New South Wales. It is known that he came from Sydney Australia, but unfortunately details of his training and postings, which brought him halfway round the world, are unknown. Whatever roads he travelled, Paul Taylor was eventually posted to No.26 O.T.U at Wing, where he met Max Bourne.

Roger Norman Humphrys was the rear gunner and came from Perth, Western Australia. Roger's father had been a sergeant in the British army, based in India with his wife Barbara, and their two children. During the early-1920s, Roger's parents moved to

The Birth of a Crew

Left: Pilot Officer Tom Brown married Daphne Baker on 20th November 1943, at St. Luke's Church, Charlton Village, Surrey. *Courtesy of Daphne Brown & Carol Artley* Right: Warrant Officer Paul Lambert Taylor, RAAF, wireless operator/air gunner, photographed wearing his flying suit during 1944. *Courtesy of Reg Heffron*

Left: A portrait photograph of Roger Humphrys, RAAF, air gunner. The picture was taken during 1945, after Roger had completed a tour of operations and had been commissioned in the rank of Pilot Officer. *Courtesy of Reg Heffron* Above: Reg Heffron, photographed in 1941, wearing the uniform of 27th Battalion, South Australian Scottish Regiment, before he transferred to the Royal Australian Air Force. *Courtesy of Reg Heffron*

New Zealand, where their younger child, a daughter, died as a toddler. Roger was born in New Zealand on 17th August 1924. During the following year the family moved again, this time to Australia, where Mr. and Mrs. Humphrys acquired a small farming allotment, under the Soldier Settlement Scheme, in the district of Manjimup in Western Australia. The name of the district, in which the family settled, like many other place names in the south west of Western Australia, is of aboriginal origin. Place names ending in 'up' indicated the presence of water, such as a stream or spring.

Roger's early education commenced at Smith's Brook, but nothing is known of how he got along there, although given the location, the school is thought to have been pretty basic.

Sometime during the thirties, the family gave up farming and the rural life, and moved to the city. They settled in the near coastal area of North Cottesloe, Perth. It was here that Roger completed his education and, eventually, volunteered for service with the Royal Australian Air Force. Like Paul Taylor, Roger was eventually posted to No.26 O.T.U.

Reg Heffron was born on 14th May 1922, at his parents' home at Eastwood, a suburb of Adelaide, South Australia. His education, which spanned between the years 1927 and 1935, was undertaken at public schools. At the age of fourteen years, Reg left school and started work in the family owned coach-building business as an apprentice upholsterer. He was still working there when he was called up for military service, with the 27th Battalion, South Australian Scottish Regiment, in October 1941.

Following Japan's entry into the war, Reg Heffron's unit was sent to Darwin in North Australia, where he received his baptism of fire in a massive Japanese air raid on 19th February 1942, which destroyed the town and its harbor facilities. Reg later volunteered to transfer to the Royal Australian Air Force and, having been accepted for aircrew, commenced training as an air gunner during the latter half of 1943. His initial training was undertaken in his home country, but on 26th November that same year he was posted overseas. Traveling via the U.S.A., on 7th January 1944 Sgt. Heffron sailed into Greenock, Scotland, on board the *'RMS Queen Elizabeth,'* which was serving as a troopship. From Scotland he was sent south by train to an RAF reception center at Brighton on the south coast of England, which is where his story really starts.

2

Operational Training Unit

Having arrived in England during January 1944 from his native Australia, Reg Heffron was sent to No.11 PDRC (Reception Center) at Brighton, Sussex, on the south coast of England. Although he had traveled half way round the world, via the United States of America, he was about to set out on another journey; albeit one that would take him into the war as a fully trained air gunner. It was upon his departure from the Reception Center that Reg commenced writing a diary about that journey.

Tuesday, 22nd February 1944
Up early in the morning, parade at 08.18am and then marched to Brighton Station, caught the 09.00am train to London Bridge where a truck was waiting to take us to Euston Station. After having some tea at the Y.M.C.A., we boarded [another] train at 12.20pm and arrived at our destination, Leighton Buzzard, Bedfordshire, at 13.50 hours.

After waiting in the snow for 2 hours a truck arrived and took us to our new quarters at No.26 Operational Training Unit, RAF Wing, Buckinghamshire. We had an evening meal and moved into our Quanson huts where we spent a very cold night. There was an alarm at 04.00am, this lasted about 45 minutes, with some gunfire.

RAF Wing, which came under the control of No.92 Group, Bomber Command, situated four miles west of Leighton Buzzard, was opened as a training airfield in 1941. It boasted three concrete runways, the longest being 2,000 yards in length, the second being 1,400 yards and the third 1,160 yards. Hard standings were provided for 30 bomber aircraft, along with temporary accommodation (Quanson huts) for the personnel. It was in a room, on this station, that Reg was to team up and become part of a crew.

Wednesday, 23rd February 1944
During the early hours we could hear London's terrific barrage in action. We spent the morning filling in forms, having a dental inspection and attending a lecture. In the afternoon there were more lectures and a period to put our anti-gas equipment in order. Today we were free to choose our own crew members, and six of us teamed up to fly together. They were the pilot, Arthur Bourne, from Western Australia, navigator, also by a strange co-incidence another Arthur Bourne, from Birmingham (met by chance), bomb aimer, Tom Brown, from London, wireless operator, Paul Taylor, from Sydney [Australia], rear gunner, Roger Humphrys, from Western Australia and myself Reg Heffron, mid-upper gunner, from South Australia. We have yet to meet No.7, a flight engineer. By the way some coal

arrived today so we will have a warm hut tonight. An alert was sounded at 10.00pm and the barrage [guns] opened [fire], flares were dropped and two brilliant red flashes indicated two raiders [enemy aircraft] were accounted for. All clear sounded at 11.30pm.

By the time Reg and those who were to become his fellow crew members had reached No.26 Operational Training Unit, they would have been well into their respective training programmes and were ready to crew up for operational training. This was done without any official pressure or delegation. The large room in which they found themselves was full of pilots, navigators, bomb aimers, wireless operators and air gunners, who mingled and chatted with each other in order to bond and form a six-man crew. The final member of the crew, the flight engineer, usually joined the crew at Heavy Conversion Unit, where the final part of their training took place.

An Australian pilot by the name of Arthur Bourne was perusing the list of navigators, when he noticed one with the same name as his own, and set off to find him. The mission was accomplished successfully and Arthur Philip Bourne agreed to join the crew of Arthur Maxwell Bourne. Either the system worked very well, or Max was very lucky, as he had soon gathered together a six-man crew consisting of those named in Reg's diary.

Thursday, 24th February 1944
Had lectures during the day on various subjects. At night we went to the mess for supper, and spent the rest of the evening by the fire in our huts. It has been bitterly cold again all day. London was attacked again about 10.00pm.

It was usually on these drab cold evenings that some airmen from the Commonwealth and Dominion Countries, who had never endured cold, damp climates like those found in Britain, wrote home to their families complaining about the weather. Some, like the Canadians who came from areas that endured really harsh winters, just wrote home about the dampness.

Sergeant Reg Heffron, resplendent in Royal Australian Air Force uniform.
Courtesy of Reg Heffron

Friday, 25th February 1944
Routine lectures on subjects concerning gunnery during the day. I met one of the instructors here, Flight Sergeant Tilbrook, who comes from Adelaide. We had supper at the mess and then [having said goodnight] turned in.

The next few days were also taken up with lectures, but there was an element of warfare on which Reg and his crew had not been lectured. One evening, relaxing in their hut, the crew tried to coax the fire in the iron stove into a blaze, but only succeeded in filling the hut with enough smoke to make the windows bulge. The result of this unscheduled war game was fire one, Reg and the crew nil. The fire was to win again a few nights later.

Monday, 28th February 1944
We'd just got the fire lit and settled down for the evening when we were called out to spread sand and salt on the runway at the 'drome. There had been a fall of snow at teatime and this had frozen into ice while the aircraft were away [on exercise]. We worked until about mid-night then had some supper and went to bed 1.00am.

Needless to say, by the time they got back to the hut, the fire had gone out.

Tuesday, 29th February 1944
The snow is still thick on the ground this morning but began to melt under [the rays of] a little afternoon sunshine. In the morning we went to the firing range for a bit of shooting, got back late for lunch, then spent the afternoon at lectures. We passed the evening in our huts doing some swatting on lecture subjects.

Notice! No mention of the fire. However, by the following morning the snow had practically all gone. Normal life [such as it was] was resumed, including the ongoing battle with the fire.

Thursday, 2nd March 1944
After breakfast we did physical training in the morning and a cross-country run in the afternoon until 3.00pm. Then I did some washing and we lit a fire in our hut before going to the mess for tea. On our return we found the fire out and so we had to get it going again. At 8.00pm it was back to the mess for supper, and then bed. I received a letter from cousin Martha Hall of Dearham, Cumberland this morning.

The ongoing battle with the Quanson hut stove was one that Reg and the crew were deemed to win, certainly over the next few nights anyway. Having received a letter from his cousin, Reg was unaware that more mail was on the way, sufficient in fact to keep him and the other lads in close proximity to the stove where they could keep an eye on the latter.

Friday, 3rd March 1944
Lectures all day today and at teatime there were six letters waiting for me at the mess, all from Australia.

One of the items of mail received, if not by Reg then certainly by one of the other crew members, must have been a parcel, as the diary entry continued ... we spent the evening by the fire in our hut, once again, with home baked cake for supper.

Letters were always welcome, as they gave that link with the folks back home. Needless to say, there were always the replies to write, which gave the crews something to do on those cold, British, winter evenings.

Saturday, 4th March 1944
Lectures again all day. Collected my laundry before having tea at the mess, and spent the evening writing letters by the fire in our hut. Snow began to fall again about 8.30pm.

Sunday, with no respite from lectures, continued in much the same way as Saturday had, although the snow had melted by 3.00pm that afternoon. It returned on Monday in the form of light snow flurries, but did not last very long.

Tuesday, 7th March 1944
We had our preliminary exams today. I came 10th with 71%. We expect to start flying at [Little] Horwood next week. It has been very cold again all day, so we lit the fire soon after tea, and huddled around it trying to keep warm. We are down to the last of our [coal ration].

Although he had received a number of letters a few days earlier, Reg was expecting further mail to arrive, but to his disappointment, none materialised. One thing that must have become available was a fresh supply of coal as, in his diary, he mentions the roaring fires in the hut stove that became too hot to sit by. This was a situation that was to last for a few days. Was the fire demon playing games again?

Thursday, 9th March 1944
No lectures today. In the morning we went swimming in the pool at [RAF] Halton, about 12 miles from Wing and in the afternoon had some practice firing from turrets at the range. We also did some clay pigeon shooting. We again spent the evening in our hut beside a roaster of a fire. It's not surprising there [are] a few chilblains in more than one pair of boots.

When the aforementioned indication that flying training was about to commence became reality, it generated much excitement amongst the young airmen, including Reg.

Friday, 10th March 1944
We leave for a months training at Little Horwood today, so as usual, there's a terrific rush to collect and exchange gear from the store, have dinner and pack. Anyway, all is ready by 2.30pm and off we go. After our arrival [at Little Horwood] we collected blankets from the store and unpacked, following which varying comments [were] passed on [the situation]. Then [we went] to bed.

Little Horwood, situated approximately five miles to the east of Buckingham, had opened two years earlier, in 1942. The base, which came under 92 Group, Bomber Command, was a training airfield that boasted three concrete runways, in the usual A-configuration, of similar lengths to those at Wing, to whom it was a satellite.

Although the base took the name of Little Horwood, geographically the airfield was closer to the neighbouring village of Great Horwood.

Saturday, 11th March 1944
After just making it to breakfast, we had a couple of talks from the 'bigwigs' and then the rest of the day free. We went for a walk through the village of Great Horwood, which adjoins the 'drome. A typical village with 2 pubs, the Swan and the Crown, an ancient church and many thatched houses [cottages], not to mention the post office, a tiny little room in one of the houses, and the postmaster with his bristling moustache and talkative wife. The villagers seem to take no notice of the bombers roaring overhead just above the housetops, but just plod the daily path as they have done all their lives. Even the fowls ignore them. After all this, we spent the evening in the mess, and then to bed late. I received three letters tonight.

All of this might have been new to Reg, but he was forgetting that by the time he and the rest of the guys arrived at Great Horwood, the villagers had endured the influx of personnel, equipment and aircraft for two years. It was part of their day-to-day lives. A little excitement did enter the crew's lives the following day, when at dusk, they saw about 50 Douglas DC3, twin-engine, transport aircraft fly over, very low and in squadron formation.

Monday, 13th March 1944
We were scheduled to fly today but the weather said "No," so we spent most of the time in the intelligence room. At 6.30pm our crew went in to the decompression chamber and saw at first hand the effects of lack of oxygen.

Due to the weather the rest of that week followed a similar pattern, with lectures followed by visits to the dispersal area for turret and other inspections, or the intelligence room. However, even when the crew's names were placed on the roster for flying, the vagaries of the English weather intervened.

Friday, 17th March 1944
After a day of messing about, we were at last detailed to fly at 4.00pm, but after taxiing out, the weather closed in suddenly and we were prevented from taking-off by control. So, we wended our way back to the mess for tea, after which we celebrated a birthday which had definitely upsetting effects on some of the celebrators, but after much persuasion they were put to bed by 11.45pm.

Unfortunately, Reg does not state whether it was the occasion that upset some of the party, or whether it was the effects of the drink consumed. Either way, there was some cause for celebration the following day.

A Vickers Wellington, twin-engine bomber, similar to the type used at No.26 Operational Training Unit, RAF Wing. *Author's Collection*

Saturday, 18th March 1944

Lectures again until 4.00pm when we took our first aerial view of England. As is usual here at this time, visibility was very poor. Our first impression on the Wellington is a good one after what we have flown in up to date. We spent the evening at the mess and turned in at 10.30pm, after opening a first class parcel I received from the South Australian Comforts Fund.

The Vickers Wellington bomber was a twin-engine aircraft of geodetic construction, designed by Barnes Wallis. Due to the nature of its construction, the aircraft had proved its worth in the early years of the war by being able to sustain varying degrees of battle damage and still get its crews home. Having been introduced to the Wellington bomber, which Max Bourne found considerably heavier than anything experienced before, the crew was taken aloft by Flight Lieutenant Belyea, one of the instructors. The weather again curtailed flying activities until the following Tuesday.

Tuesday, 21st March 1944

After a C.O's parade in the morning we had another short flip in the 'circuits and bumps' series, then some crew drill in the afternoon. [That] night, after supper in the mess, we went to our hut and talked, wrote letters and felt cold. I received five letters from Australia this afternoon.

The instructor on their second flight in a Wellington bomber was recorded as being Flying Officer Gill. Two days later they made their third flight, but it was a wonder the aircraft got off the ground.

Thursday, 23rd March 1944

We were on flying again today and were up for about three hours around mid-day. Nothing else happened except that we ate about four dozen buns and cakes which we bought from the N.A.A.F.I. wagon before taking-off. We spent the evening coaxing the fire in our hut, and a miserable effort it was until at 10.00pm we gave up in despair.

As soon as it was left alone the fire blazed up furiously and by 11.30pm it was hot enough to start opening windows so we went to bed happy.

The flying programme continued to be at the mercy of the weather, with some crews getting flying experience, whilst others sat it out on the ground. Max and the crew at least managed to complete their two allotted flights with Flying Officer Gill before the weather struck again.

Although no mention of it was made in Reg's diary, it seems the weather may have been a factor in a crash that claimed the lives of a crew out on a night-flying exercise. Thirty-three year old Wing Commander Henry Simmons, a pilot, and his crew had taken off from Wing at 19.10 hours. Later that night reports were received stating that the aircraft, Wellington bomber, LP258, had crashed at about 23.20 hours. Accounts relating to the incident implied control of the aircraft was lost as it descended through cloud, at an altitude of approximately 4,000 feet. Impact with the ground occurred a mile northwest of the village of Hardwick, between Pitsford Water Reservoir and Wellingborough, Northamptonshire. Wing Commander Simmons, from Lake Side, Lancashire, was laid to rest in Oxford (Botley) Cemetery.

A week or two before the crash, Wing Commander Simmons had approached Arthur Bourne, saying he needed a navigator and invited the latter to join his crew. Given that the crew was made up of commissioned officers and Arthur was only a sergeant, he felt it would not be a good move, especially as he would not have been able to mix with any of them away from the aircraft. With each man at his own station on the aircraft in combat situations, Arthur would never have really got to know the crew. He therefore declined the offer and stayed with his namesake. Anyway, he had already become a part of a crew, which was bonding into an efficient team. The tragedy of this event was that Arthur was in the Station Sick Quarters, when the remains of Wing Commander Simmons and his crew were brought in.

Sunday, 26th March 1944

Flying again this morning twice, but in the afternoon the weather turned bad again and flying ended for the day at 2.00pm.

A second entry in Reg's diary appears to have been made as an afterthought, which may show that as members of aircrew underwent training they got used to the tragedy that sometimes accompanied that training.

One of our course gunners, Noel Block from Australia, was killed this morning when a propeller off their aeroplane broke up [whilst flying only] 100 feet above the 'drome. The plane crash-landed off the runway, but no one else was hurt.

The young airman referred to in Reg's diary was 437364 Sergeant Noel Herbert Block, aged twenty-one, an air gunner. He came from Prospect, South Australia and was the son of Frederick Andreas and Florence Elizabeth Block. He never returned to his native land, but was laid to rest in Oxford (Botley) Cemetery, in front of the grave of Wing Commander Henry Simmons who had been killed three days earlier.

The aircraft, which was a Wellington M.III, serial BJ754, piloted by F/S R. Rodea, was forced to make a belly-landing after a defective joint on the starboard propeller caused a

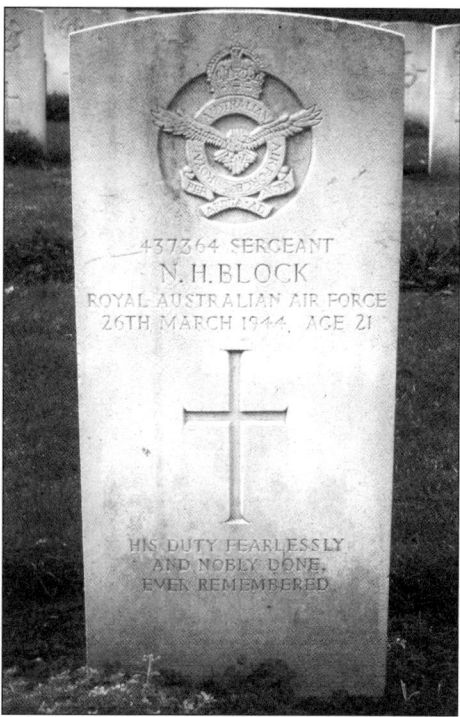

Left: The headstone marking Wing Commander Henry Simmons's last resting place in Oxford (Botley) Cemetery, Oxford. Wing Commander Simmons had joined the RAF during the 1920s and is believed to have served in Abukir as part of the RAF Middle East Air Force. *Author's Collection* Right: The headstone marking the grave of Sergeant Noel Block, RAAF, killed in a bizarre and tragic accident on 26th March 1944. *Author's Collection*

blade to become detached. Scything through the fuselage, the blade struck Sergeant Block who was occupying the second pilot's seat. No blame for this bizarre accident was directed towards the pilot, of whom it was said handled the aircraft creditably.

As tragic as the crash was, life and training had to go on. Reg and the crew flew twice the following morning; first with Flying Officer Gill as instructor and later with Flight Sergeant McKee.

Over the next few days, Reg had lessons of an entirely different nature. He was to learn a little more about the geography of England, what life was like for the ordinary working population, along with something of his own family background.

Tuesday, 28th March 1944
No flying this morning and at 11.00am I obtained a leave pass to go to Manchester to visit relatives. After hitchhiking to Winslow I went by train to Bletchley, changed there and went to Rugby, changed again and went on to Crewe, changed again and arrived at London Road station in Manchester at 11.30pm. All the last trains and buses for my destination at Irlam had gone, and at last I got a taxi whose driver demanded 25/- for the trip. Arriving in Irlam we eventually found the address I was looking for after several enquiries and much torch flashing, and the cabbie collected his 25/-. I roused my host, Joe Dawson, by liberal use of the doorknocker, and after being made welcome, had some supper. We turned in [well after mid-night].

Irlam is an area to the west of Manchester, well outside the city limits which, in those days, in a black-out situation, would have taken a long while to reach.

Although Joe Dawson opened the door to Reg the latter did not see his cousin Dorothy, Joe's daughter, until the following afternoon.

Wednesday, 29th March 1944
I rose very late and found the housekeeper had prepared breakfast, which I ate readily. After washing my dishes, [I] set off to meet Joe at Irlam Central School where he is headmaster, and had lunch with the staff, and then went by train into Manchester. I had some tea at Lyons, then visited the Central Library, a magnificent building, after which I walked down Oxford Street. It began to rain, so a visit to a newsreel cinema [seemed] quite in order. In the center of Manchester there is a large area of vacant ground left after rubble was removed after the blitz ended two years ago. The city itself is even more disappointing than London. All the buildings, even houses in the suburbs, are so blackened by smoke and soot that they appear to be painted black. The streets are very dirty and straggle all over the place. It is hard to understand why people live in such an atmosphere of smoke, fog, smells and constant rain. Anyway, emerging from the cinema, I made my way [back] to Central Library, where I had arranged to meet my cousin Dorothy Dawson, at 3.30pm. We had tea at the Mecca Café and then went to Greengate bus station and caught a bus to Irlam. Arriving home we had [more] tea and then spent the evening by the fire talking and viewing Dorothy's snaps and my souvenirs. We then had some supper, after which it was bedtime.

Joseph Dawson was dedicated to the teaching profession. He had been Assistant Master at Old Hall Drive School, Gorton, Manchester, between 1910 and 1914, but his career was interrupted by the advent of the First World War. Between 1914 and 1919, Joe undertook Military Service. He returned to teaching in 1920 when he took a position at Maryport Council School. In 1924, he was appointed Head Master at Crosby National School, Maryport, where he remained until 1930 when he became Head Master at Central School, Irlam. Joseph's own qualifications consisted of a Bachelor of Arts, London: (Hons English), a Board of Education Certificate and a University of London Intermediate Examination for B.D. Degree.

Wandering around an industrial city like Manchester probably came as a bit of a cultural shock to a young man who was used to blue skies, sunshine and open spaces. However, every city and major town in England had one place to go to brighten up the day. Lyons (Joe Lyons & Co) teashops were a chain of large teashops popular both during and after the war. They sold not only waitress served teas, but also a wonderful choice of cakes, meringues, pastries and other weight-inducing goodies, at tables where one could sit and chat with friends whilst indulging themselves and listen to gossip. Most of the outlets were situated at a main crossroads or junction, which gave them another name by which they were more popularly known; Lyon's Corner Houses. The waitresses, due to the manner in which they quickly flitted from one customer to another, were commonly known as 'Nippies.'

```
                    TEACHERS REGISTRATION COUNCIL.
                         REPRESENTATIVE OF THE TEACHING PROFESSION
                      (Established by Act of Parliament and Constituted by Orders in Council.)      E.

Register Entry concerning:  DAWSON, JOSEPH.
Date of Registration:       1st September, 1920.    Register Number: 56849.
Professional Address:       Central School, Irlam,
                            MANCHESTER.

Attainments:

                            B.A., London: (Hons. English).
                            Board of Education Certificate.
                            University of London Intermediate Examination for
                                                   B.D. Degree.

Training in Teaching:       St. John's Training College, Battersea.

Experience:                 Assistant Master -
                            Old Hall Drive School, Gorton, Manchester.  1910-1914;
                                 (Military Service 1914-1919).
                            Maryport Council School.                    1920-1924;
                            Head Master -
                            Crosby National School, Maryport.           1924-1930;
                            Central School, Irlam, Manchester.          1930 -
```

The Teachers Registration Document detailing Joe Dawson's teaching qualifications and experience. *Author's Collection*

Thursday, 30th March 1944

I rose at 8.30am and, after washing and shaving, had a real British breakfast of porridge, eggs and bacon, toast and marmalade. Then I set off for the school again, just like the days of old (except I never before had lunch with the headmaster). After lunch we went to the station, where I said my goodbyes and set off back to Wing. I went into Manchester, changed trains for Rugby, changed again for Bletchley, changed [yet] again (with a two-and-a-half-hour wait) for Winslow then a two-and-a-half mile walk to Horwood. [I] reached camp at 12.15.

With all the traveling and waiting around between trains, Reg had plenty of time to muse over his recent adventure, which included visiting a major British industrial city, meeting never-before seen relatives and taking time out in a well-loved British institution; Lyon's Corner House. However, he also had time to mull over in his mind what he was going back to, training for aerial combat in enemy occupied skies. And Reg did not have long to wait.

Friday, 31st March 1944

There was thick fog this morning, which put flying off until 11.30am. We then did a weather test flight and began our 'circuits and bumps' again, flying until 3.15 then had a late lunch or early tea (it could have been either) and then spent the evening in the mess. I have had six letters in the past two days.

'Circuits and bumps' is the term used for continuous take-offs and landings on the same runway, where the pilot takes off, completes a circuit of the airfield, lands the aircraft, but then continues to roll along the runway and immediately takes-off again. All part of the training, as they say. For this training flight, Max's instructor was recorded as being Flying Officer Nixon.

Operational Training Unit

Saturday, 1st April 1944

Clocks on 1 hour

Very foggy this morning and flying did not begin until after lunch, when we flew to Upper Heyford to bring one of our pilots back to base. We returned at 6.30pm, had tea and supper in quick succession and then went to our hut and got a good fire going.

All Fools Day (April 1st) is the one day each year when people say and do silly things, in order to catch out other people as a joke. The custom of putting the clocks forward one hour to create double British summer time, which had been induced by the outbreak of war, must have seemed very strange to a Colonial and one can imagine Reg, when being told to alter the clocks for the first time, taking the comment as a joke. However, other than recording the simple fact in his diary in four words, Reg makes no further mention of it. Maybe he had previously been made aware of the fact and knew it was not a prank.

The weather during the following week varied between fog and rain, both causing the cancellation of flying training. Reg undertook some turret drills out at dispersal on the Wednesday afternoon, but beyond that had very little to record in his diary. When flying did resume for the crew, they did not get too excited about the prospect.

Sunday, 9th April 1944

Waiting around all day expecting to fly again but nothing happened until 9.00pm, when we did two hours of 'circuits and bumps.' Then a most revolting supper and into bed at about 1.00am.

The revolting supper he had eaten the previous evening made its presence felt at 6.00am the following morning, when Reg woke up feeling very ill. Having managed see the M.O. who gave him some medicine, Reg was ordered to take the rest of the day off to recuperate. This also meant he was not allowed to eat or drink anything. Although he had not fully recovered the following day, Reg got back into the stride of things, but almost wished he hadn't.

Tuesday, 11th April 1944

Had the morning off after unhappy episode and slept in until lunchtime. We had a lecture for a couple of hours and after that free time until teatime, then briefing for night flying at 7.30pm. We were landing at 90 mph, in darkness, and heard another pilot telling control he was unable to move off the runway. We stopped just behind him with sweat on [our] brow. Then, after all the excitement was over, we had supper and turned in at 2.30am.

Having had a late finish the crew was given the following morning off. As it turned out though, due to the fact that all flying was canceled during the afternoon, they finished up having the whole day and evening off too. However, they more than made up for the time off the following day.

Thursday, 13th April 1944
Up early this morning. Flying began at 9.30am and finished in time for lunch. [This was followed by] a break until briefing at 7.30pm. [We] began flying again at 9.00pm and did not finish until 4.00am. After [having] breakfast, we got to bed at 5.30am.

Having got to bed at 5.30am, needless to say the rest of that day was a lazy one for Max's crew, once they eventually climbed out of their beds around mid-day. They wandered off to the local Y.M.C.A. where they had tea, returned to the mess for supper and then wrote some letters home.

Due to the variable weather conditions, flying was canceled again for the next three days, which left this crew, and others, at loose ends, apart from a small amount of time taken up with aircraft drills out at dispersal. However, Reg was able to fly with Flying Officer Nixon, for what was categorised as air to air firing, literally.

Although it was not recorded in Reg's diary, on 15th April, Tom Brown received confirmation of his appointment and promotion in the rank of Flying Officer. It seems odd that if a celebration of any kind was had to mark the occasion that no mention of it was made in Reg's notes.

Tuesday, 18th April 1944
The weather is much improved today and after lunch I went to do some air firing. The drogue broke its mooring as soon as it was released, and floated gently to earth, thereafter we just belted our ammo' away at the clouds.

The following afternoon, after yet another morning of inclement weather, Reg managed to get in a camera gun exercise. It was on completion of this trip that he realised that he had only one more official flying exercise to undertake before he finished the course.

Wednesday, 19th April 1944
Up bright and early this morning, but there was thick mist which kept us on the ground until 10.30 hours [I] then flew until 2.20pm on camera gun exercises.

Whilst Reg might have been up bright and early, the weather was not. However, according to his diary, Reg managed to get in at least two training flights during the day; the first with F/S Wilde and the second with F/S McKee. This still left Reg with one more flight to make before finishing the course at Little Horwood.

On this same day, according to his logbook, Max Bourne flew a bombing exercise with F/S R. Roedea as second pilot. The latter was the pilot in charge of the Wellington bomber, which three weeks earlier lost its propeller, resulting in the death of Sgt. Block.

Thursday, 20th April 1944
Up early again this morning and at 9.30am I flew for another hour and finished my flying duty here. We expect to leave for Wing tomorrow. [I] spent the afternoon bringing my log book up to date then rushing round collecting signatures on my clearance papers. After tea I did some washing, got the fire going and [then] spent the evening in our hut. [I] received another letter today, this time from an old Army mate in 27th Battalion.

Tom Brown photographed during April 1944, having received confirmation of his appointment and promotion in the rank of Flying Officer. *Courtesy of Daphne Brown and Carol Artley*

Like a bunch of schoolchildren going to summer camp, Max and his crew arose early on the morning of their departure from Little Horwood and, after breakfast, completed their packing. By lunchtime they were ready for the off, but had to wait until 3.30pm before the crew bus arrived. There was much frenzied activity as they all struggled to load their gear, and themselves, on to the vehicle, which eventually pulled away and headed back to Wing, where they arrived at 5.30pm. Once the bus reached Wing, there was further frenzied activity as luggage and equipment was hauled off the bus and piled in a heap on the ground. There, according to Reg's diary, it stayed until after they had selected beds, had tea and attended a lecture! Only then did the crew collect their gear and get settled in. For some unrecorded reason though, it seems they left one of their number behind.

Saturday, 22nd April 1944
There was not much doing all day. We should have flown in the afternoon, but our wireless operator Paul Taylor was left behind at Horwood yesterday and we could not fly without him. [However,] he did arrive at 5.30pm in time for tea.

Apart from being tested on, and passing, their crew drills, the next three days were to be taken up with a fair amount of flying; all cross-country exercises. The first took in the eastern side of Britain and lasted three hours. The route being Wing to Northampton, Framlingham, Stamford, Wainfleet, East Retford, Northampton and back to Wing. The following day they headed north, but inclement weather and icing meant that Flight Sergeant Bourne was forced to abandon the exercise after four hours in the air. However, the next day all went according to plan.

Tuesday, 25th April 1944
Up early again this morning and all ready to fly at 8.30am on our third cross-country exercise. We took off at 9.30am, the weather being much better than yesterday. Our route was via Northampton, Savernake, Conwy, Fishguard, St Judwells, Church Honeybourne and base. We did the trip at 12,000-13,000 feet and took six hours. [We] also did some bombing and gunnery exercises en-route. We signed off at 4.30pm, had lunch and tea in one [sitting] then went to the cinema.

Six hours may seem a long time to be in the air on a training exercise but, when they were finally deemed ready for operations this crew, like all other crews, could find themselves flying operational missions lasting even longer.

As there was no flying the next day, Reg decided to undertake a couple of necessary minor chores, like putting his boots and shoes in for repair. Later, during the latter part of the morning he and the rest of the crew practised some crew drills, which took them through to lunchtime. The afternoon was spent out on the airfield, where Reg undertook some gun harmonisation. The crew was not late turning in that night due to the fact they had a long day ahead of them the following day, starting early the next morning.

Thursday, 27th April 1944
We took off at 9.30am and flew until 3.30pm on another cross-country exercise. It was extremely cold above 5,000 feet and we were utterly fagged out when we finally landed. [We] had lunch and tea in one [sitting] and in the evening we went to a concert in the station theater. A very good show and thoroughly enjoyed.

Tiredness must have overtaken the crew, as the following morning they were all late in rising and subsequently were too late to partake of breakfast in the mess. Their day was to take on much the same form as the previous one, except that instead of undertaking a cross-country exercise, they did a fighter affiliation exercise against a Tomahawk aircraft. Having got airborne at 1.15pm, they met up with the fighter that made a total of thirty mock attacks on their Wellington bomber. Each time the Tomahawk was seen to line-up for an attack, Flight Sergeant Bourne threw the bomber into an evading 'corkscrew' manoeuvre, whilst the gunners tried to bring the cine camera guns to bear on the 'enemy' aircraft. After two-and-a-half-hours, all feeling exhausted, they landed back at base. Again, lunch and tea were taken in one sitting, followed by an evening of entertainment; this time at the camp theater. It is not recorded if any of the young airmen fell asleep during the show. Reg's diary implies that the evening's entertainment made them all forget their weariness.

Saturday, 29th April 1944
No flying in the morning. In the afternoon we found ourselves down on the night-flying programme, a high level bombing exercise, taking off at 11.30pm. [We] returned at 3.30am.

Anyone not fully awake, whose name was on the next scheduled night-flying exercise, was in for a bit of a shock and a rude awakening.

Sunday, 30th April 1944
We landed at 3.30am and, after a meal, turned in and slept until 1.00pm. [We] had a late breakfast and then nothing to do until briefing for night-flying again at 6.30pm. We had supper in the mess and then began our 3 hour cross-country exercise at 9.30pm. We happened to fly in the opposite direction, and at same height, as a stream of Halifaxes on their way to the Continent. It caused a lot of excitement, as some of them had no navigation lights on. After completing our exercise we got back to base at 1.00am and, by the time we put out flying gear away, it was 3.30am.

Although night-flying exercises were, by their very nature, repetitive, Reg found the one programmed for the night of 1st/2nd May 1944 different. It was the first time he had occupied the front turret of the Wellington bomber. So, instead of staring into the darkness to see where he had come from, he could stare into the darkness to ascertain where he was going! The next night he was back at his usual station in the rear turret and on this occasion, coastlines were the clue as to his whereabouts in the night sky. At this stage of his training, Reg had yet to experience the sensation of 'riding' in the mid-upper turret, high on the back of a Stirling bomber. This was to come at Heavy Conversion Unit.

Wednesday, 3rd May 1944
We slept in until lunchtime. Nothing to do after that so I spent some time writing letters, then had tea at 4.30pm, followed by briefing at 6.30pm for night-flying. We took off on a five hour cross-country flight at 9.30pm, via Goole, Carlisle, [Isle of] Man, Anglesey and Northampton. [We] landed about 3.30am.

Presumably, on this exercise and whilst they were out over the sea, Reg took the opportunity to fire off some practice rounds from machine-guns in the rear turret.

Two days later, on 5th May, the weather took a turn for the worse, with strong winds, low cloud and rain, which persisted for most of the day and night. However, around midnight, Max was given clearance to take-off for another long cross-country flight. As they crossed the Bristol Channel, one of the engines began to falter, so he decided against completing the exercise and returned to base. If the crew thought they were going to get to bed earlier than they had expected, they were very much mistaken. Having reported the problem to H.Q., the ground staff took some considerable time dealing with the problem. Also, as a result of having partaken of breakfast, Max and the crew did not finish until 5.30am on the morning of 6th May.

The following night, whilst flying out over the North Sea, where the air temperature was minus twelve degrees centigrade, the icing up of the aircraft's oxygen system caused a problem. Needless to say, once they had landed and got back to their hut, the crew gathered around the fire to get warm before going to bed. However, one bout of sleep was not enough, as Reg's diary records.

Monday, 8th May 1944
Hopped into bed at 7.00am after last night's flying, and snored noisily until 1.00pm when we stumbled out of bed. A good wash removed the necessity for matchsticks [before] lunch in the mess. [It was then back] to our hut for another sleep in the afternoon until tea time.

The flight, which had caused the crew some concern, but was to put them in good stead for future emergencies of such a nature, was their last flight at No.26 Operational Training Unit.

In spite of all their good intentions, the crew woke late the following morning, but at least did not have to worry about getting ready for another cross-country, night flight. Instead, they had to gather the necessary twenty or so signatures required on their various clearance certificates from the base, and return all equipment to the stores. After several miles of weary tramping around the station, they accomplished their mission by teatime.

There was, however, no sleeping-in the next morning.

Wednesday, 10th May 1944
[We were] up early for a change. This is our last day at Wing and we are going on leave. After breakfast we went to the pay office and caused some consternation to the staff by asking for Thirty Pounds each for the five of us. Anyway we got it and left [with our faces] wreathed in smiles [whilst] the staff sat stunned. The rest of the crew left for London after lunch, but I am leaving tomorrow morning for Manchester and then Cumberland to visit relatives. After tea, I packed my things ready for an early start. We have to take all our gear with us, which complicates things [when] traveling. Then off to bed.

Sergeant Reg Heffron was up early the following morning, had had breakfast and was ready to leave by 8.00am. He managed to hitch a ride to Leighton Buzzard station in a postman's van then took a train to Euston station. This was followed by a taxi to Liverpool Street station, where he deposited most of his kit at the left luggage office, then took another cab to the Strand Palace Hotel where he was to stay overnight. During the taxi ride he saw some of the devastation in the City of London, caused by the blitz earlier in the war, especially around the area of St. Paul's Cathedral. The sight of such destruction left him feeling very moved.

Having secured a room at the hotel, Reg went to visit the Boomerang Club, where he had lunch and spent the rest of the day taking it easy. The Boomerang Club was a social club and meeting place for Australian Service Personnel based in England. It operated from the basement of Australia House situated in the Strand, near to many of London's visitor attractions. Apart from being able to check out events, food, drink and newspapers were also available at the club. Later, during the evening, he went for a walk and saw both the Houses of Parliament and 'Big Ben' for the first time.

Given that he had a long day ahead of him the next day, he did not leave it late turning in that night.

Friday, 12th May 1944
Up at 7.30am, packed up, paid the bill and then went to Kodak House to arrange for this months cigarette quota to be sent to me. [I then] took a taxi to Euston, had breakfast at the station, then caught the Manchester train at 10.15am [I] arrived there at 2.30pm.

Reg had a very busy and enjoyable period of leave, during which time he stayed with Joe Dawson, his uncle, a widower, living in Irlam, taking in visits to Manchester, Liverpool, Chester and Southport. He then headed for Cumberland, where he met and stayed with a cousin, Martha Hall and her husband William, in Dearham Bridge. William was a farmer and Martha, apart from being a farmer's wife, was also the District Nurse. Whilst in the region, Reg visited Whitehaven, where he met another cousin, Harry Dawson.

Monday, 22nd May 1944
Up at 08.30, breakfast and out by 10 o'clock. I set off by bus for Keswick in the Lake District changing buses at Cockermouth and arriving at Keswick at 11.30am. The town is quite small, but has many quaint little shops and cafés I met two Queenslanders in Fitz Park and as they were on their own, as so was I, we stayed together for the rest of the day.

For Reg, it must have been a stroke of good fortune meeting two servicemen from his own homeland, in such an out of the way place in Britain. They walked and talked and then went to Derwent Water, where they spent some time idly rowing a boat on the water. All thoughts of the war, flying training and the future were pushed to the back of their minds as they wandered around the Lake District taking in the picturesque scenery and sights. After a sumptuous tea of sandwiches and cakes, the two Australians said their farewells to Reg and parted company. Reg returned to the shops, purchased a few items to send home and then caught his bus back to Dearham.

All too soon Reg's period of leave came to an end, and it was time to return to reality and normality. However, on his way south, he had one more visit lined-up.

Thursday, 25th May 1944
Packed my things, and after breakfast, said goodbye to William [before] Martha drove me to Dearham Bridge. I arrived at Carlisle station just in time to catch the through train from Glasgow. Changed trains at Crewe and again at Stafford for Lichfield. On arriving at the latter, I walked to No.27 O.T.U. to see John Harvey, Des Harry and Ray Giles who were all stationed there. We had a good yarn, as the last time we met was back in Australia. I stayed the night at the camp.

No.27 Operational Training Unit was based on the training airfield, situated three miles north east of Lichfield. However, Reg had not been posted there, so the next morning he set about completing his journey. Having made his way to London and collected his kit from the left luggage office at Liverpool Street station, Reg met up with Roger Humphrys, the rear gunner from his own crew. Together they put their gear on to the train for Brandon and, having half an hour to spare before their departure, decided to wander about just outside the station. Unfortunately, due to not paying attention to the time, they missed the train and had to wait four hours for the next one. Having time on their hands, the two Australian airmen ambled through the streets of the City of London's financial district, where the Bank of England is situated. It was ironic that, whilst ambling through the area of London where all big financial deals were struck, they finished up, in of all places, a penny arcade near St Paul's Cathedral. They did not make their respective fortunes, but did enjoy the interlude.

Having learned their lesson on time keeping, Reg and Roger were back at Liverpool Street in time to catch the 5.46pm train to Brandon. Arriving in the small Norfolk town, they found their luggage waiting for them but, to their horror, their respective hand baggage was missing from the pile. However, by way of recompense, the final part of the journey worked in their favour.

Friday, 26th May 1944

Who should be waiting for us at the station but our pilot Max Bourne and Paul Taylor our wireless operator, with the Rover car they had bought whilst on leave. We piled our baggage and ourselves on board and drove in style, if not in comfort, to our new camp. [On arriving I] had tea, collected blankets and four letters, then to bed.

According to Arthur Bourne, there were rumours that such was the age and condition of the car that the dealer had donated the Rover to the Australian airmen, rather than having sold it to them. Whatever the truth, the next day was the start of a new era.

Heavy Conversion Unit

The crews' destination in the car, as described by Reg on Friday, 26th May, was RAF Methwold, an operational Bomber Command station situated five miles northwest of Brandon. Max and his crew were destined to spend only six days at this base.

Apart from attending a few lectures on the use of oxygen, the dangers of flak and other flying related subjects, Reg and Roger seemed to have spent most of their week at Methwold trying to find out what happened to their lost luggage. As this task normally took them to Brandon or Norwich, they usually finished up in a theater or cinema at the end of the day. They never found the missing items, but had a great time looking for them.

It was due to the fact that Reg's diaries were in his missing luggage that he never recorded the name of Bill Vincent as the seventh member of the crew. He only had a few scribbled notes and his logbook, and had to rely on memory, for that period of time until the missing bags were recovered and returned.

Friday, 2nd June 1944
Left Methwold per R.A.F. bus after breakfast and arrived at Chedburgh about 10.30am. Spent the rest of the day with forms and signatures until tea time.

The airfield at Chedburgh was across the county border in Suffolk, situated six miles south west of Bury St. Edmunds. Like most other airfields of the period, it had three concrete runways in the usual A-Plan configuration. It was home to No.1653 Heavy Conversion Unit, which operated Short Stirling four-engine heavy bombers.

Saturday, 3rd June 1944
Had some pep talks from the "nobs" (officers) in the morning, and after lunch had a look over a Stirling bomber in which we will be flying while at this station. Their size is incredible after what we are used to.

The Short Stirling, which had been the first four-engine heavy bomber to enter service with the Royal Air Force, began operations during 1941. It had been the mainstay of No.3 Group Bomber Command during the following two years but was, in 1944, tired and unsuitable for constant nightly battles over enemy occupied territory. Max Bourne had his own thoughts about the Stirling.

Whilst there had been a few scary moments at O.T.U., they were nothing compared to the very large and heavy Stirling. This aircraft, although excellent in many respects, was not intended for the heavy duty (abuse) of repeated 'circuits and bumps.' We did thirty-eight take offs and landings in our first nine days on the type. The Stirling was being progressively dropped from front line service, as its performance in some respects was not up to scratch. They were utilised in the conversion of pilots and crews to four-engine aircraft from twins, a bit of a leap. The pilot's head was 23 feet from the ground at touch down; but we managed.

A week of lectures commenced the following day, even though it was a Sunday, with very little else happening to the crew during that week. Not much therefore to write about, except that there was some news during the middle of the week, which brought cheer to all except the enemy.

Tuesday, 6th June 1944
The air activity all last night was terrific. We had scarcely any sleep and were not surprised to hear at 9.00am of the Allied landings in Normandy. We spent the night at the mess, listening to the latest news from France, and the King's speech.

For a number of weeks prior to 6th June, the Royal Air Force had been bombing areas along both the Normandy coast and inland, in an effort to 'soften up' the German forces deployed there. However, diversionary raids and the usual bombing missions over Germany continued in an effort to draw attention away from the increased aerial activity over that part of the French coastline.

Although world changing events were happening just across the Channel, Reg had other thoughts in his mind. On the Friday of that same week exams were held, and Reg felt quite confident of the results, which were due the following day. However, for the moment he had something more pressing to deal with. Reg and Roger had been notified that their missing luggage had turned up at Liverpool Street station lost property offices a few days earlier. For their convenience, it had been transferred to Bury St. Edmunds station, from where they collected it that evening.

Reg's confidence over the exam results the next day was well founded, although receiving the confirmation still left him in a state of shock.

Saturday, 10th June 1944
Exam results 84%, and 91% for orals. [You] could have knocked me down with a sledgehammer. Very little work [was] done for the rest of the day.

In fact, very little work was done for the next two days and, whilst Reg and the crew were detailed to fly but couldn't, many others were up in the wide blue yonder.

Monday, 12th June 1944
We should have started flying on cine camera gun exercises this morning, but no aircraft were available. The weather was perfect for flying. The aerial activity during the morning was terrific, swarms of bombers and fighters passing overhead.

A Short Stirling bomber photographed at No.1653 Heavy Conversion Unit at RAF Chedburgh. Max Bourne and his crew experienced some terrifying moments flying these four-engine heavy bombers. *Courtesy of the Late Max Bourne*

It was not until late in the day on Wednesday afternoon that Reg experienced his first flight in a Short Stirling bomber, when he flew with Flying Officer Mason on a cine-camera (fighter affiliation) exercise with a Hawker Hurricane fighter as the target.

With the rest of his crew on leave, with the exception of Roger Humphrys, Reg flew again with Flying Officer Mason on a similar exercise the following Friday afternoon. Reg and Roger obviously took a school-boyish approach to the rest of the crew being given leave, and deemed to invoke their own form of retaliation.

Friday, 16th June 1944
[During the evening we] went to the drawing of the local Derby sweep, in which I am financially interested. The Derby is to be run at Newmarket tomorrow. Then at 11.00pm the rest of the crew returned from their 48 hours leave into a network of booby traps set by their enterprising gunners.

There is no record of how the two enterprising gunners took their revenge on the other members of the crew, and likewise, there is no record of how Reg's luck fared with regard to the Derby. Through the pages of his diary, it is known that Reg voiced his annoyance at not being allowed to go to Newmarket, which was only eleven miles from the base, to watch the race. Instead, he and the crew had to be content with listening to the broadcast on the radio.

Another important event not recorded in Reg's diary was the arrival of Sergeant William Vincent, who had joined Max Bourne's crew a few days earlier, as flight engineer. This omission was due to the simple fact that Reg's diaries had gone missing along with his luggage, and as such Reg was reduced to relying on a few scribbled notes and his logbook for that period, until the luggage was recovered. There is, however, no doubt that

Bill Vincent was certainly a member of the crew when Reg and the others commenced their flying training programme as a complete crew.

Tuesday, 20th June 1944
We began our flying programme this morning [starting just after] 10.00am and flew circuits and bumps until 3.00pm. [Made] my first flight in a mid-upper turret, which I am to occupy from now on and I am pleased with it.

For this flight, which lasted four hours and twenty-five minutes, Max Bourne was under the supervision of Flight Lieutenant Robert Waugh, an experienced Stirling bomber pilot who had completed a tour of operations with No.XV Squadron. On his tunic he wore the ribbon of a Distinguished Flying Cross, which had been awarded for his courage, coolness and determination in bringing his damaged aircraft home from an attack against Hamburg in July 1943. Likewise, the Stirling bomber in which they were flying, serial BK811, had seen operational service with No.90 Squadron, before being taken-on-charge by No.1653 Conversion Unit.

Wednesday, 21st June 1944
The whole crew did night vision tests all morning then, after lunch, began flying again and did not finish until 8.00p.m. During the afternoon we burst a tire while taxiing, and had to take another aircraft to finish the detail. Did our first solos in a Stirling today and we all have confidence in Max as our pilot.

Flying Officer Rhodes, another instructor, initially flew with Max, but later in the day sent the crew off on their own. Again, they completed an exercise lasting three and a half hours.
    The next day, with Max as captain of his own aircraft, the crew continued their practice of circuits and bumps. It came as some relief when the following day brought with it the culmination of the crews' circuit and bump day flying programme. This however meant that, although the ensuing week would be taken up with lectures, they still had to face the prospect of night flying circuits and bumps.

Tuesday, 27th June 1944
We did our final night vision test, taking all the morning and then, after lunch, had lectures. [Later in the evening] we walked down to our flight as we are to fly tonight. Took off at 10.30pm and flew to Woolfox Lodge, 60 miles from Chedburgh to do our first night circuits and bumps on Stirlings. We were still flying at midnight. We kept up the circuits and bumps until 3.00am then a tire went u/s, preventing our return to Chedburgh. The orderly sergeant was very decent about his unexpected guests and took us to the mess, where we had bacon and eggs, tea, toast and marmalade, while he fetched a stack of blankets, four each between nine of us. Then a bus ride to our temporary quarters.

When the crew awoke from their slumbers the following day, there was very low cloud and it was pouring with rain. Transport was provided to take them to lunch in the mess where they stayed until mid-afternoon. Due to the continuing inclement weather which canceled all flying activity, transport was again provided; this time to take Max and the crew back to Chedburgh, a journey Reg did not really look forward to.

Wednesday, 28th June 1944
The lousy weather put paid to flying for the rest of the day. So, we set off on the 100 mile, four and a half hour trip in the back seat of a bouncing bus (It's only fifteen minutes by air). Still, two stops for tea and sandwiches helped relieve the monotony. Now someone has to go back to collect the aircraft when the weather improves.

If Max and the crew thought the previous night had been bad enough, little did they know that there was worse to come the following night. As with the previous evening, the crew was detailed for night circuits and bumps, and again, these commenced at 10.30pm.

Thursday, 29th June 1944
We made our way down to flight [and] took off at 10.30pm. [It] turned out to be the most hair-raising night I've spent in the air. Twice we got caught in slipstreams and dived. Then another kite (aircraft) almost collided with ours, making the pilot dive, intentionally this time, from 1,000feet [down] to 200 feet, definitely not a safe margin with a four engine aircraft. Everything moveable, including the navigator and engineer, floated about inside the fuselage then crashed to the floor in confusion. [Fortunately] we finished the detail without further incident.

The next few days were relatively quiet for Max and the crew, then they were given four days' leave, which turned out not to be so quiet after all.

Sunday, 2nd July 1944
After breakfast, we enquired whether we were needed for duty and found we had [been granted] four days leave. Max is going to London to finalise getting his commission, which came through this morning. After lunch we packed up and set off in the car [traveling] via Bury, Newmarket and Epping Forest. We got to London at 9.30pm and ably guided by our ex-bus driver flight engineer, Bill Vincent, soon found the Codger's Club (known to all Aussies in London), where we celebrated our safe arrival (as though they needed an excuse). Bill left us [in town] and we got rooms at the Victoria League Club in Vauxhall Bridge Road, where we had the luxury of [soaking in] a hot bath.

Scarcely had Reg's head touched the pillow that night when the sirens went off, alerting the city of an impending air raid. His diary continued:

… the sirens sounded and fifteen seconds later we saw our first flying bomb, which soon after exploded some distance away. It was followed at regular intervals by about fifteen others (that we heard explode), the last one just before breakfast. [Later in the day], we had lunch at Bush House restaurant in the Aldwych. A bug (short for Doodlebug, another name for a V1 flying bomb) landed in Aldwych last Wednesday, quite close to Australia House and did a lot of damage.

The Aldwych is, as any regular visitor to London knows, not far from Trafalgar Square, the Admiralty Arch, the Royal Mall and Buckingham Palace. All are places on any tourist's agenda and, although not strictly a tourist, Reg took himself off to visit these attractions of which he had heard so much. He was not, however, very impressed with Saville Row, famous for its tailors and quality suits.

The next day Reg, Max and Paul set off in the car and headed for Chessington, Surrey, to catch up with Bill Vincent. Unfortunately, when they arrived at his home he was out, so the trio hung around in a local café for a while before returning to the house, but as Bill was still out, they drove back to London. Whilst driving through the suburbs they saw plenty of evidence of the damage inflicted by the flying bombs, from smashed windows and shattered roofs to complete destruction.

The following day, there was more V1 activity, at a very inopportune moment, as Reg recorded.

Wednesday, 5th July 1944
[We] returned to the Victoria League Club, and who should be visiting but the Duke of Gloucester. He received a very warm welcome, for just as he stepped from his Rolls [Rolls Royce car] a flying bomb landed a couple of blocks away, wrecking about eight houses and damaging about forty-five others. However, the Duke, red in face, inspected the club, asked us all in turn two stock questions and then left. [Later] we took a walk in the area west of Vauxhall Bridge Road, where the Duke's bomb went off. Some people were still buried in the rubble, while others were gathering up bedding and carrying it to the City [Town] Hall to spend the night there. The majority made light of their troubles, but some were still too shocked to know what had happened. A burst gas main [also] hindered rescuers.

Having slept soundly, and woken up at 7.00am, Reg tried to entice Max and Paul out of their beds for an early start, but to no avail. It may have been the last day of their leave, but both of them were staying put a while longer. Reg went off to wash and shave, before returning for a second assault on the sleeping pair.

Having got everything packed before they went out, they set off to conclude any outstanding items of business at the Royal Australian Air Force Stores in Kean Street, off Kingsway. Lunch at the Boomerang Club and a show at the Prince of Wales Theater followed this. After the show the trio went back to the Victoria League Club, collected their luggage and returned to the Boomerang Club to await the arrival of both Bill and Roger. Although Bill Vincent turned up soon after 5.00pm, there was still no sign of Roger by 6.30pm, so they left and headed back to Chedburgh without him.

Back at base, there was little, or nothing, for the crew to do over the next two days, apart from catch up on letter writing, do some laundry or go to the cinema. However, it was all back to normal by the following Sunday.

Sunday, 9th July 1944
At 11.00am we took off on a five and a half hour, cross-country exercise. The route took us north to the Firth of Forth, then way out over the North Sea and back over the Wash. The weather turned bad and low cloud and driving rain forced the skipper to call the exercise

off and return to base, soon after re-crossing the coast. We landed at 3.45pm sending clouds of spray off the runway as we touched down.

Although Max was a commissioned officer, with a number of flying hours to his credit the above recorded trip seems to have been undertaken with an instructor, Flying Officer Ralph, on board the aircraft. Likewise, a similar exercise undertaken the following Tuesday, may well have been carried out in the same manner, when F/O Ralph was again recorded by Reg as being on the flight.

Tuesday, 11th July 1944
We took off at 11.30pm and spent the next five and a half hours cruising about via Land's End, the Scilly Isles, South Wales and the Midlands.

The entry, re-dated 12th July, continued:

We arrived back at Chedburgh at 3.45am and without landing were sent off on a bombing exercise for nearly an hour. After debriefing, we had some breakfast before tumbling into bed.

The following Friday was a real jinxed day for Pilot Officer Max Bourne and his crew and, although it was not Friday, 13th, it was very close to being so in more ways than one.

Friday, 14th July 1944
We arrived back at base at 1.30am (from the previous night's exercise) and had to circle for two hours whilst an obstruction was cleared from the runway. We landed at 3.20am and after parking our flying gear, had some breakfast. [Later] we waited all afternoon at flight to fly on a gunnery exercise, which was canceled so we could attend briefing at 4.30pm for tonight's flying. Then everything seemed to be going wrong. The flying plan was changed five times, causing a mad rush at the last minute to get everything ready for take-off. We arrived at dispersal at 11.30pm to find the aircraft u/s and after hurried repairs, taxied out [only to have] the skipper u/s it again before take-off and return to dispersal. We changed on to the reserve aircraft, taxied out and found the radio u/s, but our wireless operator fixed it and we took off. It became evident there was something wrong before we were airborne, for the port wing failed to lift. We bounced along the length of the runway on the port undercarriage and pulled it up just in time to skip over the fence. The kite [aircraft] was almost out of control in the air. The skipper called base urgently and they had the runway cleared in record time [for] us to land immediately. The pilot and bomb aimer were both hanging on to the controls for dear life, and after a hectic half circuit made a terrific landing with a thirty foot bounce lasting ten seconds. We were all sweating and didn't waste any time in getting back to dispersal and reporting the problem.

Pilot Officer Bourne justifiably had strong reservations about the Short Stirling as a training aircraft.

Serviceability was a problem, which led to a few harrowing experiences, and we were in the serious business of long cross-country flights day and night, often with a visit to a bombing range to drop practice bombs; fighter affiliation, when we would be 'attacked' by a fighter with a camera gun. Our gunners would inform the pilot of the attack with the words "fighter, fighter, corkscrew starboard (or port), go." Sometimes in a real life combat situation, one of the words 'Fighter' might be exchanged for something more lurid. The corkscrew maneuvres were very effective if the enemy plane was seen early enough, so the vigilance of the gunners' was actually more important than their ability to aim their guns. The series of dives and turns placed a big strain on the aircraft and its occupants.

Although a one hour camera gun exercise was carried out during the afternoon of Saturday, 15th, when Max and the crew arrived at dispersal for their night flying exercise they found not one aircraft unserviceable but four! After four hours of waiting around at dispersal, they were informed that their detail had been canceled. It was 03.30 hours before they got to bed.

Sunday, 16th July 1944
Slept until 12.00 noon and then [got up] and had a greasy lunch. Later we saw yesterday's films at the projection room. At 3.00pm we took off on another cine gun exercise for an hour and a half, getting back just in time for the briefing again.

The crew had tea and then wandered back to the hut, where they all relaxed until 8.30pm, when they had to get ready for another flight. The day, which had been hot and sticky, inducing all sorts of insects to commit suicide on the perspex of the aircraft, was not over yet.

After briefing, we collected our flying gear and went by bus to [the] dispersal area. [Climbed aboard the aircraft] and took off on our last cross-country flight from Chedburgh.

This last flight from No.1653 Heavy Conversion Unit, took the crew to Newcastle via the Humber estuary, during which time they did an affiliation exercise with searchlights and T.I.'s. They arrived safely back at base at 03.30am on the Monday morning.

Monday, 17th July 1944
All slept until 12.00 [noon], then had some lunch. Later we were informed that our programme at Chedburgh was finished and we are to get five days leave.

The crew spent the afternoon rushing around getting signatures for clearance, and ensuring everything was officially in order. Then, after tea, they all commenced packing their kit, an activity that went on until midnight.

Tuesday, 18th July 1944
No one woke until 8.15am and a rush began to get breakfast [before it finished] at 8.30am. We then finalised the clearance. At 5.30pm the remaining four of us set off in the Rover for London.

Having made their own plans, Bill Vincent and Arthur Bourne left Max, Paul, Reg and Roger to set off in the car. However, Roger only went as far as Bury St. Edmunds station, where he was dropped off to catch a train. Following a stop at Newmarket for tea, Max then put his foot down and the trio headed for London, where they arrived at 9.30pm. Paul and Reg were dropped off at the Victoria League Club, whilst Max drove on to his club. However, it was not to be a totally satisfactory night for the three 'Aussies.'

Wednesday, 19th July 1944

The [air raid] sirens sounded before we got to bed [last night]. Then a flying bomb passed over at 12.30am followed by three more, [all of which] landed in quick succession, the last one rattling the windows and shaking the beds.

Having eventually fallen asleep and later awoken from their slumbers, Reg and Paul dressed, had breakfast and then went by tram and underground train to Australia House for lunch. Whilst they were there, Max rang to say that after he had dropped them off the previous evening and was negotiating his way around Trafalgar Square, the car's transmission packed up! Later that same day, Reg set off to Harpenden, south of Luton, to meet up with a cousin, with whom he was to spend a few days.

Rising early on the following Saturday morning, Reg said his good-byes and headed for the station to catch the 09.00am train back to London. Max, Paul and Roger were waiting for him at Australia House, where to his, and everyone else's relief, Reg was informed that the car had been fixed and was roadworthy again.

After an afternoon spent at the cinema in Leicester Square, and an evening spent visiting both the Boomerang Club and the Codger's Club, Max returned to his own club, whilst Reg, Roger and Paul made the way back to the Victoria League Club. The latter journey was made with Paul acting as navigator, with a map and a little help from a London policeman.

Sunday, 23rd July 1944

[We were] up at 8.00am for we are off to L.F.S. at Feltwell in Norfolk today. After breakfast we drove to Australia House to meet Max and have lunch. Then we set off and saw a block of wrecked flats in Lea Bridge Road, on the way out of London.

Lea Bridge Road is a long, straight road leading out of the east side of London, which heads in the general direction of Epping Forest; the latter being a former medieval Royal Hunting Ground for the Monarchy and a recreational area for latter day east Londoners.

The crew's route then continued out through Essex and into Suffolk, where they stopped at Bury St.Edmunds to collect some luggage which had been deposited when they had dropped Roger off six days earlier. Their journey continued on through Thetford and Brandon to RAF Feltwell, where No.3 Lancaster Finishing School was located. Unusually for a military camp, Reg recorded in his diary that the crew was actually made welcome at the guardhouse, where the sentry provided them with tea, whilst checking them in, before they went off to collect blankets for their own particular bunks, and to get settled in.

4

No.3 Lancaster Finishing School

Lea Bridge Road was not only the crew's route out of London it was also a road that led them into a completely new era, at No.3 Lancaster Finishing School. They were now on the last few days of their training and, at No.3 L.F.S., they would also learn to fly the type of aircraft in which they were to go to war, the Avro Lancaster bomber.

RAF Feltwell, situated approximately five miles northwest of Brandon, was a grass airfield that had opened in 1937. During April that same year, No.214 equipped with Handley Page Harrow aircraft took up residence and shortly afterward a flight from this squadron was taken to form No.37 Squadron. Both squadrons operated alongside each other, flying the same aircraft, for the next two years (until May 1939), when they were re-equipped with Vickers Wellington bombers. Over the next few years, various charges were made at RAF Feltwell, with regards to the base itself and the units that operated from it. At the end of 1943, with more and more squadrons converting to Avro Lancaster bombers, RAF Feltwell became the home of No.3 Lancaster Finishing School. This in turn was to become the home of Reg Heffron and the rest of the crew for just over a week.

Monday, 24th July 1944
[It was] back to camp routine today. After breakfast we began a four day ground course of lectures. At lunch time we collected the last of our gear and then back to lectures in the afternoon.

For Reg and the crew, the day was very reminiscent of their first days of training. Having endured a full day of ground lectures, the evening was spent having tea and writing letters home, followed by supper then off to bed at 11.00pm. The only thing different was that, being towards the end of July, they did not have to do battle with a fire in the hut stove.

The following few days all took the same pattern, lectures in the morning, lunch followed by more lectures in the afternoon, than catching up with some personal chores. However, on the Wednesday afternoon, there was a clay pigeon shoot, which everybody enjoyed.

Thursday, 27th July 1944
We had our final tests this morning, with good results for all of us, so we got the afternoon off.

No.3 Lancaster Finishing School

A poor quality photograph showing the Parade Ground and Barrack Blocks at RAF Feltwell, Norfolk. *Author's Collection*

Four of the crew, including Reg, wasted no time in jumping into the car and setting off for Downham Market, a small market town on a hill overlooking the Fens and situated to the northwest of Feltwell. The first thing that attracted their attention upon arrival in the town was a small shop selling baskets of strawberries. Purchases were made and the items quickly consumed. They then found a café on the main street where they consumed sausages, eggs, tomatoes and fries. This was then followed by raspberries and cream, which was equally enjoyed. Presumably feeling quite bloated, the crew then took solace in a cinema, where they sat and rested for the afternoon, whilst watching a film (ironically) entitled, 'Standing Room Only'!

By the time they left the cinema, Downham Market was deserted with not a soul to be seen. They jumped into the car and headed back to Feltwell, but on the way back the car broke down; the transmission had gone again. Leaving the stricken machine in a shed (Reg does not record whether they had the owner's consent or not), they set off on foot to walk the seven miles back to camp. However, they soon managed to get a lift in a RAF Transport vehicle, which took them to within a mile of Feltwell. Once back in the town, they headed straight for a café, where they ate platefuls of hot fries and downed cups of tea. This as Reg later recorded, "gave us strength for the last half mile back to camp and bed at midnight."

Friday, 28th July 1944
Our final lectures finished at 10.00am after which we had a talk on the Middle East by a Cambridge professor, the end of which was the signal for a rush for the lunch queue. After lunch our crew flew in a Lancaster for the first time, and gained a very good impression.

With the amount of food Max, Reg and the other crew members seemed to be consuming, it was a wonder the aircraft got off the ground, but fly it did. Their programme for the afternoon consisted of circuits and bumps, which were undertaken at RAF Witchford, an airfield a few minutes by air to the southwest of Feltwell. Initially, Flying Officer Mckenna flew as first pilot, with Max as second pilot, but later in the afternoon the roles were reversed when Max took control of Lancaster bomber, L7532. The latter was very impressed with the handling of the Lancaster and for Max, apart from the noise, it was love at first sight. There must have been a number of young airmen who thought the same as Max, but this particular 'Lady' had a chequered past. The aircraft, built by Avro at Manchester, had already seen a lot of service and was to see a lot more. Prior to being Taken-on-Charge by No.3 L.F.S, the aircraft had flown with No.44 Squadron, No.97 Squadron, No.97 Conversion Flight, No.61 Squadron, No.61 Conversion Flight, No.50 Squadron, No.207 Squadron and No.1654 Conversion Unit. After it had been Struck-off-Charge with No.3 L.F.S., it went on to serve with both No.90 Squadron and No.1656 Conversion Unit, before finally being Struck-off-Charge on 16th October 1946.

Saturday, 29th July 1944
Nothing much to do in the morning but after lunch we did some solo circuits and bumps on our own 'drome, finishing at 8.00pm. Then a late tea and back for night flying at 9.15pm.

Although the crew returned for their briefing at 9.15pm, they did not take off until around 11.00pm, when they carried out more circuits and bumps. This exercise lasted for one-and-a half hours. By the time the crew had shut down the aircraft, returned to the operations block for a de-briefing and then had a very early breakfast, it was well into the early hours of Sunday morning. In fact they did not get to bed until 03.30 hours.

Sunday, 30th July 1944
Slept until 11.00am, then off for lunch. In the afternoon, at 4.00pm, we started a fighter affiliation exercise lasting about forty-five minutes. Back in time for tea which finished the day's business. Max and Paul worked on the car to get it going again.

One of the course instructors, Flying Officer Yates, flew as second pilot to Max Bourne on the fighter affiliation exercise, and watched closely as Max corkscrewed the bomber around the skies in an endeavour to shake off the 'attacking' Hurricane fighter. The mock fight lasted for twenty-five minutes after which Max changed places with F/O Yates, who then took the crew through a similar exercise lasting a further twenty-five minutes. Although the aircraft, Avro Lancaster, W4885, in which the crew flew both these exercises, had been employed in the training role for part of its service, it had also flown in the combat role with No.XV Squadron and No.622 Squadron, prior to returning to the former role.

Monday, 31st July 1944
Had the morning off until 12.00 [noon] then [had a] briefing for a cross-country trip this afternoon. Had lunch then took off at 2.40pm.

For this exercise, having taken-off from RAF Feltwell Max turned Lancaster, L7532, onto a westerly heading, towards the Midlands. Having reached the first pinpoint, he altered course north-northeast to Darlington. Guided by his namesake, Arthur Bourne, the navigator, Max then turned the bomber out over the North Sea and flew across a vast expanse of water, as he was to do many times on operational missions in the immediate future. Again, when instructed by Arthur, Max turned the aircraft on a southwesterly course to cross the coast over the Norfolk/Suffolk border. Having reached the final turning point of Rushford, they turned in on finals to RAF Feltwell, where they landed at 6.30pm. The flight, during which Max climbed the aircraft to an altitude of 20,000,' had lasted three hours and fifty minutes. Reg recorded this milestone in his diary as being, "The highest I have been to date."

Following debriefing the crew, all of whom seemed to have voracious appetites, headed to the Mess for tea, before heading off to the camp cinema to see a film entitled, 'Best Foot Forward.' Given that Max Bourne and his crew had completed their course, flown their last exercise at No.3 Lancaster Finishing School and were declared ready for operational flying, the title of the film seemed fairly apt. It was also apt that, on this same day, Max was promoted in the rank of Acting Flying Officer.

Tuesday, 1st August 1944
This morning our crew was posted to No.622 Squadron, at RAF Mildenhall. We spent the morning getting clearances, then after lunch (3.00pm) went into Feltwell and bought a six-cylinder Wolseley on the spur of the moment. Feeling rather pleased with our selves we drove it back to camp.

Once back at Feltwell, Reg and the crew packed their gear into the waiting transport and left for Mildenhall, where they arrived at 7.00pm. Having reported in at the Guardhouse, they collected bedding, etc., were allotted billets and then had supper in the Mess.

No.622 Squadron

The RAF Station at Mildenhall, situated between the villages of Beck Row on the north side and West Row on the southwest side, was established during peacetime and, although the work had not been completed, the Station Headquarters was officially opened on 16th October 1934.

On 13th January 1937, RAF Mildenhall became home to No.3 (Bomber) Group, when it moved its headquarters from Andover, Hampshire, where it had been formed almost a year earlier. No.3 Group H.Q. was to occupy the same building on the base for thirty years, finally relinquishing its tenure when 3 Group was disbanded in 1967.

Originally, the airfield had been constructed with three grass runways, but when the base closed for refurbishment and upgrading at the end of 1942, three concrete runways were laid down. The site also had three hangars, an Officers' Mess, brick built barrack accommodation blocks for single men and brick built married quarters. It was into the latter that Reg and four other member of the crew were billeted. Reg shared a room with Roger, Arthur billeted with Bill, whilst Paul had his own room. Max Bourne and Tom Brown, having been commissioned, were accommodated in the Officers' Mess that, quite conveniently, was situated adjacent to the Bird in Hand Hotel. The allotted accommodation at RAF Mildenhall was superior to anything Max and his crew had known previously during their training. Max was so impressed he was given to write:

… [We] arrived at Mildenhall to join No.622 Squadron. What a wonderful station after some of the freezing Quanson huts we had lived in for the past year. Peacetime built brick buildings. The crew, except for Tom and me were accommodated in a 2 level flat, which in peacetime would have housed an NCO or other rank and his family. It had fireplaces, some cooking facilities and a bathroom – the boys were in heaven. Tom and I were dispatched to the Officers' Mess, much like a gentleman's club. [It was] all very civilised.

Whilst pleased with his new accommodation, Reg was less energetic in his writing, and in a matter of fact way merely noted:

… We are living in two storied houses, two or three to a room with our own bathroom and all mod cons. Anyway, after supper, we got our gear straightened out and hopped into bed at midnight …

However, the following morning there seemed to be a little more sparkle in his writing.

A photograph of the Station Headquarters at RAF Mildenhall, built in 1933, which stands adjacent to the original main entrance of the airfield. *Courtesy of Gary Wenko*

The 3 Group Headquarters building which was in use as such, with RAF Bomber Command, for thirty years. *Courtesy of Gary Wenko*

This building was completed in 1933 as the Station Headquarters and sits adjacent to the original main gate. The nearby earth-bermed building (Bldg 559) was completed prior to World War II as the Wartime Operations Centre.

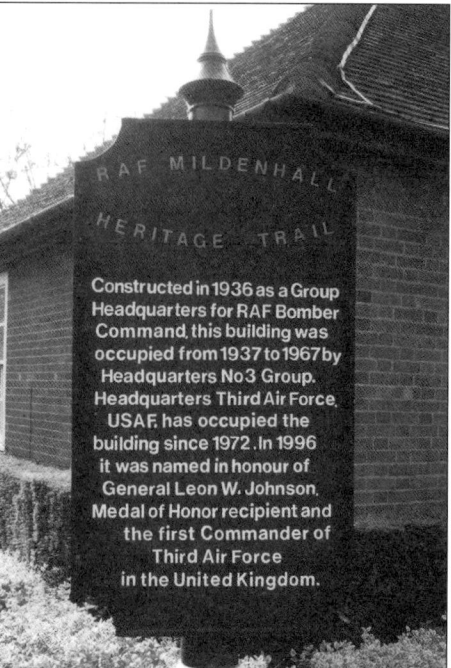

Constructed in 1936 as a Group Headquarters for RAF Bomber Command, this building was occupied from 1937 to 1967 by Headquarters No 3 Group. Headquarters Third Air Force, USAF, has occupied the building since 1972. In 1996 it was named in honour of General Leon W. Johnson, Medal of Honor recipient and the first Commander of Third Air Force in the United Kingdom.

Left: The RAF Mildenhall Heritage Trail information plaque erected by the United States Air Force to commemorate the history of the former RAF Station Headquarters. *Courtesy of Gary Wenko* Right: The RAF Mildenhall Heritage Trail information plaque gives a detailed history of the building's use, before and after World War II. *Courtesy of Gary Wenko*

Flight Sergeant Bob Kerr (extreme left), a pilot with No.622 Squadron, utilizes the fence outside a married quarters block at RAF Mildenhall for a crew photograph. *Author's Collection*

Apart from the fence being removed, and one or two other modifications, the married quarters at RAF Mildenhall remain relatively unchanged. *Courtesy of Gary Wenko*

Wednesday 2nd August 1944
Up at 7.30am for a change and made good use of our private bathroom. Then went to breakfast, after which we began the long business of interviews and arrival formalities. This went on until 4.30pm.

Reg made no further comment in his diary about his interview; however, Max well remembers his first meeting with the Officer Commanding No.622 Squadron.

[I was] called in for interview with the Officer Commanding the Squadron. I read on his door, Wing Commander I.C.K. Swales, DSO, DFC, DFM. This was no ordinary man. The DFM indicated that he had done his first tour of thirty operations, or at least part of it, as a sergeant pilot. He was on his third tour, a total of sixty-nine operations till then, when I met him. He told me that we would probably dispense with the customary 'Second Dickey' operation but would find me a nice daylight trip to do own my own. He also said, indicating his ribbons, that there were no easily won decorations on 622 Squadron. Finally, he promised dire consequences for anyone who messed up his record for putting up the most aircraft whenever a 'maximum effort' was ordered by Base H.Q. I was to find out more about this later.

Ian Clifford Kirby Swales, known affectionately as 'Blondie' due to his fair hair, was indeed no ordinary man, especially when it came to flying, fighting and qualities of leadership. He had been awarded the Distinguished Flying Medal whilst serving with No.38 Squadron, for an action that occurred on the 22nd October 1940, when his Wellington bomber was attacked by a German night-fighter. Sergeant Swales had completed his bombing run and was heading for home, when enemy cannon fire ripped through his twin-engine bomber. A shell exploded inside the fuselage, seriously injuring the rear gunner. Although the hydraulic system was rendered useless, 'Blondie' Swales piloted the aircraft over 350 miles back to its base, where he landed it successfully. The award of his Distinguished Flying Medal was published in the London Gazette on 22nd October 1940, six days after he had been commissioned in the rank of Pilot Officer. Having completed a total of thirty-two operational sorties, he was rested and posted to an Operational Training Unit as an instructor.

On 8th August 1941, P/O Swales was posted from No.11 Operational Training Unit to No.XV Squadron, based at RAF Wyton, where he flew a tour of operations on Stirling bombers. Whilst serving with No.XV, he was promoted in the rank of Flying Officer and awarded a Distinguished Flying Cross. The award of the DFC was gazetted on 13th March 1942. A month later, on 12th April, he was posted to No.15 Conversion Flight, in the rank of Flight Lieutenant.

On 1st February 1944, Wing Commander Ian Swales, DFC, DFM, assumed command of No.622 Squadron, a position he was to hold until 19th October 1944. The official announcement of his Distinguished Service Order was published in the London Gazette on 7th November 1944. He retired from the Royal Air Force on 17th January 1968, in the rank of Group Captain.

Thursday, 3rd August 1944
We were engaged at stores all morning collecting [and signing for] our gear. As we had the afternoon off, we went in the Wolseley to Mildenhall and Newmarket in search of spare parts for the car. We then went to Ely, in the Fens, where there is a beautiful cathedral.

The Wolseley had become the pride and joy of Reg and his crew, with a lot of care and attention being lavished on it. The previous evening, following their interviews, they spent two hours polishing it.

Friday, 4th August 1944
After breakfast, we collected our parachutes and harnesses and, at 1.00pm, ferried a Lancaster to Feltwell, about five minutes flying time from Mildenhall. We had lunch there and then spent about an hour reading in the mess, waiting for transport back to Mildenhall.

The crew's first flight out of RAF Mildenhall, albeit on a local ferry flight, was aboard Avro Lancaster, ED430, GI-A. This aircraft had previously seen service with No.90 Squadron and No.50 Squadron before being taken-on-charge by No.622 Squadron. It was to finish its war service at No.3 Lancaster Finishing School, before being struck-off-charge on 7th February 1947.

The trip back to Mildenhall was by RAF truck, the driver of which was cajoled into towing Max's now derelict Rover car back to their new quarters. The fact they had found a nest with two hens' eggs on the back seat shows just how long the vehicle had been standing idle.

That evening they spent another two hours polishing the Wolseley, before falling upon the Rover in an effort to find out why it would not go. By nightfall, the ground outside their accommodation was littered with wheels, an axle, drive shaft and casing, all splashed with spilt oil. They had almost completely dissected the car, but still couldn't find out the cause

Wing Commander Ian 'Blondie' Swales, DSO, DFC, DFM, Officer Commanding No.622 Squadron (seated center), with his senior flight commanders, at RAF Mildenhall. *Author's Collection*

of the problem and were forced by darkness to give up the task. There was, God willing, always tomorrow.

Saturday, 5th August 1944
Spent the morning at stores collecting more equipment, then visited the dentist and the doctor for [various] checks. After lunch, it was back to the stores for a further two hours. [After an early tea] it was back to the Rover.

Having accumulated numerous nuts and bolts to add to the already large number of parts scattered around the Rover, the cause of the trouble was eventually located, "fixed" and all the parts put back. Then came the moment of truth: Max climbed into the car, turned the ignition key and 'VROOM.' A great cheer announced the old bus was mobile again, subject of course to a test run. Finally, before turning in that night, Reg wrote in his diary "Much soap went down the drain before going to bed."

Sunday, 6th August 1944
Roger and I spent the morning cleaning guns. Then at 12.30pm we did an hours fighter affiliation exercise. After a late lunch, we took off on a practice climb with full bomb and petrol loads. [We] flew to Goole, on the Humber, then out over the North Sea and re-crossing the coast at Flamborough Head.

The fighter affiliation was carried out under the watchful eye of Flight Lieutenant Norman V. Gill, an experienced bomber pilot who had recently been recommended for the award of a DFC, which was gazetted on 14th November 1944.

The load climb exercise, which commenced at 6.00pm, was carried out solely by the crew, without an 'official' observer on board. Having reached the extent of the outward leg, Tom Brown, the bomb aimer, released the bomb load into the sea before Max turned the Lancaster onto a new heading. The flight, however, did not go without a hitch, for whilst they were flying over the sea, one of the crew noticed a petrol leak. Sergeant Bill Vincent, the flight engineer, very quickly dealt with the problem by adjusting the fuel cocks and changing the tanks. They landed back at Mildenhall, having completed a two-hour flight.

Monday, 7th August 1944
'Erk' came to our house and roused us at 8.45am and a rush began to be at the gunnery section on time. Arriving there, [we] were given D.I.'s (daily inspections) to do on our turrets, for we are listed for operational flying tonight. Then a rush began to complete the [tasks] by 12.00 noon. After lunch there were more preparations, then at teatime the operation was canceled.

The term 'erk' applied throughout the Royal Air Force to members of groundcrew who worked on aircraft, new recruits or those below the rank of Aircraftman 1st Class. There are various thoughts as to the origin of this term, one being that it is abbreviation and degradation of the words 'air mechanic.' However, in this particular case, the term 'Erk' was the 'nick-name' applied to Flight Sergeant Herbert Keith Coombe, a twenty-year-old Australian air gunner, from Broken Hill in New South Wales.

'Erk' was a particularly good friend of Arthur and Reg and was given his 'nick-name' due to his squat appearance. Being only about 5'2" tall, with a happy-go-lucky attitude, he was always smiling and was, apparently, a 'right little erk.'

'Erk' or Keith, as he was otherwise known, flew as rear gunner with George Williamson and his crew, all of whom were well known and well liked by Max Bourne and his crew. In fact, their respective friendships were made during their training days, when the two crews were posted to the same training units. Arthur Bourne, it will be remembered, first met Kenny Turner (F/L Williamson's navigator), when they were both under training at No.48 Air Navigation School, at Colindale, South Africa. Thereafter, fate took them both to Scotland, then on to Wing, where Arthur crewed-up with Max Bourne and Kenny crewed-up with George Williamson. The two crews then went via Heavy Conversion Unit at RAF Chedburgh; Lancaster Finishing School at RAF Feltwell to RAF Mildenhall, where George Williamson's crew was posted to No.XV Squadron on 5th August five days after Max's crew had been posted to the same station to join No.622 Squadron. On the same day that he reported for duty with No.XV Squadron, Sergeant George Williamson was granted a commission in the rank of Pilot Officer.

The feelings of apprehension and tension, which built up during the day, and the frustrations of waiting around for nothing, were released later in the evening by Roger Humphrys, who entered into a two-hour long wrestling match, with 'Erk.' Much to Reg's chagrin, the battling pair managed to wreck Roger and Reg's bedroom. Arthur was

Sergeant Reg Heffron (left) and Sergeant Roger Humphrys (right) pose for a photograph with their good friend Sergeant Keith 'Erk' Coombe, at RAF Mildenhall during 1944. *Courtesy of the Late Arthur Bourne*

surprised the bout lasted so long, given Keith's height against the fact that Roger was approximately 6'0" tall.

Although Max and his crew still had yet to undertake their first operational combat mission, Arthur had obviously thought about what was to come and the possible consequences. In his diary, on two adjoining pages, he wrote some precise notes which, on the first page read:

Acknowledge. Leave seat and warn W/Op.
Go forward & release A/B from turret.

Fit pack from stowage. Remove
helmet & follow A/B from rear
hatch head first

On the adjacent page was written:-

At main spar to turret. Seated facing forward,
feet braced against bulkhead.'

Warn W/Op Nav ditching.
Release A/B switch on bomb bay lights, remove
parachute harness.

Receive fix, pass surface wind velocity to pilot.
Prepare chart and pass with expected ditching
point to wireless operator.

*On reaching ditching station, slap W/Op on
shoulder and move to O.S.*

The above quoted entries obviously related to the necessary procedures required to be undertaken, by Arthur, in the event of having to bail out of an aircraft or ditching in the sea respectively.

Tuesday, 8th August 1944

Operation No.1. (Doullens)
Petrol and Oil Dump
We were told during the morning that we would be required for 'ops' tonight, so spent practically the whole day cleaning guns etc. and making preparations. After tea we went to briefing, [where] we were told the target was an oil dump hidden in a wood near Doullens in France.

The Squadron detailed fifteen aircraft for the attack, which comprised depots and storage dumps situated in the Foret de Lucheux, to the north east of Doullens. At approximately 21.50 hours, having completed his cockpit checks and received the assurances of each crewmember that both they and their equipment were 'fit for action,' Max Bourne pushed forward the throttles of Lancaster, LL803, GI-G, which thundered down the runway and climbed into the night sky. As Max later put it, "There we were, off into the wide dark yonder on our first operation."

The route out was on a southerly heading by way of Reading, Berkshire, and out over the Channel coast. Of that crossing Max recorded:

Approaching the enemy coast, we soon figured out that the twinkling specks of light ahead were red-hot shrapnel from exploding anti-aircraft shells – FLAK. We'd seen searchlights before, friendly ones of course though.

Arthur, the navigator, had other reasons to remember the Channel crossing, unfortunately much to the detriment of Bill Vincent, the flight engineer.

At the time, we were taking Cod Liver Oil tablets, one a day, but Bill thought that if one tablet was good for you, six would be even better. As we approached the French coast, the effects of the pills kicked-in. Unfortunately, Bill failed to make it to the Elsan [chemical toilet at the rear of the aircraft] by quite a distance. At one point he was seen wearing only his battle dress blouse.

To add to Bill's indignation, Arthur and Paul could not resist taking the 'mickey.' They hoped, for Bill's sake, they would not find it necessary to bail out of the aircraft, as it would have been "a bit cold around the nether-regions."

Acting Flying Officer Max Bourne could see the markers going down as he was making his approach to the target. Approximately two hours after take-off, according to the Operational Record Book, Pilot Officer Tom Brown, the bomb aimer, pressed the 'tit' and eighteen 500lb bombs rained down from 12,000.' With some trepidation, on this first operation, Max held the Lancaster steady as the on-board camera automatically took the aiming point photograph, showing where their bombs had fallen. He then pushed the control column forward and put the aircraft into a shallow dive, as for a heart-stopping moment, he flew through a belt of searchlights. Fortunately, the probing beams did not stay with the Lancaster, but swept aimlessly into another part of the night sky.

As the aircraft roared on through the darkness, and crossed the French coast, Flight Sergeant Roger Humphrys, from the tight confines of his rear turret, was able to watch the raging fires send clouds of dense smoke high up into the sky; the first time he had witnessed such a spectacle. He also saw the weaving arms of the enemy searchlights sweeping across the night sky, before the beams momentarily swept across the Lancaster. With the beams overshooting their target, Max held the Lancaster steady on a course out over the sea and headed for home.

The Channel crossing went without incident and they crossed the English coast over Worthing, Sussex. At 01.25 hours on the morning of 9th August, Lancaster, LL803, touched down at RAF Mildenhall and, following interrogation by the Intelligence Officer, the crew tucked into eggs and bacon before retiring to bed at 3.45am.

Of their first operation, Max Bourne recorded, "There were no dramas. Our target photo showed that we had scored an aiming point, i.e. an accurate drop" then added in a nonchalant manner, "There were a few small flak holes in the aircraft." It may not have been a daylight 'op' as implied by Wing Commander Swales, at Max's interview, but it was a relatively easy target, as was the crew's second mission.

Arthur Bourne simply wrote in his notebook: "Uneventful."

Wednesday, 9th August 1944

Operation No.2
Flying-bomb Storage Sites
After lunch, Roger and I went off to the gunnery section, and then to the intelligence library for an hour. [We] then went out to dispersals to check on our aircraft, E-Easy, as we are on the Battle Order for tonight. We had our pre-flight supper at 7.15pm followed by briefing at 8.00pm. We then went out to the aircraft at 9.00pm and, after a delay (to the whole Squadron) took off at 10.25pm. We crossed the French coast on the tail end of the [bomber] stream and found the target well illuminated by markers and flares. [We] got our bombs away bang on target and turned [out] across the Belgian frontier and then for home. We had two warnings of predicted flak on the way out, and also dodged a cone of searchlights and two 'strays.'

Max Bourne, piloting Lancaster bomber, LM577, GI-E, took off at 22.05 hours. The Lancaster slowly lumbered up into the darkening sky to join the formation of aircraft above, before setting course for the target.

The target comprised four launching sites and the 'flying-bomb' storage facility at Fort-d'Englos, on the outskirts of Lille, near the French-Belgian border. An attacking force of 311 aircraft, including fifteen Lancaster bombers from No.622 Squadron, set out and accurately bombed the targets. On approaching the target area Max held 'Easy' on a steady bombing run, at an altitude of 11,000.' A pall of smoke, together with a sea of burning yellow target indicators marked the aiming point. At 23.21 hours, Tom Brown released the bomb load, which joined the conflagration already burning below. With their cargo unleashed, Max hauled the Lancaster round onto a heading for home. All participating aircraft in this attack returned safely to their respective bases.

Roger Humphrys, in the rear turret, was not treated to an illuminated display to equal that which he had witnessed the previous night, when crossing the coast. Again, the flight home was without incident and they reached Mildenhall safely, where they were last to land at 01.05 hours. Having taxied Lancaster, LM577, GI-E, back to its dispersal area, Max shut down the engines and returned the aircraft to its rightful 'owners'; the groundcrew.

Thursday, 10th August 1944
Slept until lunch time and then took off at 4.00pm for an H2S exercise over East Anglia and the Wash. Landed at 5.30pm.

Although No.1 Group and No.8 Group undertook operations all other Groups in Bomber Command were stood-down on this particular day. No.622 Squadron therefore took the opportunity of detailing some of its crews for local flying or various navigational exercises etc. Max Bourne and his crew undertook an H2S exercise, flying E-Easy again, which lasted one and a half hours. H2S was an airborne radar aid to navigators, which gave a reading of the ground layout, including towns, rivers and lakes etc of an area of several miles around the overflying aircraft.

Having completed their task and had tea, the rest of the day was spent catching up with the newspapers or writing letters.

Friday, 11th August 1944

Operation No.3
Railway Yards
First thing [in the morning] we found ourselves on the Battle Order so rushed out to E-Easy at dispersal to get things in order, then to briefing at 10.00 am. The target was a railway

Image of Lancaster, E-Easy, of No.622 Squadron, painted on canvas, by the late Keith Aspinall.
Author's Collection

Aerial view of Lens, France, taken from Lancaster bomber, coded E-Easy, flying at an altitude of 15,000,' on 11th August 1944. *Courtesy of the Late Max Bourne*

yard at Lens, in France, again, near the Belgian frontier. [We] took off about 2.00pm. Our route took us over Luton, Reading and Brighton and into France between Boulogne and Dieppe.

Bomber Command amassed a total of 459 aircraft for this attack, comprising Lancasters, Halifaxes and Mosquitoes. Three railway yards at Douai, Lens and Somain, along with the railway bridge at Etaples were specified as the targets.

No.622 Squadron detailed fourteen aircraft for this operation, including Lancaster, LM577, GI-E, which was becoming Max Bourne's regular mount. Soon after E-Easy and the rest of the formation had crossed the French coast, flak started coming up to greet them and continued spasmodically until they had passed over the target. One shell burst directly beneath 'Easy' but a call for battle damage from Max soon revealed that all appeared well and, as far as anyone was able to tell, there was no damage to the aircraft. Nevertheless, the exploding shell gave the Lancaster quite a jolt.

According to the Squadron's Operational Record Book, Max made his bombing run at an altitude of 17,000,' somewhat higher than on the previous raid. He followed his bomb aimer's instructions holding the aircraft steady, until given the "Bombs gone" call from the compartment in the nose of the Lancaster. Tom Brown released the load of eleven 1,000lb bombs and four 500lb bombs, onto the clouds of smoke and dust rising up from below. Max maintained the same altitude until re-crossing the enemy coast just east of Dunkirk. Reg also noted in his diary, under the same entry as above:

Much of the countryside was flooded. There were a number of places, woods etc. and an aerodrome smothered with bomb craters.

As Max flew home, he slowly began to reduce altitude until he finally brought the Lancaster back to terra firma at 18.00 hours, when the undercarriage touched down on Mildenhall's runway. Of his second and third operations, Max recorded:

The target at Fort-d'Englos was another easy target, followed by another one on 11th August, a daylight raid to destroy railway junctions essential to the enemy's movement of supplies. These easy trips were a gentle introduction to the business, which pleased us and no doubt the British army as well.

The British army was of course on the ground, entrenched fairly close to the locations of Bomber Command's attention. But then Max continued with an ominous warning that, "Things were about to change."

Saturday, 12th August 1944

Operation No.4
Russelsheim
We left base at 12 noon to carry out an H2S exercise over the Wash and East Anglia, during which I climbed out of my turret and sat with Paul at his radio desk for a change. We [carried out] the exercise at 10,000' and then returned to base [landing] at 1.30pm. After lunch, we were informed that we were on the Battle Order for tonight, so we visited our aircraft at dispersal to make our regular checks. Briefing was at 8.00pm and take-off at 10.05pm.

The target was the Opel car factory, near Russelsheim, which was manufacturing V1 flying bombs. Bomber Command dispatched a total of 297 aircraft for this attack, seven of which were detailed by No.622 Squadron. Eight aircraft from the Squadron were also sent to attack Brunswick, whilst a further three participated in a raid on Falaise, where German troop concentrations and a major crossroads north of the town were bombed.
    Max and his crew took off at 22.05 hours and headed towards Orfordness on the east coast. As he flew out over the North Sea, he gained altitude, getting E-Easy up to 18,000' as they crossed over Belgium. Flak and fighters, the latter assisted by flares, endeavoured to hamper the progress of Bomber Command's aircraft as they fought their way across enemy occupied territory.

Diary entry for 12th August 1944, when Arthur Bourne recorded that E-Easy was attacked on four occasions by enemy fighters. *Author's Collection via the Late Arthur Bourne*

After Tom had released their load of incendiaries from an altitude of 17,000,' Max put the aircraft into a gradual descent, until crossing the enemy coast at 10,000.' On the way out, Reg, from his vantage point in the mid-upper turret, reported the sighting of three enemy fighters, none of which attempted to attack E-Easy. Whilst crossing the North Sea on the homeward journey, both Max and Reg reported seeing an enemy convoy approximately twenty miles off the Belgian coast.

Although it was reported at the time that the attack had been a great success, later reports showed that the majority of the bombs had in fact fallen in open countryside, with only the tire and dispatch departments and the powerhouse of the Opel factory being hit. Due to the defences, a total of thirteen Lancasters and seven Halifaxes were lost; 6.7% of the attacking force. Of the mission, Max wrote:

On the way to the target and on the return leg, the sky was lit up like day by parachute flares deployed by high-flying Focke-Wulf Condors, for the benefit of the nightfighters who managed to 'nail' twenty of the 297 aircraft employed.

Arthur Bourne had slightly different memories of this attack and wrote in his diary:

12th August 1944 – 4th Op.
Russelsheim
Eventful. Stooged over enemy flak ships at 3,000.' Attacked on four occasions by enemy fighters. Heavy ack-ack in the target area. Small hole in starboard wing through ack-ack.

Following the usual procedure after landing, Max and the boys went to debriefing with the Intelligence Officer, then to breakfast before falling into bed at 4.30am.

Sunday, 13th August 1944
Slept until lunch time. [We then went to lunch but] were unable to eat the meal. It was terrible. We spent the afternoon cleaning the guns and [later] did a half hour air test. While we were cleaning the guns this morning, the groundcrew were repairing a flak hole in the port mainplane, [this was] the first we knew of it.

Reg does not say why they were not able to eat their lunch. Was it cooked badly or just inedible, or were nerves from the previous nights' operation beginning to show already?

Monday, 14th August 1944

Operation No.5
Falaise
After breakfast we made our way to our respective sections by 9.15am and found we were required to attend brief for 'Ops' at 11.15am. Our target was the gap at Falaise, through which the Germans are escaping from Normandy into the center of France. We took off at 1.15pm, got into formation and set course for France at 2.45pm.

Bomber Command dispatched a total force 805 aircraft on this operation, fourteen of which were detailed from No.622 Squadron.

Having formed up, the Squadron's Lancasters headed south, via Luton, and crossed the Channel coast over Bognor Regis, Sussex. As they looked down, the aviators could see numerous convoys also heading for the French coast, albeit in their case, by sea, a longer and slower crossing. Continuing on a southerly heading, the French coastline slipped beneath the bomber, as did the town of Caen, which looked a lifeless desolate town. The fields and woods surrounding the town were pitted for mile after mile with bomb and shell craters, evidence of the fighting following D-Day and previous bombing and shelling of the area.

Oboe and visual marking, directed by Master Bombers and deputy Master Bombers at each of the seven German troop positions being attacked, signalled the start of the operation. By the time Max turned E-Easy onto its bombing run, holding the aircraft steady at 9,000' (their lowest bombing altitude to date), the target area was a billowing mass of smoke and dust, with views of the ground being obscured and very restricted.

Throughout the operation, Spitfire aircraft of RAF Fighter Command wheeled and circled in the sky above the bombers, almost inviting enemy fighters to engage in battle, but no Luftwaffe aircraft were seen.

Unfortunately, according to later reports, some aircraft bombed a quarry in which the 12th Canadian Field Regiment were positioned, whilst waiting to 'mop-up' the remaining German defences once the bombing had ceased. Efforts by the Master Bomber to rectify the error were in vain, as approximately seventy aircraft unleashed their deadly cargoes on the Allied troops below. At least thirteen soldiers were killed, whilst fifty-three were reported injured.

Avro Lancaster bombers of No.622 Squadron, flying in formation, head for Falaise, France, on 14th August 1944. *Courtesy of the Late Max Bourne*

The attack completed, the Lancasters of No.622 Squadron regrouped and flew back to RAF Mildenhall in formation. *Courtesy of the Late Max Bourne*

As the aircraft turned for home, a few flak bursts were recorded, which seemed very half-hearted and died away after a few minutes. Reg also recorded that smoke from the target area below was drifting out across the Cherbourg Peninsula, still obscuring the ground. However, the smoke did not obscure the sighting of a lone Messerschmitt Bf 109, which was recorded scuttling along at top speed below the Lancaster, which the German pilot failed to notice or just ignored completely.

As they had done on the way out to the target, the Lancasters formed up for the flight home, which for Reg held some personal excitement. The formation re-crossed the English coast and headed north, passing between Luton and Harpenden. Looking down from his mid-upper turret as they flew over the latter town, Reg was able to trace the streets and locate 'Carmel,' his cousin's house where he had stayed twice whilst on leave.

Later that evening Reg wrote some letters, but did not record whether one was to his cousin, possibly saying, "Today, I flew over your house."

Tuesday, 15th August 1944

[Roger and I] spent the morning in the hangar. After lunch [we] went out to dispersal and harmonised our guns and turrets, finishing in time to join the end of the tea queue.

It was a quiet day for Reg and the rest of the crew, with only the tasks mentioned in his diary being completed. More letters were written during the evening and, by way of a change, instead of going to the mess for supper, they prepared their own, consisting of camp pie and pickles, cake and tea. It was just as well that they had a relaxing evening at 'home,' for the next day was to prove a long one for the whole crew.

Wednesday, 16th /Thursday 17th August 1944

Operation No.6
Stettin

After lunch we found we were on the Battle Order for this evening, so visited E-Easy to check that all was well there. Briefing began at 6.45pm after which we went out to the aircraft at 7.30pm [in preparation] for take-off [which commenced] at 9.00pm. Our target was Stettin, where supplies for the Russian front are accumulated.

A total force of 461 Lancasters was detailed for the attack, including fourteen from No.622 Squadron. Five bombers from the main force failed to return, including one aircraft, Avro Lancaster, serial LM133, coded, UL-H2, of No.576 Squadron, which was abandoned by its crew over Sweden. The crew, who had bailed out, was interned in that country, except for the pilot who was tragically killed in a freak accident on landing. Flying Officer Frederick Watts, RCAF, of Toronto, Canada, died from strangulation, after the shrouds of his parachute become entangled in a tree. He was buried in Malmo Eastern Municipal Cemetery.

As navigator, Arthur was going to be busy on this mission, more so than on any of the previous operations he had undertaken thus far. Having taken-off from RAF Mildenhall at 21.15 hours, Max headed out over the North Sea at an altitude of 600.' This height was maintained until the bomber approached the Danish Peninsula, at which point Max was instructed by Arthur to climb to 1,600.' As they flew cross Denmark, the crew could see a raid in progress over Kiel, approximately 100 miles away. On they flew, with Arthur keeping a good eye on his charts and calculations, as they headed for the target on Germany's Baltic Coast.

Lancaster E-Easy approached the target at an altitude of 20,000,' but Tom Brown was unable to identify the aiming point due to cloud cover. Max descended to 16,000' from which height Tom was able to release the bomb load onto the red target indicators at 01.13 hours. The crew later reported that the bombing seemed scattered, with incendiaries burning over a wide area. The flak, which was also reported as scattered, was recorded as being very light and was of little consequence to the crew.

For one heart-stopping moment E-Easy was caught in the glare of searchlights, but by 'corkscrewing' around the sky and managing to break free of the beam, Max ensured their predicament lasted only a few seconds.

Having been thrown around the night sky over Stettin, Arthur Bourne gave his pilot a new course heading for home. They turned north-east and flew out over the Baltic coast at Kolberg (Kolobrzeg), at an altitude of 6,000,' before turning again on a north-westerly course, passing quite close to Malmo, Sweden, which was brightly illuminated. Although Max was careful to avoid neutral Swedish airspace, the ground defences opened up, peppering light flak bursts close to the Lancaster.

It was fortuitous for the crew that the rest of the journey home across the North Sea was uneventful, which was just as well as, by Reg's own admission, the whole crew experienced great difficulty in staying awake! Eventually they reached RAF Mildenhall, where they were forced to circle for some considerable time before being granted permission to land. The final comment in Reg's diary relating to this trip reads:

We were utterly fagged out, and after interrogation, had breakfast, then went straight to bed and slept until 5.00pm. We were airborne 8 hours 40 minutes.

Reg had found out the hard way why some training exercises lasted six hours or more. The only member of the crew who was not tired was Bill Vincent who, for reasons unrecorded, did not fly on this operation. Bill's place, as flight engineer, was taken by Sergeant R. Martin.

Having awoken from their slumbers, Reg and Roger carried out their necessary ablutions, dressed and went into the village at Mildenhall, where they met Keith Coombe for an evening of well-deserved relaxation.

Friday, 18th/Saturday, 19th August 1944

Operation No.7
Bremen
During the afternoon, we found we were on the Battle Order [for tonight] so went out to the aircraft to check everything was in order. [We] went to the briefing at 7.45pm, where we were informed the target was Bremen. We took off at 9.30pm and circled whilst the Squadron assembled, then set course over East Anglia and the North Sea.

The Squadron flew at a height of 1,000' whilst crossing the North Sea, but as they approached the Frisian Islands, increased altitude up to 12,000.' Having crossed the enemy coast and still gaining height, searchlights and flak batteries were very active and plotted the bombers' course across both the Netherlands and northern Germany.

A total of 288 aircraft, comprising Lancasters, Halifaxes and Mosquitoes, were despatched for the attack, including fourteen detailed by No.622 Squadron. However, one aircraft failed to take off from Mildenhall, leaving the superstitious airmen amongst the crews to contemplate the fact there were thirteen aircraft from the Squadron on this mission!

For this operation, Flying Officer Max Bourne had been allocated Avro Lancaster bomber, PD228, GI-A, a Mark I variant that had been built by Metropolitan-Vickers. It was a relatively new acquisition by No.622 Squadron, but was later to serve with No.44 Squadron.

As Max and his crew approached the target, at an altitude of 17,000,' they could see it was a blaze of light, as thousands of white incendiaries glowed and burned on the ground, shimmering like a burning sea. Brilliant flashes lit up the sky further, as 4,000lb bombs rained down and exploded amongst the already burning buildings, sending columns of debris, ash and smoke into the air. As Tom released the load in A-Able's bomb bay, at thirteen minutes past midnight, a huge explosion erupted on the ground below, but it did not prevent their 'cookie' from hitting its mark. All the while, flak burst around, above and below their aircraft, not quite being able to find its target. Chewing gum helped steady the crew's nerves and with the bombs gone, Max wasted no time in getting away from the 'hornet's nest' that the target area had become. He headed for the coast, losing altitude as he did so. They re-crossed the Dutch coast and flew out over the North Sea at 2,000.'

Although, compared to previous operations, the attacking force was relatively small in the number of aircraft that participated in the raid, the attack was (at the time) considered very successful. The center and northwestern suburbs of the city, as well as the port area, were devastated. Eighteen ships were sunk in the harbor, whilst a further 61 were seriously damaged. The commercial and industrial buildings destroyed or damaged were too numerous to record, although nearly 9,000 dwellings were burnt out. The human cost was recorded as almost 1,100 people killed, with many more listed as missing.

By the time Max and the crew reached Mildenhall, their nerves had settled down, but the emotion of the attack had left them feeling tired and fatigued. Immediately on finishing their de-briefing report, they had breakfast and fell straight into their respective beds.

Sunday, 20th August 1944
[It was] a cold and drizzly day after weeks of fine weather, and a quiet day for us. After lunch we took off on another H2S exercise. The cloud base was down to 500' and we were still in cloud at 15,000' with rain and ice which stripped paint off the leading edge [of the wing]. Max decided to turn back when 90 miles from base. We got back safely and landed at 3.00pm. At dispersal, I bought a bike from a [member of groundcrew] on the spur of the moment, and bundled it in to the back of the transport with [all] our gear.

For this training exercise, Max was allocated yet another aircraft, Lancaster, LM291, GI-F 'Freddie.' This aircraft, like A-Able, was also a Mark I variant, but manufactured by

Avro Lancaster, PD228, GI-A, flown by Flying Officer Max Bourne on 18th August 1944.
Author's Collection

Conjoined photographs showing an extended area of the devastation caused by the bombing of Bremen, by RAF Bomber Command. *Author's Collection*

Armstrong Whitworth. Unfortunately, it was to be lost on 13th September 1944, when it failed to return from an attack against Frankfurt.

Monday, 21st August 1944
We begin eight days leave this afternoon, so much packing and activity all morning. Everyone else left at 3.30pm and Max, Paul and I set off in the car at 5.00pm for Peterborough. [We] passed through Downham Market and reached Wisbech at 10.30pm. [We] decided it was too late to go any further, so got a room at the King's Head. We had a good yarn in the lounge and turned in at midnight.

This was obviously Reg's first visit to the Wisbech area, as he expressed surprise at the flatness of the surrounding countryside, known to the English as Fenland or the 'Fens,' and at how large the town itself was given its location.

Wisbech, being surrounded by orchards and bulb fields, became a flourishing area for the fruit and flower markets. This led to wealth, which in turn led to a number of the local merchants building some of the finest architecturally designed Georgian houses to be seen.

Tuesday, 22nd August 1944
We were awakened by the staff at 9.00am and, following breakfast, paid our bill and packed our gear in the car, which then refused to start. After a while, one of us [suddenly] remembered how to turn the ignition on [which we did] and off we went. We reached Peterborough at 11.30am and then drove on to Coventry, where we saw the spire of St.Michael's Cathedral, which was ruined in the blitz.

Eventually, Reg parted company with Max and Paul and went on to Birmingham by train, arriving at his destination around 16.00 hours. Having taken some refreshment at a Joe Lyons teashop near the railway station, Reg spent an hour trying to find somewhere to bed down for the night. Feeling rather tired after his day traveling, he eventually acquired a bed in, of all places, the Eye Hospital in Church Street, Birmingham! Such was the extent of Reg's fatigue that night he was in bed by 9.00pm.

Wednesday, 23rd August 1944
[I] went to New Street station to enquire about trains to Worcester, so I could visit my cousin Nellie Howitt [staying] at Broadway. I caught the 12.25pm [train] arriving at Shrub hill, Worcester, at 2.15pm. Then another train to Evesham where there was a two-hours wait for a bus to Broadway.

The bus journey took fifteen minutes and dropped Reg off outside the boarding house where his cousin was staying, she being an evacuee from London. Nellie was waiting by the front door of the house and after greeting Reg ushered him inside. Having had tea, the landlady of the 'establishment' joined them but, when the talk became very one-sided, and they couldn't get a word in edgeways, they decided to go for a stroll in the park where they could talk more freely. Before too long, having had a long day, as well as a long journey, Reg set off to find suitable accommodation in which to spend a couple of nights.

Thursday was spent with Nellie, shopping in the local village stores or talking about respective families in England and Australia, during which Nellie gave Reg a message that she asked him to send to her relations on the latter continent, by airgraph letter.

On Friday, having had lunch together, Nellie accompanied Reg to Evesham, where he caught a bus back to Birmingham. Whether Reg thought the bus would be quicker than the train is not known, but it did not work out that way as the bus broke down two or three times during the journey. Eventually, the bus arrived at its destination, where Reg was supposed to meet up with Roger at the Grand Hotel, but the latter failed to materialise. It was not until around 10.00am on the Sunday morning that Roger re-appeared. Where he had been for the last two days was discussed by the two friends, but was not recorded in the diary!

Having taken a train to London on Monday morning, Reg and Roger spent all day in the capital, enjoying themselves, before catching a train back to Mildenhall late that same night.

6

Return to Operational Flying

The period of leave from which Reg and the rest of the crew returned was the first they had been granted since being posted to RAF Mildenhall a month earlier. For eight days they had been able to put the war behind them, but it was now time for a return to operational flying.

Tuesday, 29th August 1944

Operation No.8
Stettin
Had the morning off, so '*Erk*' [Keith Coombe], Paul, Roger and I exchanged stories about our respective adventures whilst on leave (still no details recorded as to where Roger had been for two days). After lunch [Roger and] I went out to the aircraft to check all was well, for we are on the Battle Order for tonight.

Bomber Command ordered an attacked against Stettin that night, for which a total force of 402 aircraft were despatched. No.622 Squadron detailed fourteen Lancasters for the operation, but one failed to take off. Reg and the crew had attended their briefing at 6.45p.m, where they were informed of the target and the route. The latter was out over the North Sea, across the north of Denmark, across the Kattegat and southern Sweden and the island of Bornholm.

Having completed his cockpit checks, Max Bourne taxied out ready for take-off. On receipt of the green Aldis lamp signal, at 9.17pm, the throttles were pushed forward, the brakes released and Lancaster E-Easy lumbered down the runway and climbed gingerly into the air. They crossed the North Sea at a height of 1,000,' but increased altitude after being fired on by enemy flak ships. Crossing over Denmark at 8,000,' a German night-fighter swung in to attack the Lancaster, but the pilot thought twice about giving chase after Max threw the four-engine bomber into a corkscrew manoeuvre. The German pilot's actions could possibly have, inadvertently, saved the crew of E-Easy, as Arthur recorded in his diary, "Attacked by fighter over Denmark with rear gunner's guns u/s." However, the navigator on Flight Sergeant Neilson's crew, who were flying on Lancaster, GI-L, was not so lucky when his aircraft was attacked by a night-fighter, as he was severely wounded. During this period of the flight, Reg recorded the loss of two Lancasters, which crashed in flames and blew up, and a third which went down in Sweden. Although light flak from

Swedish artillery was in evidence, it was felt that this was fired more as a warning to the bomber crews, rather than attempts to shoot them down.

Having lost altitude during the evasion manoeuvre, Max put the aircraft into a climb and only levelled out when he had reached 17,000,' the altitude at which he crossed the Baltic and from which he commenced his bombing run.

With heavy flak bursting around them, and searchlights sweeping backwards and forwards across the night sky, Max held the aircraft steady as Tom Brown guided his pilot to the aiming point. At six-minutes-past-two in the morning Tom flicked the bomb switches, pressed the 'tit' and their load cascaded down to explode in the already shimmering sea of fire below. As the bombs tumbled out of the bomb bay, the aircraft lurched upwards, lightened in weight by a few thousand pounds. Receiving a course alteration from Arthur, Max turned the Lancaster on a heading for home, flying over Jutland and Lim Fjord. Crossing the latter at a height of only 3,000,' they drew the attention of two searchlights and a violent burst of light flak. Max called for a damage report and, having ascertained that all was well with his crew, continued the flight out over the North Sea. They crossed the English coast in daylight at 06.45 hours, tired but still vigilant. By the time they landed at Mildenhall half-an-hour later, they had been airborne nearly ten hours.

Following debriefing and breakfast, they went straight to bed and remained there until 5.00pm when they were awoken by 'Erk.' Being the friend he was, Keith had brought with him some camp pie, a tin of pineapple and some jelly, which saved the boys the bother of 'sprucing up' in order to go to the mess for tea.

Thursday, 31st August 1944

Operation No.9
Abbeville
Paul came dashing into the house at 11.30am to tell us we were on an 'op' in the afternoon.

The target that afternoon was at Pont-Remy, to the southeast of Abbeville. It was one of eight V-2 rocket storage sites in the north of France, which drew the attention of Bomber Command. A total of 36 Mosquito aircraft, 147 Halifax bombers and 418 Lancaster bombers participated in the attack. No.622 Squadron detailed twelve of the latter aircraft.

Max Bourne hauled E-Easy off the runway at 3.35pm, circled round and climbed to a height of 12,000.' The route was designated as via Lakenheath, then south over Reading, Berkshire, the Channel and crossing enemy-occupied coast over the Somme Estuary.

As Max cross the enemy coast he could see a short distance ahead, thick flak arcing up into the sky. From his vantage point in the mid-upper turret, Reg was also able to see the flak, but disregarded it with the thought that it would not prevent them from completing their task and he was right. With Tom lying full length on the bomb aimer's couch in the nose of the aircraft, bomb release button held in his right hand, he guided Max on the bombing run. At ten-minutes-past-six, keeping his nerve, Tom pressed the button and called, "Bombs gone" as the bombs rained down from an altitude of 18,000.'

Max turned the Lancaster away from the target and put the aircraft into a dive, just as five flak shells burst directly in front of them, causing a certain amount of alarm amongst the crew. A sudden violent manoeuvre of the control yoke by Max, whilst unnerving for those on board, assured the continued safety of the aircraft, which made its return journey across the English Channel without further incident.

Having left the heat of battle behind them, for Max, Reg and anyone else who wanted to look, there was, for most of the journey back, a glorious view of the cliffs along the south coast of England, gleaming white in the late summer sunlight. Ironically, having crossed the coast over Worthing, the Lancaster endured the buffeting of several rainstorms before landing at Mildenhall at 7.30pm.

The following day Reg and Roger spent the day cleaning and harmonizing their respective guns and turrets. The former even took the opportunity of changing the ammunition in his turret. No stoppages (hopefully) in the middle of a fight for him.

Although not on 'Ops' over the next three or four days, Max and his crew did not leave camp. The 'Easy Boys' did not feel like going anywhere anyway, as the weather had deteriorated and it would not stop raining. In fact, on Sunday morning, Roger saw no point in getting up and therefore refused to leave his bed. Reg took advantage of the fact that Tom's gramophone was on a visit from the Officers' Mess, and continually played the records which came with it, albeit that, according to Reg's diary, "Most of them were cracked." Monday was spent in much the same vein as the previous few days, although the rain had eased up. Reg and Roger took the opportunity of going out to dispersal to check on the condition of E-Easy, but returned to the house where boredom continued to be the name of the game.

Tuesday, 5th September 1944

Operation No.10
Le Havre
After breakfast we did our daily inspections on the aircraft then prepared for an H2S exercise, which was canceled just before take-off. We found our [names] on the Battle Order for the afternoon and at briefing [learned] the target was Le Havre, where 5,000 Jerries are trapped by the army's drive to Antwerp and the Channel coast.

After the last few days of inactivity, the return to operations came for Max and the crew when E-Easy lifted off the runway at Mildenhall at 16.25 hours, and climbed up over the Suffolk countryside. E-Easy was one of thirteen Lancaster bombers detailed by No.622 Squadron to join a total attacking force of 348 aircraft, comprising 313 Lancasters, 30 Mosquitoes and 5 Stirling bombers.

Flying Officer Bourne, having received navigational details from Flight Sergeant Bourne, turned onto a south-westerly course and headed towards the target via St. Albans, where he climbed to 13,000,' then on to Chichester and out over the English Channel.

In the early evening light the crew witnessed the spectacle of hundreds of Lancasters streaming towards the enemy occupied port, where the bombing was reported as accurate. At the allotted moment, Max turned his aircraft on to a new heading in preparation for the bombing run. As Tom Brown, situated in the bomb aimer's compartment in the nose of the aircraft, called, "Left, left, left, steady, ri-i-i-ight," Max endeavoured to hold Easy on a straight and level course, not an easy task with flak bursting all around. Below clouds of dense smoke and dust billowed up into the air, but fortunately a strong wind kept the target area visible. Then were heard the two words from Tom that the rest of the crew were always pleased to hear, "Bombs gone." As the bombs rained down, the crew could see the dock area and half the town awash with flame from the many fires burning below. Following release of the bombs, Max held E-Easy on a straight and level course long enough to get their aiming point photograph, before diving and turning away from the target.

After having endured the flak, which although not intense was fairly accurate, the return flight was uneventful, except for one near mid-air collision caused by the formation getting a bit ragged and out of hand.

The official verdict on the raid was that it was an accurate attack, made in good visibility during which no Bomber Command aircraft were lost.

Wednesday, 6th September 1944

Operation No.11
Le Havre
We were on the Battle Order again from early morning, but the briefing was delayed until 1.30pm. We went out to E-Easy to carry out our daily inspections before lunch and also had time to spend an hour in the intelligence library. [Later we went] to briefing which eventually started at 2.15pm.

The target was again Le Havre, where the German troop concentrations were still holding out. A similar number of aircraft, comprising the same types as the previous day, were despatched during the late afternoon. Max Bourne took off a couple of minutes after 16.00 hours and climbed to join the formation over Lakenheath. The route to the target, again, was the same as the previous day.

Over the Channel, as the attacking force approached the French coast, visibility began to deteriorate, forcing the bombers down to 7,000' in order for them to see the target. Fortunately, possibly due to the previous days action, flak was not evident, which cheered the crews immensely.

The bombing was considered to be good and Tom Brown, after guiding Max up to the aiming point, dropped their bombs which straddled a road, a railway track and part of the docks facility. A great pall of smoke and dust again hung over the docks and town, adding to the visibility problems, which meant great care had to be taken to avoid collisions with aircraft both going into and out of the target area.

Amongst all this confusion, especially having kept a constant watch for other aircraft in the target area, Max lost his own formation and flew back out over the Channel alone. However, having crossed the English coast over Portsmouth, which was congested with all manner of ships, the crew caught up with, and re-joined, the formation. An impressive sight awaited those on the ground at RAF Mildenhall, as all fourteen aircraft detailed by No.622 Squadron flew into view in perfect formation and then broke away for landing. The first aircraft down was E-Easy, touching down at 19.45 hours. The crew hurriedly shut down their respective stations on the aircraft and rushed off for de-briefing, ahead of everybody else. They were also the first into the Mess for the post flight meal and the first to hit their respective beds.

Reg and the others in the crew may have been the first in for their meal on their return from Le Havre, but they overslept and missed breakfast the following morning and made do with a slice of toast until lunchtime. As a result of this indulgence, they only just made roll call.

Friday, 8th September 1944
[After] lunch we went flying on an H2S exercise for a couple of hours, [during which] we landed at Snitterfield near Birmingham to drop off a chap going on leave from Mildenhall. The intrusion of a Lancaster bomber on an Avro Oxford training station caused open mouth gaping amongst the locals. We struck some sticky weather on the return trip, with very low visibility and heavy rain so made a wide detour to reach base.

RAF Snitterfield was an airfield well known to Max Bourne, who of course flew from there when attached to No.35 Course, No.18 (Pilots) Advanced Flying Unit. The airfield came under the command of No.23 Group, the headquarters of which was at RAF South Cerney on the Gloucester side of the Gloucestershire/Wiltshire border.

The following day the crew was detailed to undertake a fighter affiliation exercise, but panic ensued when it was realised that half of the crew did not know what the other half were doing, or where they were. Calm was eventually restored when the 'absentees' were rounded up and the crew once more became the efficient team they had become. But, frustration set in again when, after having taken off, they had to wait twenty minutes for the fighter to turn up.

Sunday, 10th September 1944

Operation No.12
Le Havre (Troop Concentrations)
Today's attack seems to be intended to obliterate the place, for 900 Lancasters [dropped] 5,400 tons of bombs over [a period of] three hours.

Reg was slightly adrift with the figures in his diary entry with regard to the number of Lancasters participating in the attack. A total of 992 aircraft participated in the operation, but this figure was made up 521 Lancaster bombers, 426 Halifax bombers and 45 Mosquito aircraft.

No.622 Squadron detailed sixteen aircraft for the attack, including LM577, GI-E, piloted by Flying Officer Max Bourne. Max hauled E-Easy off Mildenhall's runway, at 15.20 hours, and climbed to join the ever-expanding formation. When all participating aircraft were in place, the formation set course by flying south over St. Albans, Chichester on the south coast and out across the English Channel.

The target for No.622 Squadron was one of eight German strong points, each of which was independently marked by the Pathfinders. There was no fighter opposition and nothing in the way of flak; in fact the only gunfire seen was that from Allied artillery around the town, adding to the German garrison's discomfort with a continuous barrage.

The "Easy" Boys

Nine hundred and ninety-two aircraft of Bomber Command took part in the bombing of Le Havre on 10th September 1944. The columns of dense smoke rising from the ground indicates they found their target. However, the German ground forces' smoke screens probably added to the confusion.
Courtesy of Reg Heffron

As the aerial armada, still in formation, crossed over the estuary and port area, those members of aircrew who had the opportunity to do so, looked down. Below them they saw the flashes of light as the artillery shells erupted from the barrels of each gun, in a brilliant ball of fire, arced and whined their way through the air and exploded in another ball of fire as they detonated on impact. Holding formation, the bombers droned across the target area with bomb doors open. Then, adding to the whining noise of the artillery shells, the bombs whistled as they fell earthwards, adding to the carnage below. Great clouds of smoke and dust rose up into the air and drifted out over the Channel, as if to follow the bombers home.

Following de-briefing, the crew learned that the attack had been a great success, with all participating aircraft returning to their home bases.

Monday, 11th September 1944

Operation No.13
Kamen (Oil Plant)

[After] roll-call, we went out to dispersal to do our daily inspections. [Whilst there] we had a chat with *'Tubby'* and his ground crew. At mid-day we found our names on the Battle Order for later that afternoon. We went to briefing at 2.00pm where we learned the target was Kamen, near Dortmund.

The operation planned by Bomber Command for this particular afternoon involved three separate forces of bombers, totalling 379 aircraft, attacking the synthetic-oil plants at Gelsenkirchen (Nordstern), Castrop-Rauxel and Kamen, north-east of Dortmund. Whilst the targets at Gelsenkirchen and Kamen were easily identifiable, that at Castrop-Rauxel was partially hampered by the use of a smokescreen that proved a hindrance to the bombers.

Amongst the 154 Lancasters that participated in the attack, twelve were from No.622 Squadron, including E-Easy, piloted by Max Bourne. Following the usual procedures, the latter took off at 15.55 hours, got into formation over Lakenheath and then set course via Stowmarket, Orfordness and the North Sea to the Netherlands. Having reached the enemy occupied coast, where a large part of the coastal area of Holland was seen to be flooded and villages submerged, the bombers followed the River Rhine to the German frontier.

Riding in his mid-upper turret, high on the back of the Lancaster, Reg could see the attack developing over Gelsenkirchen, where heavy flak bursts turned the sky black with smoke. Flak began to arc up into the sky around E-Easy as the aircraft approached the target, with one or two bursts getting a little bit too close for the crew's comfort. Arthur Bourne, the navigator, was the lucky one on the crew as he could get engrossed with his charts and course calculations and pretend that all was well. As on twelve previous occasions, Max guided the bomber on to the aiming point following Tom Brown's instructions and, at the appropriate moment from an altitude of 16,000,' Tom pressed the 'tit,' checked the switches and called, "Bombs gone."

Max turned 'Easy' on a homeward course but just as they flew over the outskirts of Hamm, to the northeast of the target area, the German defences opened fire with bursts of flak. Max continued in the turn and as he did so the crew witnessed a large explosion in the target area from whence a huge mushroom shaped cloud of smoke erupted. It grew in size and rose up in to the sky, to a height of approximately two and a half miles.

The flak continued to follow the bombers and although Reg recorded that E-Easy came through unscathed, Arthur recorded in his diary that their aircraft was 'hit in two places by flak.' Lancaster bomber, DS787, JI-G, of No.514 Squadron, was not so lucky. This aircraft was hit by flak and crashed onto the road at Lerche, southwest of Pelkum, approximately three miles from the center of Kamen, at 18.42 hours. Although the flight engineer and both air gunners managed to bail out safely, the remaining four crewmembers were killed. The latter were later laid to rest in Reichswald Forest War Cemetery. Having witnessed the crash, Reg later wrote in his diary that one wing tore off the Lancaster just before it hit the ground.

An aerial view of the remains of the synthetic-oil plant at Kamen, following attacks by Bomber Command. *Author's Collection*

Avro Lancaster bomber, LM115, GI-C, of No.622 Squadron. This aircraft was lost during an attack against Rostock, Germany. All seven crewmembers, including three from the Royal Australian Air Force, were listed 'Missing' in action. *Author's Collection*

Twenty-six squadrons of fighters had escorted the three bomber formations, but as no enemy fighters were encountered before, during or after the attack, the escort pilots must have had an easy day.

The return journey went without incident. The bombers decreased altitude down to 12,000' as they crossed the Dutch coast and were flying at 3,000' by the time they crossed over the east coast of England. Max landed at RAF Mildenhall at 20.30 hours and, after debriefing and a cup of tea, followed by a late meal in the mess, the crew finally got to bed at 11.30pm.

An hour before E-Easy landed, Lancaster bomber, LM511, GI-C, piloted by Flight Sergeant E. Devine, RAAF, had taken-off from Mildenhall, along with five other aircraft from No.622 Squadron, for a mine-laying (Gardening) operation in the Baltic. Unfortunately, this aircraft failed to return. The seven members of its crew, which included three members of the Royal Australian Air Force, would never feel the warmth of their respective beds again.

Tuesday, 12th September 1944

After roll-call we went out to dispersal and did the usual jobs. [We then] amused ourselves by making a [sledge] with some bomb roller conveyors and generally acted like kids until lunch time. In the afternoon we were on the Battle Order as reserves but after standing by were not needed.

With little else to do, Reg, Roger, Bill and Tom spent the rest of the afternoon in and around the village of Mildenhall, trying to locate spare parts for the car Tom had recently acquired, but all to no avail. Given their behavior earlier in the day, it may well have been that the members of the ground crew thought that the two air gunners, the bomb aimer and the flight engineer were missing a few parts themselves! However, the 'Brothers-in-arms' were not perturbed about what anybody thought and continued their childish fun the next morning when, after having completed their daily inspections, Reg, Roger and Bill had a few rides on their sledge, much to the amusement of all.

The merriment continued on into the afternoon, but in a more grown-up sort of way. Having been stood down, Reg, Roger and Bill set off on bicycles to Mildenhall, Barton Mills and Newmarket, where, having first made enquiries about another car, they partook of a meal of hamburgers, onions and potatoes, all washed down with cups of coffee. After their meal they set about cycling home, but stopped halfway back to have a snack at a roadside café. Continuing their journey, they managed to get back to Barton Mills where they decided to drop in at the Bull public house and make merry for a few hours. The result of this latest decision being a hectic, if not hilarious, bike ride home. However, before reaching the base two more stops were made; the first being in order to purchase some fish and chips, whilst the second stop was made to pick Keith 'Erk' Coombe up off the road. Unfortunately, Reg does not record what 'Erk' was doing lying in the road, although records show that it was on this same day that George Williamson, 'Erk's' pilot, was promoted in the rank of Acting Flying Officer. Had the little guy overdone the celebrations?

The following day, Max's crew were detailed to undertake a H2S exercise to Leeds and back flying on E-Easy, but given the amount of food and drink consumed, it was a wonder they were not instructed to undertake a 'loaded climb' exercise!

During the afternoon of Friday, 15th September, the crew undertook another H2S exercise, again to Leeds and back. Having landed at 17.00 hours, three of them jumped into one of the cars and drove to Mildenhall, still chasing the elusive spare parts they needed for the fleet of cars they now appeared to be acquiring. The following day normality was almost resumed.

Saturday, 16th September 1944
I took my guns to the cleaning room and [stripped] and polished them before lunch. [Then] Roger and I took them back [to the aircraft], mounted them and harmonised the mid-upper turret. [Later in the afternoon] we ferried a squadron leader to Desborough and, on the way back, tested the H2S over the Wash from 15,000.' [We] landed at 5.30pm and had tea.

Although it was now getting late in the day, the 'Three Newmarketeers' as they began calling themselves, set off in Tom's car to visit the garage where they had previously made enquires about another car. However, by the time they got there they had acquired three punctures, but not necessarily all in the same tire. The proprietor of the garage very kindly fixed the punctures, thereby allowing the 'Newmarketeers' to get home via Mildenhall, where they stopped for food at Morley's café.

Sunday, 17th September 1944

Operation No.14
Boulogne
We are on the Battle Order this morning and were woken by the Service Police at 6.30am for an early breakfast, [followed] by a briefing at 8.15am.

The target was German positions in and around the port of Boulogne, for which a total of 762 aircraft were detailed. No.622 Squadron despatched sixteen Lancasters, including HK615, GI-Z, piloted by Flying Officer Max Bourne.

Max took off at 10.40 hours, joined the formation over Lakenheath before setting course for France. The route took them south over the Thames Estuary, over Dover and the very familiar waters of the English Channel. By the time the formation reached the target area, the attack had been in progress for over three hours. Much to the crew's delight, there was no enemy opposition.

Running up to the target, at an altitude of only 3,000,' Tom Brown prepared for what was his lowest bombing run to date. The attack went without incident, but as Max began to bank the Lancaster away on a turning point, a crescendo of loud bangs startled the whole crew and tossed the aircraft around with considerable force. It transpired that this cacophony of noise was the result of their own bombs exploding almost beneath the aircraft. Because the bomber was in a banking turn at the time, Roger almost had his hair parted down the middle when another stick of bombs, from a Lancaster flying nearby, rained down from above at almost the same time. However, luck was on their side and the bombs whizzed past the top of Roger's turret without causing any serious damage or injury!

Lancaster, HK615, GI-Z, taxiing out for take-off. Although Max Bourne flew this aircraft on 17th September, during an attack against Boulogne, the photograph above was taken on 25th October, when it participated in a daylight raid against Essen. *Author's Collection*

Over three thousand tons of bombs were dropped on Boulogne, which was left smoking due to the large number of fires burning. The German troops garrisoned in the town surrendered a short while after the attack.

Monday, 18th September 1944
At 11.30am we took off on another H2S exercise, this time to Gloucester, Leeds, the Wash and back to base. During the trip I [spent] about twenty minutes at the controls, my first attempt [at flying a Lancaster bomber].

The aircraft which both Max Bourne and Reg Heffron flew on this exercise was Avro Lancaster, PD225, GI-D. The trip lasted approximately two-and-a-quarter hours and passed without incident. There is no comment or mention as to whether Max stood over the 'second pilot' during the twenty-minute period that Reg flew the aircraft. However, having landed back at Mildenhall, presumably with Max at the controls, the crew had a late lunch before Reg and Roger retrieved their respective guns from PD225 and returned them to E-Easy. The following day, Reg and Roger spent time cleaning the guns, but later in the day the latter also took the opportunity of harmonising the mid-upper turret.

Wednesday, 20th September 1944

Operation No.15
Calais
Found we were on the Battle Order, so had lunch early and then went to briefing at [midday]. The target was Calais, a Jerry stronghold surrounded by the Army. We took off at 2.30pm and got into formation on the circuit in bad visibility. We set course from over Lakenheath an hour later after climbing to 8,000.' Ten minutes later [whilst] approaching a cloud bank the formation leader, without warning, turned across the front of us. Max put the nose down and passed under him and in front of the following formation, which went into the cloud in disorder. A few minutes later I saw two Lancs in collision, locked together, [with] their noses pointing vertically upwards. Then they were lost in cloud.

An aerial photograph taken over Calais on 20th September 1944. Note the numerous bomb craters.
Courtesy of Reg Heffron

The incident recorded in Reg's diary related to the mid-air collision of Lancasters, LM167, GI-N, and LL802, GI-M, both of No.622 Squadron. The former, piloted by Flying Officer M. Hogg, had taken-off at 14.35 hours, five minutes after Max Bourne had taken-off, whilst the latter, piloted by Flying Officer C. James, had taken-off at 14.36 hours. They both impacted with the ground at Wormingford, to the northwest of Colchester, Essex, killing all fifteen airmen who made up the two crews.

Having witnessed the grotesque spectacle, which was enacted out in front of them, the other members of aircrew had no choice but to continue with their allotted mission. As the formation continued southwards out over the Thames Estuary and across Kent to Calais, each man sat at his crew station, silent with his own thoughts. Maybe, due to the fact he was older than the rest of the crew, was married and had a young daughter, Bill Vincent was deeply disturbed by what he had seen. The incident was something about which he never spoke, either then or later in life.

A total of 646 aircraft, comprising 437 Lancaster bombers, 169 Halifax bombers and 40 Mosquito aircraft, were despatched on the raid, seventeen of the Lancasters being detailed by No.622 Squadron. Reg recorded that seventy-nine other aircraft were bombing at the same time when Max Bourne held E-Easy on her bombing run. Blasts from the bombs exploding below continually shook the aircraft as Max fought to hold 'Easy' steady, at an altitude of between two and three thousand feet. Dust, debris and smoke added to the situation.

With their task completed and the aiming point photograph taken, Flying Officer Bourne turned the Lancaster onto a heading for home, swinging south before turning north-west. Looking down from his vantage point Reg could see the paradoxical situation of Allied Army vehicles traveling along the roads, whilst French farmers went about their business working their fields. Turning over Le Touquet, the evidence of war was more obvious with the town being badly damaged and the two road bridges across the river being inaccessible.

Max and the crew returned to base via Reading and landed at RAF Mildenhall at 17.40 hours. After de-briefing, where more than one report was made about the mid-air collision, the crew went to tea and then spent the rest of the evening relaxing in the Mess.

The raid, which lasted for a total of two and a half hours, was recorded as the heaviest attack against Calais with accurate and concentrated bombing.

Fifteen Down, with Fifteen to Go

It is not recorded in Reg's diary whether, during their musing in the Mess after the attack on Calais, the crew realised that they were exactly half way through their tour of operations. Their mission tally was fifteen down, with fifteen to go.

As no operations were scheduled over the next few days the crew was able to relax, although they were not given leave. Apart from carrying out daily inspections on the aircraft and a few other small jobs at dispersal, time was very much their own until 23rd September.

Saturday, 23rd September 1944

Operation No.16
Neuss
We took off at 7.15pm and set course from base via Clacton, Ostend, Liege and Aachen to the target, [where] there was complete overcast at 12,000' and the only indication we had of [the target] was a faint red glow on the cloud. We did a wide orbit to starboard and dropped our bombs on the second run onto an invisible target.

Bomber Command sent a total of 549 aircraft to attack the railway yards and docks at Neuss, on the southwestern outskirts of Dusseldorf. Seven bombers were lost during the operation, which was considered a success, although the count could have easily been eight.

Avro Lancaster bomber, LM577, E-Easy, was undertaking its 47th operational mission and was beginning to show signs of 'battle-fatigue.' During the flight out, Max Bourne had a fight on his hands as the bomber struggled to maintain height at 18,000.' but, as Reg recorded, they managed to reach the target and drop their deadly cargo. As they turned away from the target, four enemy fighters were spotted but, much to the crew's relief, they made no move on the ailing bomber. Then, at that same moment, the hydraulics serving Roger's rear turret failed, as did his intercom. The problems were further compounded when, according to Arthur's diary, the starboard fixed aerial was damaged by flak and continued to flap back and forth, against the cockpit, in the wind. Added to all of this, Paul and Roger almost lost consciousness due to lack of oxygen whilst trying to repair the intercom.

Over the Belgian frontier, on the way out of the target area, the aircraft began to lose altitude again and was down to 4,000' as the bomber passed over Lille in France. Max fought with the controls and managed to climb to a height of 10,000' in order to cross the 'enemy' coast and the North Sea.

However, even when they reached base at 23.30 hours, their troubles were still not over. Firstly, they had to circle for half an hour before being given permission to land at 00.05 hours then, having reached terra-firma, Max had to taxi around the remains of a crash-landing in order to reach his dispersal!

The aircraft that had crashed on the runway at Mildenhall an hour before Max landed was PD285, LS-Z, of No.XV Squadron. It had been piloted by Flying Officer George Williamson, RAAF, who had requested a priority landing due to the fact his flight engineer, Sergeant Arthur Piggin, had been taken ill. According to the official accident record card (A.M. F1180), Flying Officer Edward Winton, the bomb aimer, assisted the pilot during the landing procedure, but failed to lower the undercarriage when ordered to do so. The pilot was held responsible for not checking that the undercarriage had been lowered as ordered, and this action was recorded as being due to faulty cockpit drill. The crew escaped injury and the aircraft, which sustained Category B damage, was repaired and eventually returned to operations.

Avro Lancaster Mk.I, PD285, LS-Z, had originally been taken-on-charge by No.XV Squadron on 25th August 1944. A week later, on 1st September, the aircraft was taken-on-charge by No.622 Squadron, only to be returned to No.XV Squadron two days later. Following its accident, PD285 was returned to A.V. Roe, where it took four months to repair the damage. Finally, on 21st January 1945, the aircraft was taken-on-charge by No.50 Squadron. It was finally struck-off-charge during October 1946.

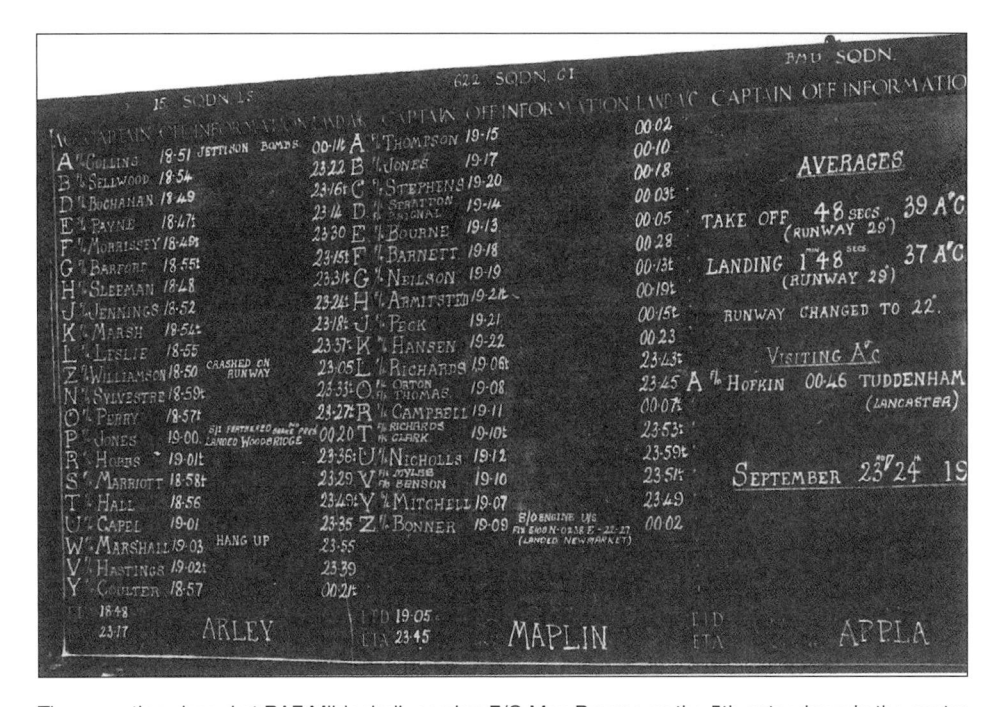

The operations board at RAF Mildenhall, naming F/O Max Bourne as the 5th entry down in the center column. F/O Williamson's name, in the left-hand column, records by the side of it that his aircraft 'Crashed on runway.' *Author's Collection*

It had been a long, tiring and fraught day for the crew, which had started when they missed their breakfast. Then, having carried out the daily inspection on the aircraft, they found that they were to undertake an H2S exercise encompassing Mildenhall, Norwich, Yarmouth and Lowestoft, during which Reg nearly froze to death, followed by the fact they were listed on the Battle Order. It was one trip they would not forget!

Monday, 25th September 1944

Operation No.17
Calais
We were awoken at 4.00am by the Service Police and told we were on the Battle Order, so dashed up to the Mess, got an early breakfast and [then] made our way to the briefing room. [Following the briefing] Roger and I then began a wild dash round in the darkness to collect our guns and put them in the turrets. We took off in daylight at 7.00am got into formation in the circuit and set course from Lakenheath via the Thames Estuary and Kent at 8.45am. Visibility was good at first, but over the Channel was a cloud layer that hid the target. We had to orbit for nearly half-an-hour, then we heard by R/T the mission was canceled.

Bomber Command detailed a total force of 872 aircraft to attack Calais, where German defensive positions were still defiantly holding out. However, the speed with which the cloud layer moved in meant that only 287 aircraft were able to bomb the target before the attack was called-off.

All nine aircraft from No.622 Squadron were ordered to jettison three bombs each into the English Channel so as to attain a safe landing weight back at RAF Mildenhall. Having carried out this order safely, the formation returned to its Suffolk airfield via the south coast and up across Reading, Berkshire.

As far as Max and the boys were concerned, the only good thing to come out of the abandoned operation was that the crew, having had an early breakfast, also managed to secure an early lunch!

As far as Bomber Command was concerned the day was not completely wasted as seventy Handley Page Halifax bombers of No.4 Group were detailed for use in a transport role. The crews' allotted task was to ferry petrol across the Channel to Belgium to assist the Allied ground forces, who were experiencing a severe fuel shortage. Each aircraft carried approximately 750 gallons of fuel, contained in about 165 petrol cans, on each flight. Over an eight-day period, commencing on this particular day, approximately 325,000 gallons of petrol were delivered.

Tuesday, 26th September 1944

Operation No.18
Cap Griz Nez
Once again we were awakened by the Service Police, this time at 6.30am and after dressing hastily went to an early breakfast. Briefing was at 8.00am and our target was a long range gun battery at Cap Griz Nez used for shelling the English coast. We took off at 10.15am got into formation, and set course from Mildenhall at 8,000' a little over an hour later.

We reached the French coast [where] bombing was well concentrated and made without any opposition. The countryside in the area is scarred with bomb craters for miles, and in two places patches of ground covering about a quarter of a square mile were devoid of everything but churned up earth, [due to] the bomb craters overlapping each other.

Two separate raids, both in the same area, were ordered by Bomber Command for this day, with 191 aircraft being detailed to the bomb areas around Calais, whilst 531 bombers attacked four targets at Cap Griz Nez. No.622 Squadron dispatched eleven aircraft on the latter operation.

Having reached the target area without incident, Max Bourne eased E-Easy onto the bombing run and at four-minutes-past-mid-day Tom Brown released the bomb load from an altitude of 9,000.' The bombs rained down and exploded on impact, sending dirt, debris and mud high into the air, thus adding even more craters to the already battle-scarred landscape, of which Reg and Roger had uninterrupted views from their respective turrets.

During the bombing Max had, somehow, lost the formation and had to wait until he was out over the Channel, well clear of the target area, before making a circular orbit in order to locate the remainder of the Squadron. His aim achieved, Max rejoined the formation and flew home.

On landing at RAF Mildenhall, instead of taxiing E-Easy back to the aircraft's dispersal area, Max taxied to one of the hangers where the bomber, which three days earlier had shown signs of 'battle fatigue,' was to undergo an overhaul.

Following the de-briefing, Reg and Roger returned to the hanger where they stripped the guns from their respective turrets and returned them to the cleaning room. With a feeling of a job well done, Reg, accompanied by Tom and Arthur, set off for the cinema, where they watched a film entitled, 'Millions Like Us.' This was not, as may have been thought, a film about military personnel at war, but a film about two young women, working in an aircraft factory, caught up in the turmoil of the war as endured by civilians. The main feature was followed by a newsreel film showing the destruction of flying bombs over southern England, which appealed to Reg.

With a lack of operational tasks to keep them occupied over the next few days, certain members of the crew reverted to that period of their training when they did nothing but eat! However, this basic human activity seemed to get the better of Roger on one occasion. Four of the boys decided to jump in the Rover and drive to Mildenhall for tea at Tilly's Café, where Roger caused much suppressed amusement by depositing a plate full of scrambled eggs, fried tomatoes and toast upside down in his lap. Nobody knows how this was achieved, or saw the plate do a backward somersault, but there Roger sat bemused by the sight of his tea having reached his stomach without him even opening his mouth. Even Tilly had a grin on her face as she assisted in the clean-up operation.

The following day, the eating marathon continued when the lads decided to have lunch at Morley's Café, thereby giving Tilly's a wide berth. On this occasion, Roger managed to keep the plate and its contents of a pile of fried tomatoes, eggs, and that wartime delicacy Spam and fries, on the table. This was followed with a large bowl of stewed apples and custard.

Smoke rises high into the air during an attack against the coastal defenses at Cap Griz Nez on the Channel coast of France. *Courtesy of the Late Arthur Bourne*

Feeling somewhat bloated, they helped each other out to the car and drove back to camp, just in time for roll-call. Roger and Reg then spent the afternoon cleaning their guns before going to the Mess for tea! This was followed later in the evening by supper, also taken in the Mess.

For a third day in succession, food seemed to be the main agenda with which to occupy the day. Having been dismissed after roll call, Reg, Roger and Paul jumped into the Rover and drove back to Morley's Café for breakfast. Although no description is available as to the content of this meal, it must have been quite hearty as the guys spent the rest of the morning sitting in the car reading the newspapers; that is until lunchtime! Both tea and supper were again taken in the Mess.

Feeling somewhat aggrieved that they had missed breakfast the next morning, the crew made up for it by tucking into platefuls of bacon and fried tomatoes, followed by marmalade and toast. The proprietor of Morley's Café must have been rubbing his hands eagerly together with this constant flow of regular customers.

Fifteen Down, with Fifteen to Go

Although feelings of contentment followed their breakfast, the aggrieved feelings they had started the day with, returned later in the morning out at dispersal, when they found another crew taking the beloved E-Easy on an H2S exercise. As this situation was beyond their control, Reg and the others headed for the Mess where they sat down to what Reg described as a tripe curling lunch. However, this experience did not prevent them from visiting Tilly's Café during the late afternoon!

On their return to camp, the crew found they had been detailed to fly that night but, on entering the briefing room at 7.00pm, they were informed the exercise had been canceled. Big smiles burst onto each of their faces as they left the briefing room headed back to their billet, where they sat down to boiled eggs, toast and tea.

The eating bonanza went into a fifth day and was only broken when Reg paid a visit to the petrol issuing officer to inquire about the availability of petrol for a car he intended to buy. Unfortunately, much to his chagrin, Reg received a very polite, but negative answer, so he withdrew from the situation feeling somewhat baffled with the outcome.

Monday, 2nd October 1944
[After] the daily inspection at dispersal, [we] spent the rest of the day chasing after leave passes and filling in cards and forms. [Later] Roger and I went by bike to the Bull at Barton Mills for an hour or so. [Whilst there] the lights over the whole district failed so all the cafés were closed and the only place we could get supper was at the Mess.

Whilst Reg and the others were getting ready for bed that night (by torch light), F/S Keith Coombe arrived, having returned from six days' leave. They had not seen 'Erk' for some time, so sat chatting with him, catching up on all his news whilst eating mouthfuls of the chocolate he had brought with him.

Morley's Café, Mildenhall. The man about to enter the premises has been identified as Flight Sergeant 'Butch' Harris, a bomb aimer serving with No.XV Squadron. *Author's Collection*

Eventually 'Erk' took his leave and, as the door slammed behind him and the sound of his boots thumped down the stairs, Reg and the others tumbled into their respective beds. Poor Keith then had to ride his bike back to his own billet in total darkness.

Tuesday, 3rd October 1944
Much rushing about to dress, collect passes and pack, for the whole crew goes on leave today. We got a taxi to Shippea Hill station and caught a train there for London at 12.15pm. We had to ride in the guards van with some crates of fowls, prams and bikes for the first part of the trip. [We] got into Liverpool Street station after 3.00pm and took a taxi to Australia House; where Roger and I dumped our bags [before hitting the town].

Having spent the evening, first at the cinema, followed by a visit to the Boomerang Club and later at Codgers, Reg and Roger eventually found some sleeping accommodation at the Gordon Club in Victoria.

The following morning, having booked a room at the Victoria League Club and transferred their luggage there, the inseparable pair set off by tram for Streatham, South London, where they wanted to buy a car. Unfortunately, Reg and Roger were unsuccessful in this venture so preceded to another dealership at Clapham Junction, where they found a Morris 8/40 at a price which did not do too much damage to their wallets and would, they were told, be ready for collection two days later.

Thursday, 5th October 1944
Roger packed a bag and set off for Brighton, intending to return in time to pick up the car tomorrow. I went [first] to the Boomerang Club for lunch, then to Kodak House in Kingsway, to collect a walletful of money, after which I went to County Hall to purchase a driver's license.

Whilst sitting in his room later that evening, the air raid sirens wailed into life, followed very quickly by the chug-chugging noise of two flying bombs in quick succession. Reg heard the explosions as both fell to earth in the nearby vicinity but, thankfully, not too close.

Like an excited child, Reg was up early on Friday morning and went to the Boomerang Club, where he was to meet Roger. The latter materialised at mid-day and together the pair set off by bus to Clapham Junction to see if the car was ready. To their dismay it was not. However, before they could legally drive the car there was a small technicality that had to be overcome; the issue of a Motor Vehicle License. This problem was easily resolved by Reg and Roger who made their way to the Motor Vehicle Licensing Office in Tooting where, having paid the appropriate fee, the document was handed over.

Saturday, 7th October 1944
Much fooling about, dragging of bedclothes off [the beds] and throwing them about the room, etc. before we went to breakfast.

The excited, childlike, playfulness started the day as it had done the previous morning, however, it was a bit more exuberant on this occasion as Reg had somebody with whom to share the excitement.

Having first paid a visit to Kodak House to place an order for cigarettes, the mischievous pair boarded a bus to Clapham Junction, to see what progress had been made with their car. As the vehicle was nearly ready, they decided to wait for it. Eventually, after handing over a large wad of one pound notes, the car was theirs. With some trepidation, Reg carefully reversed the car off the parking lot and out into the road, before beginning the hectic journey through London's traffic to Vauxhall Bridge Road. It was the first time in three years that Reg had driven a car and nine miles of traffic lights, trams, buses, cars and trucks, plus the pedestrians and a maze of streets (some one-way only) left him a nervous wreck. Having parked the vehicle in the car park near the Victoria League Club, Reg was spared the trauma of undergoing any further driving (even if he had felt able to), due to the lack of petrol in the car.

After a well-earned lunch, Roger and Reg made their way by train to Tom's home in Charlton, South London, in the hope of begging some petrol coupons with which to purchase petrol. Unfortunately their luck, like Tom, was out, so having made the journey for nothing they had to retrace their steps back to central London.

Sunday, 8th October 1944
Had breakfast then began a day long hunt for enough petrol to get us back to camp. We began by calling at a [barrage] balloon site, then went to a garage near Vincent Square and were rebuffed. From here we took a taxi to the Air Ministry building in Woburn Place and tried to get coupons, but were politely sent on our way once more. Then another taxi ride to Charing Cross, where we got a train to Charlton once more, in the hope of begging some coupons from Tom.

Ironically, the 'scrounging pair' met Tom in a street near his home, where he was trying to get his car to start. After many attempts the engine 'fired,' they all climbed in and drove the short journey back to Tom's house.

Back at the house, Reg and Roger informed Tom of their dilemma, no doubt adding a few heart wrenching performances into the bargain, whilst Daphne prepared lunch for them. Having partaken of lunch, and secured two half-gallon coupons from Tom, the 'scrounging pair' took their leave, with Tom giving them a lift back to the railway station.

Later that evening, under the cover of the blackout, and armed with the two cherished petrol coupons, the scheming pair set off in search of the elusive fuel. They went back to the balloon site they had visited earlier where, to their utter amazement and delight, they achieved their objective, albeit with a young W.A.A.F, with whom they stayed long enough to have a cup of tea and a chat!

Monday, 9th October 1944
We raced round to the car park to collect our precious Morris, then drove back to the club, packed our bags, and set off for Tom's place at Charlton, via Old Kent Road and New Cross Road.

Having scrounged lunch from Daphne Brown the previous day, the two incorrigible rogues had Tom's poor young wife making them tea before they departed on the journey back to Mildenhall.

After stopping for more tea at Newmarket on the way back, the trio also made a stop at the Bull Inn at Barton Mills for sustenance of a stronger nature, before the final few miles to the camp. To their surprise and delight, they found 'Erk' awaiting their arrival. The details of what they got up to whilst on leave, including the saga of purchasing the car, were all related to 'Erk' over supper taken at Morley's Café.

Tuesday, 10th October 1944
After lunch and [a second] roll-call, Roger, *'Erk'* and I drove into Mildenhall to do some shopping, for which we used our [left over] leave coupons to buy food for future suppers in our house at camp.

The first part of the morning was spent, needless to say, polishing the car, before they went shopping. The return journey to camp was made with Roger at the wheel, which caused Reg to record in his diary, "we got there safely."

During the day, a new Lancaster bomber flew into RAF Mildenhall, to be allocated to No.622 Squadron. As this type of event was a somewhat regular occurrence, no mention of its arrival was made in Reg's diary. However, unbeknown to them, the crew would soon get acquainted with this same aeroplane.

The Sheffield Incident

Not having been airborne for two weeks, it was time for Max and the crew to make a return to flying which, given the nature of the weather, did not rest well with them.

Thursday, 12th October 1944
[We] made our way out to dispersal to clean the guns and make the usual inspections. We had a chat with the ground crew, which took us up to lunch time, [then] Roger had a driving lesson in the Morris. After lunch we gathered at the section [where] we found we were to fly in spite of the bad weather and low cloud.

Having completed all the necessary cockpit checks, Max lifted E-Easy off Mildenhall's runway at 15.30 hours and climbed up into the low, gray clouds. The nature of the flight was an air test during which all the equipment on board the aircraft was individually tested, this presumably following the Lancaster's overhaul whilst the crew were on leave. Having cruised around in the driving rain for an hour, and satisfied themselves that all the equipment was in good working order, they finally returned to base. Having confirmed to a relieved groundcrew that all was well, the 'Easy Boys' stood down.

During the early evening, some of the crew went to the cinema to see a film entitled, 'Heaven Can Wait,' an epithet with which the whole crew, plus many other airmen, would have agreed. It was certainly a 'phrase' which came to mind when they had to return to the fray on the following Saturday.

Saturday, 14th October 1944

Operation No.19
River Port
We were awakened at 3.00am as we are on the Battle Order for today. [We] went to breakfast at 4.00am and then to briefing [half-an-hour later]. About this time a flying bomb passed over and exploded nearby. Our target was Duisburg in 'Happy Valley' [the Rhur], a large inland port on the Rhine.

At 06.30 hours, before the first light of dawn penetrated the morning sky, the green Aldis lamp signal flashed in the darkness. Flying Officer Max Bourne pushed the throttles forward, allowed the power to build in the four Rolls Royce engines and, with that same power

A poor quality aerial photograph of the docks at Duisburg. *Author's Collection*

surging through the aircraft, released the brakes. The Lancaster moved forward, slowly at first, but then gathered pace. With Bill Vincent sitting watching his pilot's movements, whilst at the same time keeping an eye on the instruments, Max guided E-Easy down the runway with ever-increasing speed. As Max eased gently back on the control yoke, the heavily laden Lancaster lumbered up into the air at the start of his flight to Duisburg.

Sergeant Arthur Bourne, from the seclusion of his navigator's compartment behind the cockpit, passed course details to his pilot. Initially, they headed east, but then flew what was referred to as the 'Kings Lynn triangle' while waiting for other bomber aircraft to join the formation. As they flew the 'triangle,' they gained altitude, flying through cloud until Max levelled out at 18,000.' One-hour-and-twenty-two-minutes after E-Easy had taken-off, the formation finally headed out over the sea towards its target. The sky was a mass of aircraft; twenty-one of which were detailed by No.622 Squadron.

This raid, however, was not just an attack against the world's largest inland port. It had been given the special code-name 'Operation Hurricane' and involved the use of 1,013 bomber aircraft, supported by a large fighter escort. Its purpose was to evince to the enemy that both the RAF and American Eighth Army Air Force had overwhelming superiority in its ability to attack such targets.

During the outward flight there was little or no opposition, but that was to change as the formation approached the target, where heavy flak peppered the lightening sky with angry black bursts of shrapnel. Such was the intensity of the flak that it was later revealed that thirteen Lancaster bombers and one Halifax bomber failed to return.

Whilst the gunners had no choice but to scan the skies and watch the scenario unravel around them, Paul Taylor, the wireless operator, and Arthur Bourne, the navigator, could if they so desired, keep their heads down. Although this was something the latter admitted to on more than one occasion, Arthur did not take this stance during the attack. Instead, he climbed up into the astrodome and effectively became a spare pair of eyes for the gunners. Paul on the other hand, who had little to do at this juncture of the mission, sought his pilot's permission to be allowed to climb down and join Tom in the bomb aimer's compartment. Given that he did nothing to impede Tom in the execution of his duty, Paul's request was granted. However, having climbed down into the confines of the bomber's nose, Paul's stay there amounted to less than a few seconds, after which he was observed hurriedly retracing his steps back to the confines of his own station on the aircraft, muttering basic Anglo-Saxon expletives!

It was into this maelstrom of fury that Max flew, holding the Lancaster on a steady course, endeavouring to fly straight and level whilst being buffeted about by exploding anti-aircraft fire. The urge to get out of that 'corner of hell' was immense, but Max concentrated on the slow, deliberate tones of Tom Brown issuing his instructions on the bombing run. At the appropriate moment, Tom pressed the bomb release button, checked the switches as usual and then called, "Bombs gone." The deadly cargo rained down from an altitude of 18,000' and exploded amongst a churning mass of smoke, cloud and dust, between a built up area to the west end of the docks and the river, at three-minutes-past-nine-o'clock.

With the aiming point photograph taken, and their luck still holding against the continuing torrent of flak, Max Bourne pushed forward on the 'stick' and put the aircraft into a diving turn. Luck stayed with the crew as they made their return home, even when they passed close to a German flak battery situated in a pocket on the Scheldt. However, given that the shells were not radar predicted and the German gunner's aim was not very good, the crew of E-Easy did not show too much concern. Their attention, however, was drawn to the island of Walcheren, which was almost completely flooded as a result of recent action by the Royal Air Force.

Having crossed the Dutch coast, Max decreased altitude down to 5,000' and remained at that height as he crossed the North Sea. Re-crossing the English coast at Orfordness, they reached base at 11.00 hours and, to the crew's delight, were given an early turn for landing. They wasted no time in 'closing down' the aircraft and then hurried off to de-briefing.

Following a quick lunch five of the crew, of whom it must be remembered were up at 03.00 hours that same morning, decided to jump in the Rover and head off to do some shopping in Mildenhall. Needless to say, being in the town, they rounded off the day by having dinner at Tilley's Restaurant.

On returning to camp, two shocks awaited the five airmen. The first one came when they found that their names, along with those of Max Bourne and Tom Brown, plus nineteen other crews' were on the Battle Order for an attack that night; the target was another strike against Duisburg! Unfortunately, the second shock came later, when circumstances were to dictate that Max and his crew would not undertake the mission after all; in fact, they did not even get as far as taxiing out for take-off.

Following his return from the earlier attack, Max followed the normal procedure of taxiing straight in to the dispersal area, opening the bomb doors and shutting down the engines, with the tail of the aircraft facing the exit of the dispersal pan. Normally a tractor would have turned the aircraft around but, with two maximum effort raids in one day requiring bombing up, re-fuelling and re-arming it seems that either there was insufficient

A photograph showing part of the devastation following action by the Royal Air Force, in an effort to flood areas of Walcheren Island, Netherlands, with a view to driving enemy forces away from the area. *Author's Collection*

A rare and poor quality photograph of 'Tubby' Hiscock posing for a photograph with Flying Officer Tom Brown. *Courtesy of the Late Arthur Bourne*

time to turn the aircraft or no tractor was available for the task. So, when taxi time came, the Lancaster had to turn on the concrete dispersal, under its own power. Of the episode, Max Bourne later wrote:

We had taken part in the morning effort and were on the Battle Order for that night. Having completed all of the routine checks, started the engines and run them up for testing, the time came to taxi out to the take-off point. The ground crew chief, Flight Sergeant *'Tubby'* Hiscock, directing me with his signal torches, had me heading for a large muddy puddle off the edge of the dispersal hardstanding. Afraid of bogging, I took my eyes off him for a few seconds and did my own thing, aiming to leave the dispersal via the concrete 'driveway' as usual. Bad decision, [I] should have bogged the ruddy thing. As I swung to port again to line up with the 'driveway,' one of the crew yelled, "Stop." Too jolly late! At the same instant was heard the clatter of my starboard outer airscrew chewing up the wingtip of an aircraft which should not have been within a hundred yards, let alone with his blasted wingtip poked into our dispersal.

Somewhat taken aback by what had just happened, Max shut down the engines. The sound of silence that followed was eerie after the banshee-like screaming they had just encountered. Gradually the crew became aware of noises outside the aircraft as members of ground crew raced forward to see what had happened, the beams of their torches flashing back and forth as they hurried to the scene.

On clambering out of their aircraft, Max and the crew were able to ascertain exactly what had occurred a few minutes earlier. It became apparent that as E-Easy edged forward off the dispersal pan the aircraft collided with another Lancaster taxiing past far too closely.

One of the first to arrive on the scene, apart from the ground crew who were already there, was the workshop engineering officer, to whom Max suggested the aircraft could still undertake its allotted task as there appeared to be no visible damage to the propeller. Unfortunately, Max received a reply that the aircraft was grounded due to the fact the prop would have to be shock tested.

Bearing in mind the part played by 'Tubby' Hiscock in the episode, Max was quick to vindicate the latter of any blame, informing the engineering officer that the ground crew chief was out of sight, having disappeared from view behind the port inner engine at the moment of impact.

After having faced many 'visitors' all armed with torches and questions, which they were duty bound to answer, Max and the crew were packed off in a vehicle back to the locker room, where they disrobed from their flying kit whilst wondering what would happen next.

Sunday, 15th October 1944
At 10.30am Bill came in to wake us up. Events had moved fast during the night after our accident, and we (the whole crew) had to be ready to leave for a disciplinary camp at Sheffield at 3.15pm there to dote on our misdeed for the next three weeks.

That morning, prior to leaving RAF Mildenhall, Flying Officer Max Bourne stood in front of a desk, with memories of his initial interview on being posted to No.622 Squadron, at the forefront of his mind. Behind the desk sat a stern-faced Wing Commander Ian Swales. In the latter's view, the Australian pilot who stood before him was responsible for messing up his reputation for top response to a call for 'maximum effort.' A warning had been issued at that initial interview, and now would come the unpleasant consequences.

Max was told that he and his crew were to go immediately to the Sheffield disciplinary camp, for a period of three weeks. When Max, in an effort to spare his crew being punished, suggested that the ultimate responsibility was his, he was told that the crew should have been keeping a lookout on the blind side of the aircraft.

In one final attempt to avoid their fate, Max pointed out that the collision occurred whilst his aircraft was still in its own dispersal area. He added (having discovered after the incident) that the other aircraft had been parked on the grass, running up her engines without the benefit of chocks or brakes and had rolled forward in the dark to a position alongside E-Easy's hardstanding. Wing Commander Swales paused for a moment then looked at Max and said, "Oh well, you had better go, all of the arrangements have been made."

On learning they were still going to disciplinary camp, Reg Heffron, ever philosophical, remarked that they should consider the fact that one of the operational missions they were to miss whilst at Sheffield might just have been their 'chop' trip. Everyone concurred that this was a reasonable thought.

Monday, 16th October 1944
We arrived at Sheffield at 2.30am (having travelled via London) and spent the next two hours hanging about the station waiting for transport to captivity.

Feeling cold, unhappy and somewhat aggrieved, the crew finally arrived at the camp at Norton, south of the city, at 04.30 hours. Much to their consternation and anger, they were told that there were no beds available so they would have to sit in the Mess all day until beds became available later during the afternoon.

Having had only eleven hours sleep over the last three days, Reg and the rest of the crew did not feel too bright, which added to their annoyance. Furthermore, not that they really expected any but, there was a total lack of sympathy for their plight.

Tuesday, 17th October 1944
A pleasant little voice bawled us out of bed at 6.00am and after washing, making our beds and sweeping up, we marched off to breakfast. Then back to the hut to get coats and notebooks.

The first hour of the day consisted of drill. They were then taken by transport to the swimming pool in Sheffield (compulsorily) to fill in the next hour. This activity was then followed with lectures until they broke for lunch. Another hour's drill took up the first part of the afternoon, followed, again, by more lectures. The afternoon concluded with an hour-long physical training session. However, although they may have thought it, the crew's day was not yet over as, after tea, they were to attend a night study class.

The Sheffield Incident

The ensuing days consisted of much the same type of routine, with one or two additional activities like window cleaning, floor polishing and C.O.'s inspections thrown in to keep the crew on their toes. The final indignation being that they had to be in bed by 10.30pm.

Sunday, 22nd October 1944
We had to go on church parade today at 9.45am all done up like sore toes to please the C.O. We marched a couple of miles to the village church at Norton, and then returned to camp at 12.30pm.

After lunch, the crew were allowed out of camp and immediately headed into Sheffield by bus. It was the first time they had seen the city in daylight and were shocked by the devastation they saw following attacks by Luftwaffe bombers. Many buildings were pretty badly damaged, whilst others were either burnt out or completely destroyed. Having spent the afternoon walking around the streets, Tom, Bill and Reg decided to go to the cinema, whilst Roger and Arthur went off in search of other activities. They all met up again at 8.00pm that evening, and according to Reg, both Roger and Arthur were both 'in a slightly disabled state.' No prizes for guessing where the latter spent their evening, but then who could blame them.

Whilst Reg and the others were wandering around Sheffield, unbeknown to them, Flying Officer George Williamson and his crew, including Keith Coombe, were packing their bags having been posted to No.186 Squadron, based at Tuddenham, approximately six miles from Mildenhall. The move must have come as a bit of a shock for the crew as, by

Flying Officer George Williamson and his crew, photographed at No.1653 Heavy Conversion Unit, flew with No.XV Squadron, RAF Mildenhall, before being posted to No.186 Squadron, at RAF Tuddenham. *Courtesy of the Late Arthur Bourne*

this particular time, they had completed a total of eighteen operational missions and were over half way through their tour of 'ops.'

No.186 Squadron had originally been formed at East Retford as a night flying training unit, producing pilots for the Home Front and Western Front during the First World War. After the Great War, during the inter-war period, it became a Torpedo Development Unit, based at Gosport, Hampshire, where it was re-numbered as No.210 Squadron. Reformed as a fighter-bomber unit during the Second World War, it was again re-numbered, on this occasion as No.130 Squadron.

On 5th October 1944, No.186 Squadron was reformed yet again, this time from 'C' Flight, No.90 Squadron, which was already based at Tuddenham. The new squadron did not, however, undertake its first operational mission until the 18th October, four days before the arrival of Flying Officer George Williamson and his crew.

On Wednesday, 25th October, an application was made by Max Bourne for an interview with the Senior Warrant Officer at the Camp to see if some of the restrictions levied against the crew could be lifted from their innocent shoulders. The application was granted and an interview came the following day.

Thursday, 26th October 1944

At it again all day, drill, swimming, P.T. and lectures until 4.00pm when our interview materialized. Paul did the talking on our behalf and [the outcome was] we were put on a modified course which allows us out on five nights a week. We were deliberating over our new found freedom on our beds when somebody remembered that this was one of the other two nights. We raced to the lecture room in a body. We will know tomorrow if we got away with it.

They got their answer after lunch the next day, when they were given the job of moving hundreds of three-gallon petrol cans from one part of the camp to another; a task which kept them busy all afternoon.

During the early evening, a visit was made to the hospital where Tom Brown had been admitted a day or two earlier. Due to the fact he was suffering from a duodenal ulcer, and on his being transferred to a hospital in Blackpool, the others all felt more than certain that they would lose him from the crew. This is exactly what happened as, on 28th October, F/O Tom Brown was officially posted to No.32 Base, RAF Mildenhall, where he was to undertake non-flying duties.

The drudgery and monotony of the day-to-day existence in the camp continued as October gave way to November. Relief came in the evenings, when they could go to Sheffield or visit a local pub near the camp, where on more than one occasion they almost had one too many drinks. Then a glimmer of hope appeared on the horizon.

Saturday, 4th November 1944

We are due to go back to Mildenhall on Monday or Tuesday, but have to pass some exams to get away from here. The first is a P.T. test, which we did this morning and I put up my best performance so far. We spent the afternoon playing floor hockey in the gym then everyone else disappeared, this being a general night off.

Sunday was a lazy day for all after church parade, which was held in the N.A.A.F.I. and finished at 10.00am. Roger and Arthur set off again for the pleasures that Sheffield had to offer, whilst the rest of the crew either read the papers or snoozed until teatime.

Monday brought forth the final two exams that the crew had to complete, which consisted of drill and admin. With the exams out of the way, the afternoon was spent getting the accommodation tidy, packing and getting the clearances approved ready for them to leave the camp the following morning.

In the evening a last visit to Sheffield was made by all, but when they got there Paul, Arthur and Reg set off for the pub. The intrepid trio, having drunk their fill, caught a bus back to camp via Gleadless, just north of Norton. Unfortunately, they stepped off the bus into a terrific storm with hailstones that nearly took their ears off! Having bought some fish and fries from a local shop, which they mournfully devoured in the shelter of a friendly wall, they finally set off on the long walk uphill back to camp.

Tuesday, 7th November 1944
Much bustle and activity first thing in the morning, for we were to be ready to leave for Mildenhall by 8.00am. We finally left those grim gates behind us at 8.30am.

Max Bourne and his crew, with the exception of Tom Brown who was still on sick leave, were taken to the railway station in Sheffield by truck, where they caught a train to London. Having arrived at St. Pancras, they took the underground train to Liverpool Street station, where they caught a main line train to Shippea Hill, traveling via Ely. The station at Shippea Hill was in a remote location, surrounded by fenland, approximately five miles northwest of the airfield at RAF Mildenhall. On reaching their destination, it fell to the captain of the crew to telephone the camp and request vehicular transport for his men. The time spent awaiting its arrival was put to good use in the local pub.

Wednesday, 8th November 1944
Needless to say we were in no hurry to step out of bed into the freezing cold, but were forced to eventually, as the C.O. wanted to congratulate us on our safe return. After seeing the 'old boy' we returned to our billet to continue last night's straightening out process which took the rest of the morning. After lunch we went flying for an hour or so to get us used to the idea once more.

It seems from the entry in Reg's diary that the 'flying lesson' was a good idea especially as, due to the bad visibility, Max experienced problems getting the aircraft down and was forced to overshoot twice before making a safe landing on the third attempt.

Thursday, 9th November 1944
Max, Roger and I flew with another crew on a fighter affiliation and bombing exercise. After lunch, Bill, Roger and I went to the village to get Tom's car and drove into Mildenhall to collect the Morris from the garage where we had left it before going to Sheffield. Had to get a tow to start both cars then took them back to camp. We found '*Erk*' in our billet, on leave after his crash-landing in Holland, and had a good yarn.

Avro Lancaster, PB223, GI-B. Max Bourne flew this aircraft on a fighter affiliation exercise on 9th November 1944. The aircraft is seen here taxiing out for an unrecorded war operation. *Author's Collection*

For the fighter affiliation and bombing exercise, during which Max flew as first pilot, he took the controls of Lancaster bomber, PD223, GI-B. The flight was uneventful and lasted just over one hour.

Although there had been no mention of it in Reg's diary, mainly because he had been away on an enforced stay at the disciplinary camp, 'Erk's' aircraft had been forced to make a crash-landing on 2nd November. Sergeant Keith Coombe along with his pilot, Flying Officer George Edward Williamson, RAAF, and the rest of the crew had been participating in an attack against Homberg. Their aircraft, Lancaster, LM618, AF-U, of No.186 Squadron, was hit by flak whilst approaching the target area. Both the port engines were disabled and, to add to the problem, only one propeller could be feathered. The port wing and part of the fuselage were doused with fuel as petrol seeped in due to the tanks being 'peppered' with shrapnel and, although the aircraft was losing height, F/O Williamson continued with his bombing run and completed a good attack. Having completed their task, course was set for home, but the aircraft continued to lose altitude. As though they did not have enough problems to contend with, the aircraft was hit by flak a second time, and with fuel diminishing at a fairly rapid rate, Flying Officer Williamson had no choice other than to put the stricken aircraft down. This he did, in a minefield, in Allied territory, near, Woensdrecht, south of Bergen op Zoom, Holland, at 15.10 hours. Having affected a 'safe' landing without injury to his crew, the next major task for George Williamson was to get them out of the minefield safely. Fortunately for all of them, this was achieved with the help of British troops who were in the vicinity at the time. For this action Acting Flight Lieutenant Williamson, RAAF, was awarded a Distinguished Flying Cross, notification of which he received on 17th November. The crew all returned safely to Tuddenham from where, after a short period of leave, they were to fly again.

Saturday, 11th November 1944

Operation No.20
Castrop-Rauxel
We were awakened at 6.00am for an early breakfast and briefing at 7.00. Our target was a synthetic oil plant and chemical works at Castrop-Rauxel near Dortmund, and our first

experience of G-H Bombing. We took off at 8.15am and set course from East Dereham at 9.09am at 8,000.'

Bomber Command dispatched a total of 122 Lancaster bombers for the attack, all of which were from No.3 Group. Sixteen of the aircraft were detail by No.622 Squadron. For this raid Max was piloting Lancaster bomber, PD229, GI-K.

The formation flew out over Suffolk and Norfolk following a course that took them over Bury St.Edmunds, Diss and Orfordness. Having crossed over the North Sea the formation (according to Reg's diary) continued over Antwerp and Nijmegen, where the participating crews could see the famous bridge spanning the River Waal. Turning south, the formation began the run towards the target. It was fortuitous that no enemy fighters appeared as, just prior to reaching the target, the hydraulics on Roger's rear turret failed when an oil line in the mainplane burst, spewing its contents over the port fin and tailplane.

When they reached Castrop-Rauxel the crews found the visibility less than 100% due to ground haze, but this did not impede the attack as all aircraft were fitted with the relatively new navigational aid G-H. This new system, which had been introduced in a fully operational trial only a week earlier, worked on the basis of a radar set installed on an aircraft, emitting signals to two receiving ground stations. After a given interval, the ground stations responded with distinctive signals. Measurement of the time-interval and the response enabled the navigator to fix the position of his aircraft.

A few minutes after 11.00am, flying at an altitude of 20,000,' Max commenced his bombing run. Momentarily, he was taken aback when a strange voice over the intercom began issuing the usual bombing run instructions. Due to the fact F/O Tom Brown, had been posted to No.32 Base, RAF Mildenhall, Flight Lieutenant H. Middleton was flying with the crew as a replacement bomb aimer. At eight minutes past eleven, bombing on instruments, F/L Middleton called, "Bombs gone," but the results were not observed although the bombing was reported as being fairly close.

The fact the bombing was reported as being fairly close was an understatement as far as Reg was concerned. As Max was holding the aircraft steady, in straight and level flight on the bombing run, a cluster of bombs cascaded down from above them, just missing the starboard wing. Although Reg was scanning the sky around him, watching for the possibility of fighter attack, he did not see the bombs being released from an aircraft flying directly above them and was therefore unable to issue a warning.

Although flak was scattered and inaccurate, it had been in constant action the whole time the formation was over enemy territory. Some bursts were closer than others, but nothing that close as to worry Reg that was, until later, when a piece of shrapnel was found embedded in the perspex canopy of his turret.

They re-crossed the North Sea at 20,000,' dropping down to 3,000' over Orfordness on their return to RAF Mildenhall, where they landed at 12.55 hours. After de-briefing, where they had a little more than usual to report, the crew went off for a well-deserved lunch.

Sunday, 12th November 1944

We were on the Battle Order all day, but eventually were not required and had a stand down until midnight.

Reg, and one or two of the others, passed the time talking, reading and doing some odd jobs on one of the cars. The following day was almost a repeat of Sunday, with the exception that the eating 'bug' seems to have struck again!

Being on the Battle Order for Monday, they arose early and hurried off to breakfast at the Mess. Following the first meal of the day, they then made their way to the briefing room where they learned the operation had been canceled. From the briefing room they went out to the dispersal area, where they chatted with 'Tubby' Hiscock and the other members of their groundcrew and, although Reg and the others got on very well with 'Tubby' and his lads, one cannot help but think the aircrew had an ulterior motive for sticking around. That motive possibly being the impending arrival of the N.A.A.F.I. wagon, which brought with it the promise of hot, steaming mugs of tea and a wad (sandwich, cake or bun). Having savoured the delights of the N.A.A.F.I van, Reg and the crew took their leave and returned to the house, where they awaited the arrival of lunch.

During the course of the afternoon, four of the crew piled into the Rover car and drove into Mildenhall, where tea and cakes were taken. This mission having being satisfactorily completed they returned to camp just in time for tea in the Mess. Supper was taken in Paul's room later during the evening.

Tuesday, 14th November 1944
Got up just in time for roll-call then went off to Morley's Café for breakfast. [We] got back to [camp] to find briefing about to begin. [We] went through all the usual instructions, meteorological, take-off details, formations etc. and were just collecting [our] flying gear [when] the effort was scrubbed. Naturally this caused some cheering and happy smiles for it is very cold today. [It is] the type of day when everyone should be huddled around fires and not flying.

The rest of the morning was spent in Arthur's room reading the newspapers until lunchtime. It was not until the afternoon, when they returned to Arthur's room, where Arthur sat writing letters home that Reg got to sit in front of a fire. That is until somebody announced it was time for tea, so off down to the Mess they trotted.

Wednesday, 15th November 1944

Operation No.21
Dortmund
The target was a synthetic oil plant and storage depot on the outskirts of Dortmund. Take-off was delayed until 12.30 [then], after circling base, we flew to Newmarket to meet the G-H aircraft and set course at 1.45pm via Bury, Diss and Orfordness, at 12,000.' We crossed The Belgian coast near Bruges at 20,000' leaving a great mass of vapour trails. The ground was completely obscured by cloud and we did not see any part of the continent during the whole trip. Approaching the target we ran into some bad visibility, which scattered the stream, and after this our fighter cover of Mustangs arrived. They did their best to go slow enough to keep with us. There was no flak until we reached Dortmund. During the bombing run the formations were straggling all over the place. The flak was very scattered and light, and did not cause much trouble. One Lancaster had an engine on fire, but was still flying straight

Flying Officer Max Bourne (third from left) and his crew with E-Easy. Note the aircraft identification letter under the front turret and the mission tally under the cockpit housing. Courtesy of the Late Max Bourne

and steady. We got our bombs away [but] had one hang-up, which we later dropped in the sea off Southwold. The return journey was uneventful, except for a few mysterious smoke puffs and streamers, which came up through the cloud. Over the target a flash of flame was probably a spoof (fired by A.A. guns on the ground) as we saw no wreckage falling. We maintained height until reaching the Belgian frontier, and then came down gradually over the North Sea, and got through a gap in the cloud near Orfordness. It was just getting dark as we reached base, and had to circle for half-an hour awaiting our turn to land.

One hundred and seventy-seven Lancaster bombers from 3 Group, nineteen of which were detailed by No.622 Squadron, participated in the above-described attack and although the crews could not see the target, the results were thought to have been fairly accurate.

Flying Officer Max Bourne was once again at the controls of E-Easy, but on this occasion the 'Easy' he was flying was a replacement aircraft for LM577. Lancaster bomber, LM577, GI-E, had sustained serious flak damage during a daylight attack against Bottrop on 31st October, whilst Max and his crew were still at Sheffield. The aircraft was repaired and returned to service with No.622 Squadron on 9th December 1944. However, four days later, the aircraft was transferred to No.218 Squadron.

The new E-Easy was Avro Lancaster bomber, Mk.I, PD366, built by Metropolitan-Vickers. Apart from one bomb refusing to budge from the bomb bay during the operation, the new aircraft flew without any other snags. It is not known whether F/O P. Titchener, who was flying with the crew as bomb aimer, felt any embarrassment about the hang-up situation; he should not have done as it was not his fault.

Two aircraft, HK595, KO-A, and NN706, KO-B, both from No.115 Squadron based at Witchford, were lost during the attack with, sadly, no survivors from either crew. The former aircraft was piloted by Squadron Leader Hugh Castle, RAFVR, age 30, of Beddington, Surrey, whilst the latter was flown by Flight Lieutenant John Davidson, RCAF, aged 21, of Ontario, Canada. It is not known whether either of these two aircraft was the one Reg saw flying with an engine on fire.

Thursday, 16th November 1944

Operation No.22
Heinsberg
We were awakened for an early breakfast, and then briefing, which was then delayed until 10.30am. The target was the town of Heinsberg, 16 miles from Aachen, the object being to destroy the roads and buildings being used by the Wehrmacht.

The attack, in support of the American First and Ninth Armies and the British Second Army, was carried out in two phases, with the United States Eighth Army Air Force undertaking the first aerial phase.

The operation was against a number of towns to the north and east of the Aachen area, including Heinsberg, Julich and Duren, which were all near the German lines, against which plans were prepared for a major assault. Apart from 'softening up' the area, the objective was to cut communications behind enemy lines.

At 11.15 hours on the morning of 16th November, a force of 1,239 American heavy bombers, comprising Liberators and Flying Fortresses, escorted by approximately 450 fighters, flew over the designated target areas and unleashed a cascade of bombs, their attack being timed to coincide with that of the ground forces.

Phase two of the operation was carried out later in the day by a total of 1,188 Bomber Command aircraft, comprising of Lancasters, Halifaxes and Mosquitoes, who continued the work commenced earlier by the United States Eighth Army Air Force. An escort of approximately 250 fighters protected the aircraft of the Royal Air Force.

Of the 188 Lancaster bombers participating from No.3 Group, who had specific orders to attack Heinsberg, eighteen were detailed by No.622 Squadron. Amongst the latter was Lancaster, E-Easy, with Max Bourne at the controls.

Max took off at 13.00 hours in very poor visibility, formed up over Lakenheath and set course with the formation one-hour-and-twenty-five-minutes later. Their route took them via Orfordness, the North Sea and Ghent, Belgium to the target area. The blanket of cloud, which had beleaguered them since take-off, began to break as they crossed the enemy occupied coast and flew over Belgium. Looking down, they could see traffic moving along the roads.

The run-up to the target, at an altitude of 7,000' was, as Reg put it, organised confusion. The target indicators were dropped in the wrong place and course corrections to the aiming point had to be made at the last minute by the Master Bomber, over the R.T. This resulted in a disorganised formation of Lancaster bombers arriving over the target at the same time. The entry in Reg's diary, relating to this episode reads:

'The stepped up formations bombed in layers and we were in the bottom layer. [We] had a hectic few minutes as the bombs came hurtling down around us. Our bombs went during all this disorder, and although we were at 7,000,' the blast from the 4,000 pound 'cookies' was plainly felt. We landed in poor visibility at 5.37pm. After de-briefing, we went to the Mess for tea and then to our house, [when] *'Erk'* arrived on a visit from RAF Tuddenham, his base.

Having carried out their allotted task, with yet another newcomer, Flight Sergeant J. Gambell, flying as bomb aimer, Max wasted no time in hauling E-Easy out of the stream and getting away from the melee that surrounded them.

The route home took them over Beveland and Walcheren, where they could clearly see the gap in the dyke and subsequent flooding, created by an attack by the RAF a few weeks earlier. They crossed the east coast of England at an altitude of 500' before climbing to 2,000' in preparation for landing at RAF Mildenhall at 17.37 hours.

Only one aircraft, Lancaster bomber, PB137, LS-U, of No.XV Squadron, piloted by Flight Lieutenant Frederick Sanders, RNZAF, was lost during the attack against Heinsberg, but it was to prove a significant loss. Apart from the pilot and crew, this aircraft also carried Wing Commander William Watkins, DSO, DFC, DFM, Officer Commanding No.XV Squadron, an observer/navigator who was acting as Master Bomber. Watkins was an experienced airman who had already completed a tour of operations with No.149 Squadron, on Vickers Wellington bombers.

Wing Commander William Watkins, DSO, DFC, DFM, Officer Commanding, XV Squadron, RAF. *Author's Collection*

Flight Lieutenant Sanders, a New Zealander from Timaru, on the east coast of South Island, had taken-off at 13.35 hours, thirty-five minutes after Max Bourne. Two hours later, at approximately 15.30 hours, F/L Sanders held Lancaster, PB137, on a steady approach to the target but, having made a safe bombing run, the aircraft was hit by flak. Although sustaining some damage the aircraft continued to fly on, but suddenly it was hit by heavy flak and exploded in mid-air. The bomber disintegrated and fell to earth, killing seven of the eight-man crew. Wing Commander Watkins, although badly burned about the face was the only survivor. He was later captured and taken prisoner of war.

Flight Lieutenant Sanders was also an experienced pilot. This particular sortie was his twenty-eighth, meaning that he only had to complete two more operational missions before being declared "Toured Expired" and sent on a rest from operational duties.

Having been through the usual ritual of debriefing following the operation, and tea at the Mess, the lads headed back to the house until suppertime. As they were preparing to go back to the Mess for supper, 'Erk' arrived and was invited to join them, which he did.

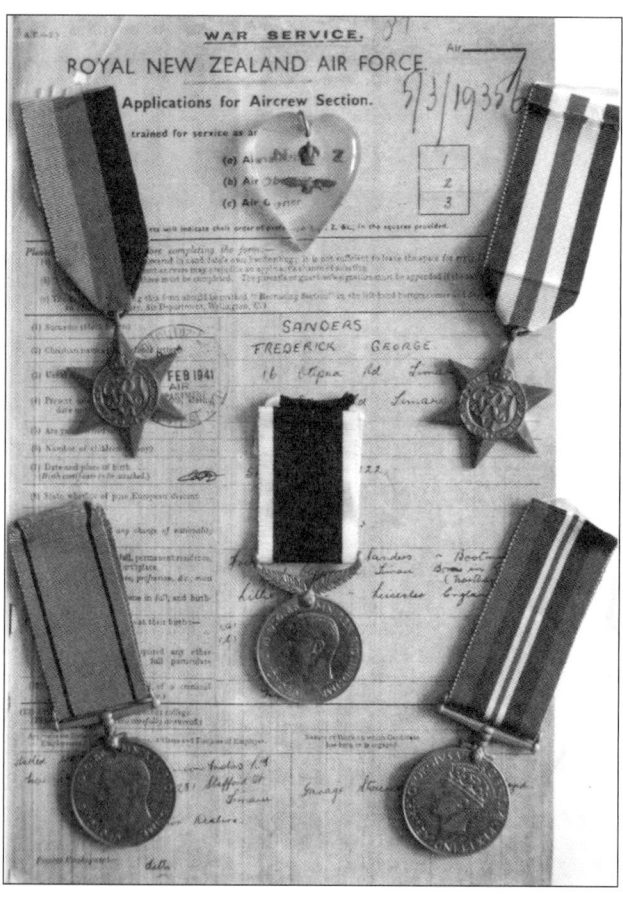

Left: Flight Lieutenant Frederick Sanders, RNZAF, photographed when a newly commissioned Pilot Officer, was killed in action on 16th November 1944. *Author's Collection* Right: Medals and memorabilia. A copy of Frederick Sanders' 'Application for Aircrew' with the Royal New Zealand Air Force, together with a sweetheart brooch and the Campaign Stars and War Medals he never saw or got to wear. *Author's Collection*

Following the meal, they adjourned to the Mess anteroom, where they played a few games of 'Housie, Housie,' which in postwar years was to be reinvented as Bingo. Later in the evening they ventured back to the house, where they sat in front of the fire in Paul's room, chatting over old times, the operations and the future until 'Erk' had to leave at midnight. Although they did not realise it at the time, this was to be a very poignant meeting.

Friday, 17th November 1944
No one came in to wake us up this morning so we slept in until 11.30am and had to get up then as lunch would not wait for us. After lunch we went to our section and then out to dispersal, in the pouring rain, to clean the guns.

The rest of the day was spent fairly close to the fire, in their room, listening to the radio, eating various varieties of food and drinking tea. The following day passed in much the same vein, except for the fact that some of the crew went in to Mildenhall for their meals.

After lunch on the Sunday, having had their photographs taken for new I.D. cards, which were to be issued soon, five of the crew piled into the Rover and headed for Tilly's Restaurant for tea. This was followed by a visit to the Comet cinema, where they saw a film entitled, 'Mr Lucky' a title which, having completed a total of twenty-two operations to date without too many hair-raising experiences, each member of the crew probably felt applied to him. However, from one line entered in Reg's diary for the following day, he may well have had second thoughts.

Monday, 20th November 1944

Operation No.23
Homberg
We are still on the Battle Order from yesterday. [We] cleaned our room and then went to briefing. The target was a synthetic oil plant at Homberg in the Rhur. The target has a reputation for deadly flak.

Bomber Command despatched a total of 183 Lancaster bombers from 3 Group, seventeen of which were detailed from No.622 Squadron.

Having completed the cockpit and other checks, Max released the brakes on E-Easy and let the aircraft roll forward and followed the snaking line of Lancasters in front of him along the taxiway towards the end of the runway. A final check of the engines and crew and, on the given signal, he turned the Lancaster onto the runway and pushed the throttles forward. The aircraft vibrated and shook as it gathered momentum, before finally lifting into the air at 12.35 hours. Suspended from the racks in the bomb bay were one 1,000lb bomb and sixteen 500lb bombs.

Not for the first time, Max endured the problem of having to climb up through cloud to join the formation at 16,000' to rendezvous with the G-H Leaders over Newmarket. One hour and twenty minutes later the formation set course via the usual route of Bury St. Edmunds, Diss, Orfordness and out over the North Sea.

The cloud persisted and on the way to the target the visibility deteriorated. The crews also encountered stratus and some very heavy convection cloud, which caused the formation to disperse. Unfortunately, things were not going to improve. The target was not visible and the bomber stream was divided in two by a large cloud which disorganised the bombing run and, consequently, the bombs went down all over the place.

A permanent replacement for Tom Brown had still not joined the crew, and Max was once again flying with a spare bomb aimer on board. On this occasion the position was occupied by Flight Sergeant O.M. Chaplin, RAAF, who released the bomb load at 15.30 hours. To his chagrin, one 500lb bomb refused to leave the comfort of the bomb bay, and remained there until further efforts were made on the way home to dislodge it and it finally fell into the North Sea. Flight Sergeant Chaplin's bombing run was made at an altitude of 21,000,' but even then they were not above the level of the highest cloud tops.

To Reg's joy, the flak was not as heavy as expected, but to his discomfort it was spot on for height and, just after leaving the target area, there was a huge explosion at 20,000,' which Reg believed to be a direct hit on a Lancaster bomber. His belief may have been well founded as Lancaster bomber, PB689, AA-X, of No.75 Squadron exploded in the air over Baerl, approximately four kms northeast of Moers. The entire crew, led by Flying Officer Ronald Gordon, was killed.

Concentrating on the job in hand, Max pushed the control column forward and E-Easy began to decrease height, passing through several banks of high cloud en-route. Then the cloud began to disperse allowing the crew to see the ground for the first time since they had taken-off. By the time they crossed the Belgian coast, Max was down to an altitude of 18,000,' but still flying in several smaller banks of cloud. However, in the time it took them to cross the English Channel, conditions had deteriorated once again and, in order to make a safe landing, Max was forced to fly at an altitude of 500' in order to keep the ground in sight.

Having safely reached the airfield, Max was required to remain in the circuit for thirty minutes before being giving permission to land. Even then, he had to endure a forty-five mile per hour crosswind.

Although nothing was recorded in Reg's diary, one cannot help but think that he really did think he was 'Mr Lucky,' unlike some others.

Five aircraft were lost during the attack against the synthetic oil plant. Apart from Lancaster, PB689, AA-X mentioned above, two other aircraft from No.75 Squadron also failed to return. The latter two aircraft were Lancaster Mk.III, PB520, AA-G, piloted by F/O H. Rees and Lancaster Mk.III, ND911, AA-Y, piloted by F/O P.L. McCartin, RAAF. Flying Officer Rees and his crew managed to bail out of their aircraft, but were all captured and taken prisoners of war. Flying Officer McCartin and his crew were less fortunate. One member of the crew survived, whilst the remaining six all paid the supreme sacrifice. Two of them are buried at Reichwald Forest War Cemetery, whilst the other four rest at Rheinberg War Cemetery. Flying Officer Patrick Leo McCartin, RAAF, aged 28 years, was the son of Michael and Anastatia McCartin, of Brunswick, Victoria, Australia.

Two more aircraft, one from No.514 Squadron and one from No.186 Squadron, also never made it home. The aircraft from No.514 Squadron, Lancaster bomber Mk.I, LM286, JI-F2, piloted by Flying Officer J. Harland, crashed in the target area with the loss of the whole crew.

9

The Loss of a Friend

The aircraft from No.186 Squadron, lost over Homberg, was Lancaster bomber, HK622, AP-Z, piloted by Flight Lieutenant George Williamson, DFC, RAAF. The aircraft was hit by flak whilst passing over Moers. It continued on a northeasterly course for a couple of kilometres, before crashing near Baerl. The entire crew, including Flight Sergeant Keith '*Erk*' Coombe, RAAF, was killed. Just as they had trained together, flew together and died together, they now all lie at rest together in the Reichswald Forest War Cemetery, Germany.

The loss of a friend is never an easy thing to bear, but the loss of seven friends at the same time brings with it much heartfelt sadness. These were no ordinary friends, they were brothers-in-arms with whom one had literally laughed, played, joked, trained and fought alongside. Such friendships could only be forged in a time of conflict, but the real tragedy was that those remaining had to put the loss of these friends to the back of one's mind and get on with the job in hand. This was the predicament that faced Reg and the crew when they received the news of the loss of '*Erk*' and his crew.

Tuesday, 21st November 1944
Much rush and bustle to pack and get ready for 6 days' leave with the assistance of the Morris. Roger's uniform had not arrived from the cleaners [by the time] we were ready to leave. So after lunch we set off for Bury to collect it. Left Bury and set off for Sheffield via St Ives, Huntingdon, Stilton and Stamford, where darkness overtook us.

Having to go and collect Roger's uniform had cost traveling time and, by the time Reg and Roger got to Stamford, they were forced to seek overnight accommodation. A task not as easy as one would have thought, as Reg had to try three pubs before finally securing a room for the night at the ancient George Hotel.

They were in no hurry to rise the following morning and it was 10.30am before they were ready to go. They duly complied with the request to "Pay at the desk" before departing in the direction of a nearby café where breakfast was taken. The Morris was not ignored either, having been given a drink of oil before the start of the long haul to Sheffield.

Upon arrival in the industrial city, Roger found suitable accommodation, whilst Reg continued his journey across to Manchester; a journey he could well have done without. It was very rough across the moors, with the wind almost blowing the car off the road at times. Gripping the steering wheel tightly, and changing down to second gear, Reg steered the car for many miles through the howling wind, knowing to some small degree how Max felt when he endured high winds when flying.

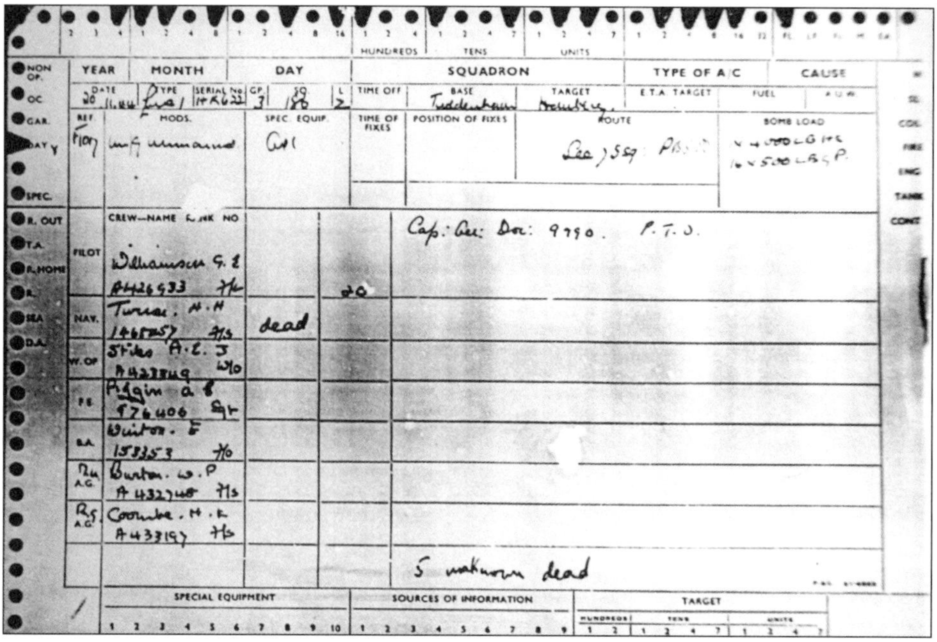

The caption reads:

The Operational Loss Card for Avro Lancaster, HK622, AP-Z, which Flight Lieutenant George Williamson, DFC, RAAF, was piloting on 20th November 1944. Reg Heffron's friend, Flight Sergeant Keith 'Erk' Coombe, RAAF, was one of the crewmembers killed when the aircraft crashed at Baerl. *Author's Collection*

Unfortunately for Reg, his troubles were not yet over. It was dark by the time he reached Manchester, and only by giving a lift to a stranger who knew the route did he manage to find his way to Irlam, where his relation Joe Dawson lived. However, a mile or so from his destination the car ran out of petrol and he was forced to beg a gallon of fuel from two old cronies sitting around a fire puffing on horrid pipes.

By the time Reg arrived at the house Joe had gone out, but as he had been expecting the young airman, he had left a key in a suitably, pre-arranged secret location. Reg took advantage of this fact, let himself into the house and made himself comfortable in front of the fire. Joe, who was a widower, and his daughter Dorothy returned home later in the evening, whereupon the kettle was boiled, bread, jam and cakes materialized and life became even more comfortable.

The next four days were spent talking, eating, doing odd jobs, visiting friends in the locality and visiting Manchester, usually all finished off with supper in front of the fire.

Sunday, 26th November 1944
After lunch I packed my bag and got the car ready for the road, for I have to go back to Sheffield to meet Roger and then return to Mildenhall tomorrow.

Having said his good-byes, Reg left Irlam at 3.30pm and headed off across the Pennines. If he thought the journey to Irlam was bad enough, he was in for a shock on the return journey. Crossing the 'Spine of England' he ran into a snowstorm and spent an anxious hour sliding all over the road. To add to his problem, the windscreen was coated with ice and visibility was down to a hundred yards. All he could see of the road was the tracks of the vehicles that had preceded him.

As with his outward journey, it was dark by the time he reached his destination, but he found Roger waiting for him at the Albany Hotel. They spent the evening together, first at the cinema and then at the Grand Hotel, before returning to their own accommodation.

The journey home the following day went without incident, that is until the front fender fell off the car as Reg was driving through Huntingdon. The diary does not record what expletives, if any, Reg used at the time.

Tuesday, 28th/Wednesday, 29th November 1944

Operation No.24
Neuss

We had been on the Battle Order all day and while waiting for the briefing in the evening I wrote some letters and we sampled a cake I received today. The pre-flight meal was delayed until 11.30pm and after that briefing began at 12.30am on Wednesday the 29th. The target was a railway yard, which we visited once before. We got out to dispersal and Max had to declare the aircraft u/s at the last minute and fly in a spare, Q-Queenie.

It was a little ironic that the first operation to be undertaken by Max and the crew since learning of the loss of 'Erk' and his crew, was against Neuss, the target they attacked when F/L George Williamson crashed on the runway at RAF Mildenhall, returning from a former operation on 23rd September.

The attack against Neuss on this occasion was on a much smaller scale, with Bomber Command detailing a total of 145 Lancaster bombers from 3 Group and eight from 1 Group. The aircraft piloted by Max Bourne being Avro Lancaster, HK617, GI-Q.

During the spring and late summer of 1944, any aircraft serving with No.622 Squadron which carried the code Q-Queenie had been considered a jinx. This situation was due to the fact that bombers carrying the 'Q' code regularly failed to return from operations or incurred severe battle damage. If Max or any other member of the crew were aware of this phenomenon it was not recorded in Reg's diary.

Max took off at 02.45 hours and climbed steadily to an attitude of 7,000,' where he joined the circling formation. It was a bright night, with light from a full moon illuminating the sky, thus making it easier to form up.

The route to the target was to the south, via Reading and Beachy Head continuing out over the Channel, across the French coast, over Lille and turning on to the last leg for the approach to the target. By the time the formation reached the latter part of the outward journey, it had climbed to an altitude of 20,000' in preparation for the bombing run. Initially there was no flak, but the ground defences commenced firing once the bombing had started and, as on a previous occasion, it was not heavy but was accurate as far as height was concerned.

Flying with yet another 'new' bomb aimer on the crew, Max lined Q-Queenie up in straight and level flight for the bomb running, whilst F/O W.A. Mildren issued instructions. From the bomb aimer's position in the nose of the aircraft, came the call that all but one hang-up had tumbled down onto well placed concentrated markers. Apart from seeing the glow of fires radiating up from the ground below, Reg recorded that he could also see an attack on Essen thirty miles away.

Returning via the Scheldt Estuary and Walcheren, Max flew out over the North Sea where, after some 'friendly persuasion,' the lone bomb still hung-up in the bomb bay detached itself and fell into the icy waters below. Apart from this one slight misdemeanour, Q-Queenie brought her crew home safely to fight another day.

Needless to say, after debriefing and a meal, the crew retired to their beds, where they spent all day sleeping.

Thursday, 30th November 1944

Operation No.25
Bottrop
We were awakened at 6.45am to go to breakfast early, and then briefing at 8.00. The target was a factory area at Bottrop, near Gladbach in the Rhur. [We] took off at 11.00am, formed up on the circuit and flew the Kings Lynn triangle until [we] set course at 11.46am. The route was from base at 10,000' via Diss and Southwold, across the North Sea climbing all the way to bombing height at 19,500.'

This attack was small by normal Bomber Command standards, with only sixty Lancaster bombers from 3 Group being despatched on the operation. No.622 Squadron detailed sixteen aircraft for the attack, including E-Easy.

Flying in the first formation Reg noticed that, a few minutes before they had even reached the target area, flak bursts began peppering the sky ahead of them. The angry red balls of fire turned to black bursts of smoke as they marked their presence before dissipating on the wind. Furthermore, it was predicted flak, and accurate.

Being in the forefront of the attack, Max's formation had no cover from 'Window,' which were strips of aluminium foil, each cut to half the length of the wavelengths of the German radar. When dropped, 'Window' created a snow blizzard effect on the screens and confused the enemy radar operators. Although bundles of 'Window' were being carried on E-Easy, and were dropped, it was the aircraft following on behind that really benefited from the cover it provided.

However, Max and the first formation continued with their bombing run, during which Reg reported two aircraft going down in flames, one of which broke up before disappearing into cloud.

Although no official reports confirm the loss of two aircraft on the Bottrop attack, there were a number of similar small operations in the same region. The two aircraft reported by Reg may well have been participating in one of those attacks. Reg was certainly right about one thing though: the accuracy of the flak, which was to prove to be a little too close for comfort. As shells exploded around them the aircraft bucked and bumped around on the vortex of each blast, but Max persevered and fought to hold the aircraft as steady as possible on the bombing run. Arthur recorded that E-Easy was holed in the elevator and starboard wing.

Down in the bomb aimer's compartment, trying to ignore the angry red and black flashes bursting around the perspex nose blister on the front of the Lancaster, Flight

Lieutenant H. Middleton endeavoured to guide Max up to the aiming point. Middleton, who was an experienced bomb aimer and had flown with Max and the crew on a previous occasion, released the bomb load at 13.11 hours. Unfortunately, there was yet another hang-up, which apparently caused some problems when they endeavoured to get rid of it over the North Sea on the way home. Due to the target being obscured by cloud, the results of F/L Middleton's labours were not observed.

Having completed the homeward run, still in formation and without incident (apart from the hung-up bomb), Max touched down on the runway at RAF Mildenhall at 15.15 hours. He taxied to his dispersal area, shut down the engines and, after checking all was in order, hauled himself out of the pilot's seat. As he climbed down from the Lancaster, his attention was drawn to the groundcrew, who were engrossed in conversation and obviously talking about the aircraft. Max, Reg and the others wandered over to see what was going and found, to their utter amazement, that E-Easy had sustained flak damage to the underside of the mainplane, the elevators and the fuselage. The aircraft had sustained Category A/C damage, which was repaired on site by A.V. Roe. Although E-Easy returned to No.622 Squadron on 9th December, it was taken-on-charge by No.218 Squadron four days later. The crew took the damage in their stride and, after debriefing and a late lunch, Roger and Reg jumped into the car and sped off into Mildenhall to get the fender, which had fallen off three days earlier, fixed. Paul followed them in the Rover, so as to give them a lift back to camp. It is a sure bet they did not tell the mechanic they had very recently returned from a bombing operation over Germany, which could so easily have been their last.

Friday, 1st December 1944
Slept until 11.30am. Went to lunch at 1.15pm and then out to dispersal at 2.30 to bring some of the guns to the cleaning room.

It took Reg and Roger three hours to complete their task, after which they adjourned for tea before going to the cinema later in the evening. It was around midnight when they finally retired and, not being listed for operations the next day, Reg and the others slept in until 9.30am the following morning.

A leisurely breakfast was taken at Morley's Café, until they all realised that they were detailed for a fighter affiliation exercise. The breakfast table and its contents were very nearly sent flying as a hurried exit was made from the establishment. However, much to their chagrin, when they arrived back at camp they found the aircraft had been recorded as 'unserviceable' and they were told to go and have an early lunch!

The bomber, having got off to an inauspicious start at the beginning of the day by not being airworthy, gave Reg further cause for concern later in the day, once they had got airborne for a fighter-affiliation exercise. During the one hour and twenty minutes flight, Reg's hands froze as he sat in the mid-upper turret. Lucky not to have succumbed to frostbite, approximately two hours were to pass before he got all feeling back in them.

Having extricated themselves from their flying clothing, Roger, Paul and Reg ventured into Mildenhall to retrieve the Morris which, having been reunited with its front fender, was ready for collection. Having got the car safely back to camp, the three crewmembers, including Reg, teamed up with 'Tubby' Hiscock for a few games of cards.

Sunday, 3rd December 1944
Missed breakfast, so went to the Rosemary Café at 10.00am for tea and toast. After [an early] lunch Paul and I set off in the Morris to gather firewood and came back with a load.

Rosemary's Café was a two-storey house, originally built of timber, with a tiled pitched roof. An extension to the side and front of the house was added, probably in the 1930s, constructed in brickwork. It was the latter part of the property that housed the café, which many airmen from the airbase across the road would visit for various forms of nourishment. Sadly, this building was demolished during the late-1980s.

The airfield at Mildenhall was originally constructed in a heavily forested area, some of which still remains. Therefore Paul and Reg would not have needed to travel far in their quest for fallen branches and deadwood. The task completed by 2.30pm, Reg teamed up with Roger and spent the rest of the afternoon cleaning their guns.

Monday, 4th December 1944

Operation No.26
Oberhausen
On the Battle Order first thing. Briefing was at 9.30am. The target was a marshaling yard and factory area at Oberhausen. Our bomb load consisted of 1x4,000lbs ['Cookie'], 6x1,000lbs and 6x500lbs bombs. We took off at noon, climbed to 12,000' on the Kings Lynn triangle, setting course from base at 12.54pm via Bury, Diss and Orfordness. [We] crossed the North Sea, climbing to bombing height at 20,000' on the way [and] crossed the Dutch coast just west of the Scheldt. There was no flak until the target area then it came up accurately among the first wave.

Rosemary Café was one of the establishments in and around RAF Mildenhall that catered for hungry and thirsty airmen. Although situated down a lane, off the main thoroughfare through Beck Row, it did not lack for customers. *Author's Collection*

The Loss of a Friend

Sergeant Pat Wilson and Pilot Officer Robert Skilbeck (seen here in the rank of Flight Sergeant) were killed when their aircraft, Lancaster, HK626, LSW, of No.XV Squadron, was blown from the sky, following the detonation of a 4,000lb bomb. The bomb, which they had just dropped, exploded having been hit by flak. *Author's Collection*

Arriving over the target, Flying Officer D.G. Mackenzie, a member of the Royal Canadian Air Force, who was flying as bomb aimer to Max and his crew, prepared for the bombing run. Following the same procedure as Tom Brown had done on numerous previous occasions, F/O Mackenzie guided the Lancaster up to the aiming point. Due to low 10/10th cloud over the target, bombing was carried out on instruments, from an altitude of 20,000.'

Whilst the pilot and bomb aimer were engaged in their respective tasks, the rear and mid-upper gunners watched the skies around them. Traversing his turret back and forth, sweeping the cloud-laden sky for enemy fighters, Reg was able to see other aircraft flying all around and above them. He could also see the angry red bursts of anti-aircraft ground fire, searching for those same aircraft, exploding and then dissipating in black plumes of smoke on the wind.

As Reg's eyes continued to sweep across the sky he saw a 4,000lb bomb fall from the bomb bay of an aircraft flying ahead and slightly above them. As it began to fall, the bomb received a direct hit from a burst of flak and exploded in a violent ball of red, orange and crimson flames. The blast encompassed the aircraft from which the bomb had just been released, igniting the remaining payload in its bomb bay. The resulting explosion tore the Lancaster apart, killing the entire crew in the process. A second Lancaster, flying behind, was unable to take evasive action and had no option but to fly through the wreckage that punctured the airspace around.

The first aircraft is believed to have been Avro Lancaster, HK626, LS-W, of No.XV Squadron. It was a Mk.B.I variant piloted by Flying Officer Vincent Davis, a 22 year-old, Royal Australian Air Force pilot. Apart from the pilot, there were three other members of the Royal Australian Air Force flying on the aircraft, including P/O John Furness, navigator, P/O John Lowe, bomb aimer and P/O Robert Skilbeck, wireless operator. The remainder of the crew consisted of Sgt. John Shewen, flight engineer, Sgt. Stanley Taylor, air gunner and Sgt. Patrick Wilson, air gunner. All three were members of the Royal Air Force Volunteer Reserve.

The wreckage of Lancaster bomber, PA170, LS-N, of No.XV Squadron, piloted by Flying Officer Robert Ostler, DFC, which crash-landed having flown into the debris of Lancaster, HK626, LS-W, which exploded in mid-air. *Author's Collection*

Avro Lancaster bomber, HK626, LS-W, which was built by Vickers-Armstrong at Castle Bromwich, had originally been taken-on-charge by No.622 Squadron on 25th September 1944, but did not fly any operational missions with the unit. A week after its arrival at RAF Mildenhall, on 1st October, the aircraft was taken-on-charge by No.XV Squadron, with whom it was to undertake a total of eighteen operational missions before being lost. Although a number of pilots were to fly this aircraft operationally, by some ironic quirk of fate, for both its first and last missions Lancaster bomber, HK626, was piloted by Flying Officer Vincent Davis. The second aircraft involved in the incident is believed to have been Lancaster bomber, PA170, LS-N, piloted by Flying Officer Robert Ostler. Although PA170 sustained damage to the flying controls, having flown through the debris of the exploding bomber, F/O Ostler managed to effect a safe crashlanding behind Allied lines, from which he and his crew walked away without injury.

Tuesday, 5th December 1944

Operation No.27
Schwammenauel Dam
We were awakened at 5.30am and went to breakfast at 6.00 [then] off to briefing at 7.00. The target was a dam on the Roer River, near our lines. We were given much detailed information and instructions for bombing. [We] took off at 08.50, got into formation on the circuit and flew the Kings Lynn triangle, gaining height until we set course at 09.47 hours.

Having crossed the Suffolk coast over Orfordness, the route out was across the North Sea and over the Belgium coast. The formation, comprising fifty-six Lancaster aircraft from 3 Group, continued on passing two miles to the south of Brussels, where many of the aircrews were able to look down upon the city.

Approaching the dam and flying at an altitude of 14,000,' the target became obscured by a blanket of cloud, thus necessitating a call from the Master Bomber instructing the participating crews not to release their bomb loads. Although the two G.H. Leaders did release their bombs, no results were observed. On receiving the instruction not to bomb, Flying Officer Mackenzie, who again was flying as bomb aimer with Max Bourne, shut down the bombing systems and prepared for the journey home, although his task was not entirely completed.

Although there was no flak, Reg did notice a couple of enemy jet fighters appear in the distance, zooming towards the formation. He was not unduly worried though as, glancing upwards he saw the comforting sight of several squadrons of American P.51 Mustangs and British Spitfires circling above the bombers.

With the attack called off, the bombers broke formation and turned, in twos and threes, for home. Re-crossing Belgium, they began to lose height until out over the North Sea, where each aircraft was ordered to release three 1,000lb bombs in order to gain a safe landing weight. This still meant that, in the case of the fourteen aircraft detailed by No.622 Squadron, they would be landing with ten 1,000lb bombs on board. Arriving back at RAF Mildenhall, Max landed 'Easy' a few minutes after 13.00 hours, taxied back to dispersal and shut down all the aircraft's systems.

The debriefing, which did not take very long, was followed by a late lunch after which Reg and Roger drove into Mildenhall village in the Morris to get some petrol and oil for the car. The rest of the afternoon was spent cleaning the vehicle.

Wednesday, 6th December 1944

Operation No.28
Merseberg

We were up at 04.45am and had to be at briefing at 05.00, so no breakfast. The target was the dam again, but by the time the transport came to take us to dispersal, the operation was scrubbed and we wasted no time getting back to bed. [We were] on the Battle Order again in the afternoon and went to briefing at 3.00pm. The target was the Leuna [synthetic] oil plant at Merseberg, 5 miles from Leipzig, a round trip of 1,700 miles.

Weather-wise, the day commenced with a severe hoar frost and small amounts of cloud that built up as the morning progressed. By noon there was a blanket of 10/10th cloud over the Suffolk countryside, but visibility was recorded as good.

However, although the attack on the Schwammenauel Dam had been canceled, plans for attacks that same day against Leuna, Osnabruck and Giessen were being finalised. A total force of 475 Lancaster aircraft and 12 Mosquito fighter-bombers from 1, 3 and 8 Groups were detailed for the attack against Leuna, whilst a similar number of mixed bomber aircraft from 1, 4, 6 and 8 Groups were to attack Osnabruck. A smaller number of Lancasters and Mosquitoes from 5 Group were detailed to attack Giessen.

For its part in the operation against Leuna, the first major attack on an oil plant in eastern Germany, No.622 Squadron detailed twelve aircraft, all of which took off safely commencing at 17.00 hours. However, one of the Squadron's Lancasters, HK617, GI-Q, piloted by Flight Lieutenant Armitstead, was destined to return early due to a defective rear turret. The guns would not fire when tested.

The remaining eleven aircraft, along with the rest of the main formation continued on the pre-arranged course settings. The route out was on a southerly heading, via Reading and Beachy Head. Having crossed the English Channel, the attacking force continued on over the Belgium coast and then headed south of Charleroi, battling against bad weather all the way. With the force attacking Osnabruck taking much the same route as that heading for Leuna, there were several near mid-air collisions, as the two bomber streams flew on through the low cloud blanket and the ever-darkening night sky.

Crossing over the Allied front line, in the region of the Roer River, the formation heading for Leuna, climbed to 17,000,' where the cloud thinned out and visibility improved. Continuing on across Germany, the formation gained further altitude up to a height of 22,000,' in preparation for bombing.

As 'Easy' approached the target area, flying at an altitude of 20,500,' the crew could see the first batch of marker flares glowing brightly through the blanket of cloud below. They could also see the bright flashes of the barrage of heavy flak, which arced up into the night sky and burst in and around the invading bomber force. Reg was later to record that this was the heaviest concentration of flak the crew had encountered for some weeks.

Endeavoring to ignore, to the best of his ability, the bursting flak, Flying Officer Mackenzie, by now an established member of the crew, released the bomb load at 20.56 hours, noticing as he did so that the target below appeared to be well alight.

The glow of the fires, cast upon the clouds, enabled Roger and Reg to see the darkened shapes of Lancaster bombers flying over those same clouds both behind and below them. Suddenly, and without any warning, the enormous dark shadow of a Lancaster bomber turning sharply behind them, loomed into view as it missed their aircraft by about fifty feet, giving both the rear and mid-upper gunners' almost instant heart failure. Recovering their composure, the two gunners soon settled back into the task in hand, that of searching for enemy fighters and not supposed friendly bombers.

Having escaped the melee over the target area, Max began to lose height and dropped down to an altitude of 6,000.' Whilst flying at this level, they skirted Geissen, which was well ablaze with great columns of smoke rolling up above the clouds. A huge explosion erupted from one of the fires, sending up a great sheet of flame. On the port side of the aircraft, a few miles away to the southwest, one of the crew noticed a large concentration of searchlights, which they kept well away from.

The night was full of activity. Having regained altitude in order to fly over the front line at a safe height, the crew witnessed the spectacle of gun flashes as the Allied armies pounded those enemy fractions not receiving the attention of the bombers overhead. The spectacle was short-lived as E-Easy flew on into an electrical storm whilst over France and was forced down to an altitude of 1,000.' Static electricity covered the aerials, perspex and guns with blue and white sparks as St. Elmo's fire danced across the upper surfaces of the Lancaster for a period of approximately fifteen minutes. Towards the end of this period, Max was forced to bring the aircraft down to a height of about 500,' so as to keep the ground in sight.

Once out over the North Sea the cloud broke and the conditions improved, but they were not home yet. Having reached base at 12.20am, Max was forced to circle for twenty minutes before being given permission to land. The latter having been granted, 'Easy' touched down, cleared the runway (although it is reported a portion of the trailing aerial was left on the end of the runway) and taxied round to the 'Easy's' allotted dispersal area only to find another Lancaster parked there! According to Reg's diary, they left their aircraft on the edge of a turnip field where, by the time dawn broke, it had sunk into two feet of mud.

Thursday, 7th December 1944
Slept in until lunchtime, then spent the afternoon repairing the fireplace in our room, before going into Mildenhall in the Morris to have tea at Tilly's.

No mention was made in Reg's diary of any recriminations with regard to the bogged down Lancaster. Neither was there any clue as to what damage had been done to the fireplace or how it had occurred. It was in all essence a very lazy day following a long and hazardous night. After tea at Tilly's, Reg and Roger paid a visit to the local cinema accompanied by 'Tubby' Hiscock, with whom they later had supper before retiring at midnight.

Friday, 8th December 1944
Slept in until 10.30 then made a cup of cocoa [before] rushing off to do a fighter affiliation at 11.30 which was canceled because of the weather which grew worse during the afternoon.

The rest of the day was almost a repeat of the previous day, except for the fact that neither Roger nor Reg went to the cinema. They did however finish up sitting in front of the repaired fire writing letters home, whilst devouring toast topped with salmon and drinking more cocoa!

Saturday, 9th December 1944
It is very cold with ice on the ground and a nippy wind blowing. Had lunch, cleaned up a bit and then went to briefing at 2.15pm.

The target, for which the crews were being briefed to attack, was listed as Merseberg again, but it did not take place. Having gone through the usual pre-operational routine of having a meal, getting kitted-out in flying clothing, being transported out to dispersal, carrying out pre-flight checks of the aircraft (both externally and internally) and running up the engines, news was received that the operation was scrubbed. One would have thought that having gone through all that procedure, the participating aircrews would have been somewhat downhearted, but no, the vehicles transporting them back to the briefing room were filled with much joviality and laughter.

Reg and Roger wasted no time in getting changed, seeking out the whereabouts of 'Tubby' Hiscock and driving off in the Morris to Mildenhall. Tilly's, as usual, was the first stop, where the trio took tea. This was followed a short while later with a stop at the Bell Inn, also in Mildenhall, where they stayed and downed quite a few 'bevvies.' Around 8.00pm that evening, the need was felt for some sustenance of a more solid nature, so it was agreed to 'hot-foot' it back to camp for supper. Given that the Sergeants' Mess also had a bar, the rest of the evening was spent in decidedly merry circumstances.

As no operations had been scheduled for the following day, the guys found there was little to do apart from playing various games in their billet, going to the cinema and having supper. The only entry in the Reg's diary for this day, relating to drink, was a cup of cocoa at bedtime!

Monday, 11th December 1944

Operation No.29
Osterfeld

On the Battle Order again. We were awakened at 5.30am for breakfast [with] briefing at 6.30am. The target was a railway yard at Osterfeld, six miles from Essen. The bomb load consisted of one 4,000lbs bomb and nine 1,000lbs bombs. We got off at 8.35am, formed up on the [Kings Lynn] triangle and climbed to 12,000.'

Max set course at 09.39 hours, via Bury, Diss and Orfordness, climbing through thin cloud until they reached the Belgian coast over Blankenburg, by which time they had reached 20,000.' As their journey progressed the cloud cover increased, allowing the crew only occasional glimpses of the ground.

One hundred and fifty Lancaster bombers from 3 Group had been despatched for a G-H led raid against the marshaling yards at Osterfeld, fourteen of which had been detailed by No.622 Squadron. A further fifty-two Bomber Command aircraft had been ordered to attack the Benzol plant, also at Osterfeld.

There was no opposition from the enemy fighters, or flak, until the bomber stream reached the target area, then the predicted heavy flak peppered the sky causing the bombers to break formation. Such was the intensity of the barrage that Reg later wrote in his diary:

"… It was the worst we had struck so far and it chased us for seven minutes"…"

Pilot Officer Mackenzie had a good but somewhat unpleasant view of the whole scenario unfolding around the Lancaster. From his position in the bomb aimer's compartment in the nose of PD366, he faced the exploding shells, as Max held E–Easy on a straight and level course for the bombing run whilst flying through the dissipating black balls of smoke. At one minute past eleven o'clock, having guided Max onto the aiming point, Mackenzie pressed the 'tit' and released the bomb load.

E-Easy was carrying a bomb load totalling 13,000lb in weight, comprising one 4,000lb 'cookie,' six 1,000lb bombs and six 500lb general-purpose bombs. With flak bursting on all sides of the aircraft the crew were relieved to feel the aircraft lurch upwards as the bombs left the bomb bay, although it was recorded that one 1,000lb bomb was 'hung-up' and refused to move.

Having completed their task, Max prepared to leave the target area and as he did so, another Lancaster flew into the airspace E-Easy had just vacated. From the confines of his turret, Reg watched in horror as the Lancaster exploded in a ball of fire and fell from the sky, with flames trailing behind it like a comet, through the cloud towards the ground.

Seven young men, two of whom were only nineteen years old, were killed. Their aircraft, Lancaster Mk.I., NG350, JI-C, of No.514 Squadron, piloted by Flying Officer Ellis Hill, crashed onto a house in the area of Sterkrade. The two nineteen year olds who died were Sergeant John Balman, flying as mid-upper gunner and Sergeant Alan Bowen, who was occupying the rear turret. The rest of the crew was made up of Sergeant Norman Readman, flight engineer, Sergeant Cyril Atter, wireless operator, Flight Sergeant Frank

Grouped around the crew entry door of Lancaster, PD366, GI-E, are (L to R) Ground-crew; Tubby Hiscock; Ground-crew; Paul Taylor; Roger Humphrys; Ground-crew; Ground-crew; Arthur Bourne; Bill Vincent; Ground-crew. Reg Heffron is center in the doorway & Max Bourne is on the right in the doorway. *Courtesy of Daphne Brown & Carol Artley*

Guest, bomb aimer, and Flying Officer Reg Cowles. Flying Officer Cowles, who was flying as navigator, had been awarded a DFC only six months earlier, whilst serving with No.10 Squadron.

Reg, watching the Lancaster go down, was brought back to the reality of his own situation with a bump, literally, as flak hit the starboard outer engine and wing of E-Easy. Oil spurted out and flew back in the slipstream covering the nacelle with black greasy slime, but the Merlin engine continued to function properly. Unfortunately, Reg's turret did not as the hydraulics were severed, rendering it useless.

Following receipt of a course from Arthur, the navigator, Max turned the Lancaster for home. Although during the course of the journey back to base, whilst out over the sea, two or three attempts were made to dislodge the 'hang-up' still in the bomb bay, the offending ordnance would not budge. Therefore Max, had no option, he ordered the bomb doors closed and returned to RAF Mildenhall with the bomb still on board!

The journey back went without incident. E-Easy crossed the English coastline over Orfordness, at an altitude of 2,000,' and reached base at 12.43pm, where they were informed by ground control they were 20th in line for landing.

Although no verbal comments were recorded as having been made, each member of the crew had their respective thoughts about the bomb and hoped the landing would go without incident. Eventually Max was given permission to land and E-Easy touched down at five-minutes-past-one.

The Lancaster's main undercarriage made contact with terra firma and rolled along the concrete runway. As the speed dropped away, the tail-wheel did the same, E-Easy, had made a safe landing. Max taxied back to the dispersal area where he completed his cockpit checks, shut down all the systems and, in compliance with standing orders, opened the bomb doors. As he did so, there was a loud, dull, metallic thump as the 1000lb bomb fell and made contact with the concrete hardstanding. This was all the crew needed to finish off the trip's effect on their shattered nerves.

All but one of No.622 Squadron's aircraft returned safely. The aircraft that did not make it home was Lancaster bomber, LM235, GI-C, piloted by Flying Officer W. H. Thorbecke. With two engines feathered and a third overheating, the pilot managed a safe forced landing at Gilze Rijen, a former Luftwaffe airfield now in Allied held territory. The airfield, situated south-west of Tilburg, in Holland, was the same one that P/O L. Burpee, DFM, crashed his crippled bomber onto, during the outward journey of the famous Dambusters attack, in May 1943.

Tuesday, 12th December
Slept in until 10.30am then went to our sections but there was nothing doing, so we went to lunch at 12 o'clock then cleaned our room. [Later] we went out to dispersal to clean our guns and harmonise them and fill [the] ammo bins. [After] we went in the Morris to Mildenhall, where we paid a visit to the garage for a headlamp globe, [followed by a visit] to Tilly's for tea.

Over the next few days the weather continued to be frosty, with a heavy fog hanging around, which in turn meant there was little again for the crews to do. Reg and Roger took advantage of the situation and undertook further work on the Morris, which led to the occasional jaunt into either Bury St. Edmunds or Mildenhall for spare parts for the car. This automatically led to the two air gunners visiting suitable establishments where tea and cakes or other forms of sustenance, were available for purchase. On one of these jaunts, Reg and Roger treated 'Tubby' Hiscock to an early supper at Tilly's Café, followed by an evening in front of the fire at their billet. However, before the evening was out, another supper, consisting of tea and toast, was served amongst much merriment and laughter, the cause of which was unrecorded. Although they were on the Battle Order for the following morning, the lads did not go to bed until 1.00am that same morning.

Saturday, 16th December 1944
We were awoken at 7.30am, rushed up to breakfast then found it was a false alarm, so [made] our way back to the house and lit a fire. [Later] Roger and I went to dispersal to check G-George, our workhorse for tonight, for we are still on the Battle Order.

After lunch at the mess, followed by a relaxing period sat in front of a fire, the crew made their way to the briefing room, where they learned the forthcoming operation was a mine-laying sortie in the Baltic, to the northwest of Stettin.

At the appropriate time they went through the ritual of having their pre-flight meal, changing into their flying-clothing and then taking the crew bus out to the dispersal area where Lancaster, PD223, GI-G, waited in the dull, dreary, late afternoon, December weather.

Max Bourne and the rest of the crew, having been wished good luck by 'Tubby' Hiscock, clambered aboard the four-engined bomber, settled at their respective stations and set about their individual pre-flight checks. With Max and Bill Vincent in the cockpit working together, one by one the four huge propellers coughed, belched smoke from the exhaust stacks, and burst into life, causing vibrations the length of the fuselage as the propellers gathered speed. With the aircraft straining against the chocks wedged under the tires of the main undercarriage, Max increased the power to each engine and with them roaring at almost full power, the pilot received a message over the intercom, 'Shut down engines, the operation is scrubbed.' Slowly the noise and vibration died down as the propellers ground to a stop and peace reigned again as it had done shortly before. With mixed feelings of emotion, the crew clambered out of the aircraft and climbed back into the bus that was to take them back to the crew room.

The 'scrubbing' of the operation worked in 'Tubby's' favour, as he was again taken out to supper by Reg and Roger, before spending another evening with them in front of the billet fire. They were joined, just after midnight, by Max and some of his friends, when yet another supper materialised. Again, it was the early hours of the morning before they finally turned in for what was left of the night.

Monday, 18th December 1944

Slept in again until lunchtime, when Tom came and woke us up.

Tom Brown, the crew's former bomb aimer who had been taken ill back in mid-October, was on leave following his spell in hospital and had caught an early train from London, whilst his former crewmates were still asleep.

Having got themselves together, the crew, including Tom, all went to a café in Mildenhall for lunch. Needless to say, there was much chatter and many questions asked as there was an awful lot of news to catch up on from both sides.

As a result of his illness, Tom had been grounded permanently and was therefore on alternative duties. To his delight, he was posted to the Intelligence Section, at No.32 Base, which was in fact RAF Mildenhall, so, although he would not be flying with them, there would be future opportunities for Tom to catch up with his former crew.

Tuesday, 19th December 1944

Operation No.30
Mine-Laying

Up [early] for a change. We took the Morris to three garages in Mildenhall and Barton Mills to get a small job done, but no luck. On the Newmarket road we came across a heavy tank and had a word with the driver. He showed us over it and explained everything of interest. [We] then went to Tilly's for lunch and then on to the camp [arriving there] at 12.30pm.

An hour and a half after their arrival back at the airfield, Max Bourne's crew, along with that led by Flight Lieutenant John Cox, also of No.622 Squadron, together with two other crews from No.XV Squadron, were called to the briefing room at short notice. The four crews were detailed for a mine-laying operation in the Rostock approaches of the Baltic Sea.

Flight Lieutenant John Cox (later DFC) and his crew consisting of, back row, left to right, F/O 'Titch' Titchener, B/A; Sgt Ken Matthews, MUG; Sgt 'Gil' Gilroy, R/G; F/S 'Taffy' Hughes, F/E. Front row, left to right, F/S Brian Shine, W/Op, RAAF; F/L John Cox, DFC, Pilot; F/O Joe Taylor, Nav. *Courtesy of John & Elisabeth Cox*

Earlier in the day, twelve other crews from No.622 Squadron, together with a further twelve crews from No.XV Squadron, had also been instructed to report to the briefing room, where they learned they were scheduled for an attack against Trier. However, although a total of thirty-two aircraft from Bomber Command carried out the attack, only one Lancaster out of the twelve detailed by No.622 Squadron managed to take off from Mildenhall, due to the adverse weather conditions which had closed in after the aircraft of No.XV Squadron had taken off.

The weather cleared sufficiently for the four mine-laying crews to take off a couple of hours later. Max hauled Lancaster, PD223, GI-G, off Mildenhall's runway at 15.30 hours, with four Mk.6 mines secured in the bomb bay, and immediately climbed up above the cloud layer.

Setting course out over the North Sea, Max headed for Scandinavia. Their course took them across Denmark and the southern tip of Sweden, where they crossed the Swedish coast over Landskrona. Although they did not endure flak from the ground defences, three red tracer flares arced up into the sky ahead of them as a warning.

Cloud cover began to increase over Sweden and, as Max turned G-George onto a heading towards the dropping zone, whilst flying through this cloud, his quick reactions narrowly avoided a mid-air collision with another Lancaster. Fortunately, having completed the course change safely, the rest of the operation went without incident. The mines were 'planted' in the allotted area of sea, between Zealand and Jutland. Although there was 10/10ths cloud over the drop zone the mines were released on instruments from an altitude of 10,000.'

As the aircraft flew over Jutland, in central Denmark, two bursts of light flak arced up into the sky, fired probably more in hope than anger, but no damage was recorded. Crossing out over the west Danish coast, Max decreased altitude down to 2,000' for the long flight to RAF Lossiemouth; a distance of 400 miles. By the time they reached the airfield on the exposed northeast coast of Scotland, the weather had cleared, enabling Max to make a safe landing at 22.05 hours.

Following de-briefing, the weary crews were treated to a meal before being transported to the accommodation, where beds had been reserved for them. The total trip having taken seven hours and twenty five minutes, and there were twenty-eight tired and weary airmen who fell into their respective beds at 01.30 hours the following morning.

Of this same mission, Flight Lieutenant John Cox, DFC, recalls:

On 19th December 1944 we were briefed to drop four 1800lb Mk.VI mines in Rostock Bay. The route from Mildenhall was to cross the North Sea to a position 56 degrees North, 7 degrees East, then eastwards along the 56th parallel – this entailed crossing part of Sweden. Then south to Rostock Bay, dropping the mines 10 miles off the German coast; the return route was across Denmark and then the North Sea. We were not using our usual aircraft (GI-R) but GI-N. The flight took 7 hours and 25 minutes. There were two aircraft from No.622 Squadron and a total of 12 aircraft from the Command. Navigation was done by the newly installed H2S [an early form of search radar] which showed us the coastlines. Mines were dropped from 10,000.' We saw nothing of the other aircraft, [which was] not surprising as it was at night and we were in and out of cloud all the time. There was no reaction from the Germans but quite a lot from the Swedes. Both times as we crossed the Swedish coast we could see numerous searchlights just north of our track, they were pointing vertically upwards and their anti-aircraft guns seemed to be firing in the same direction – they were certainly not trying to damage us. On the way back we received a radio message to say Mildenhall was covered with fog and that we should divert to Lossiemouth. We landed there after a tiring flight and received a warm welcome and the usual bacon and eggs. [We] returned to Mildenhall two days later. This was our 28th operational sortie.

Amongst his items of memorabilia, Flight Lieutenant John Cox still has a copy of the navigator's chart used on this particular operation.

Wednesday, 20th December 1944
Slept until 9.15am and then taken to breakfast by bus. [We then went] to the watch office, but [as] the weather was still duff, take-off was put back another day.

With nothing planned, and new places to explore, Reg and one or two of the others set off, first to the fishing village of Lossiemouth, just up the road from the base, and then into Elgin, some six miles away in the opposite direction. Naturally, in both locations, they were able to seek out cafés and other establishments, including a local church hall, where food, tea and cakes were served.

Thursday, 21st December 1944
Up at 7.30am, had breakfast at the mess and, after waiting at the watch office until 10.00am, were taken by bus out to dispersal.

Having completed his cockpit checks, Max called the tower to request permission to taxi out ready for take-off; this he duly received. Easing the throttle gently forward, G-George

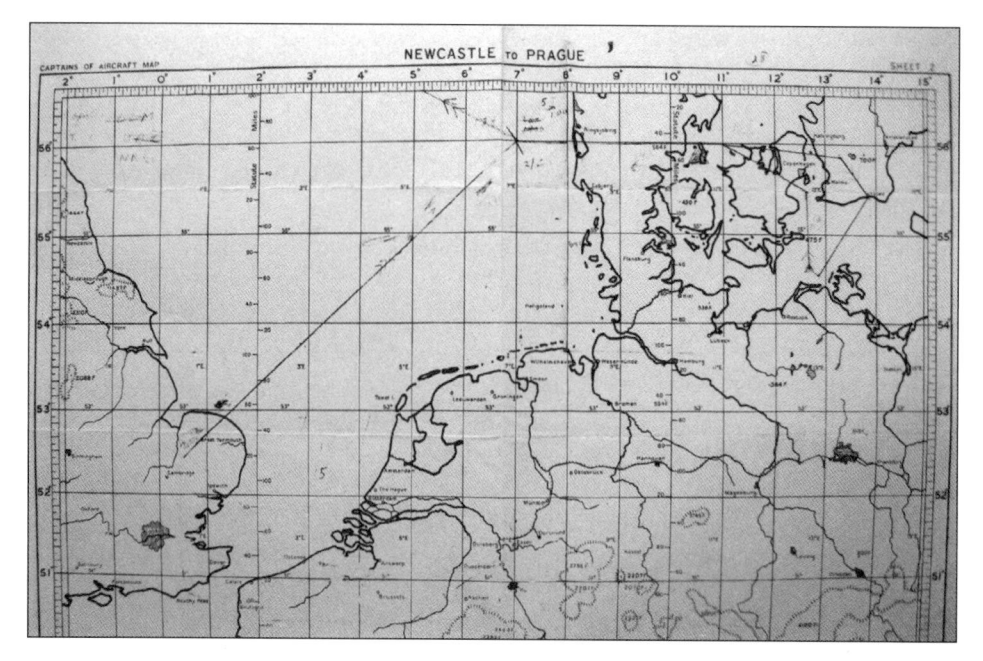

Photograph of the chart used by F/O Joe Taylor, the navigator on F/L John Cox's crew, for the mine-laying operation in the Baltic Sea, on 19th December 1944. *Courtesy of John & Elisabeth Cox*

made its way towards the threshold of the runway, where the crew became aware of a de Havilland Mosquito aircraft, flying very low over the sea, shooting up some rocks on the coastline, just off the beach adjacent to the airfield. Suddenly, and without warning, the twin-engined fighter-bomber cartwheeled into the sea, sending up a great plume of spray, through which pieces of wreckage flew as the timber-constructed aircraft broke up. Some pieces of debris floated on the surface of the water, but the main part of the wreckage sank immediately.

The Lancaster crew reported to the tower by radio, describing what they had just witnessed, before requesting, and being granted, permission to take-off. Max turned the bomber into the wind, opened the throttles and raced off down the runway. Being lighter in weight than usual, the aircraft climbed easily up into the air, leaving the drama below behind.

The route back to base followed the coastline, flying out over the sea, via Peterhead, Flamborough Head down as far as the Wash, with visibility gradually worsening. By the time they landed at Mildenhall, visibility was down to an estimated 300 yards.

Friday, 22nd December 1944
Slept in again until 11.00, had lunch at the mess and spent the afternoon getting pay and the first of a long series of signatures on our clearances from this station.

After tea the whole crew, together with the ground crew, made their way to the White Horse Inn to celebrate the completion of their tour of operations. The first half-hour was fairly quiet and subdued, but then things suddenly began to liven up as the beer flowed faster and faster. By closing time, at 10.00 pm, the place was in uproar, with beer running over the tables and floor, and everybody falling over upturned chairs. The playing of the piano added to the general bedlam of noise, as an epidemic of tie-ripping spread rapidly through the pub.

With some encouragement from the landlord who wanted to close up, everyone finally staggered out into the street. It was then decided that the 'party' should continue at Morley's Café, so eighteen inebriated souls piled into, and onto, the Rover, which then swerved and swayed all over the road on its way to its destination.

Even at this late hour the café was packed and the hungry revelers soon realized there was no hope at all of getting a meal. Reg decided the best policy was to make his escape and head back to camp, which he did and set off alone on foot, leaving the rest of the group to clamber aboard the car once more.

It is not recorded whether Reg cut across country, or whether there was a misdemeanour with the car on its way home, but Reg beat the latter by twenty minutes, enabling him to get a decent fire going by the time the mob crashed in through the door. Following a meal of toast and herrings, the group began to disperse in ones and twos until finally Reg and Roger had the room to themselves.

Saturday, 23rd December 1944

Arthur and Bill went off on leave during the day, but the rest of the crew are staying in camp for Christmas. After tea, *'Tubby,'* Roger and I went to the flicks [cinema] to see *'Stage Door Canteen,'* then to Morley's for supper at 9.00pm. [Then] back to our room to talk. Shortly after midnight there was a terrific explosion, which shook the house. The sky was brilliantly lit for several seconds by the flash.

Whilst Arthur headed off to the Midlands to see his family, Bill went down to Surrey to spend his last wartime Christmas with his wife and young daughter Ann.

The film which 'Tubby,' Roger and Reg went to see was an apt film for servicemen to go and watch, as the plot revolved around the exploits of a group of young American soldiers on leave in New York City, before they head to Europe to fight in the war. The film, which starred a host of British and American film stars, including Gracie Fields, Ginger Rogers, Helen Hayes and George Raft, was a semi-musical production, based on the famous American Servicemen's Club named 'Stage Door Canteen.' It was in this film that Betty Davis, who in later years was more widely known for appearing in dramatic and sinister films, performed her only song on celluloid.

The enormous explosion which shook Reg and Roger's billet to its foundations was caused by a German V2 rocket, which fell to earth in open countryside, close to the Judes Ferry Inn. It was somewhat of a close call, as the Judes Ferry Inn, where the film crew who made the 'Lion Has Wings' in 1939 had stayed whilst filming at RAF Mildenhall, was only about half-a-mile from the camp.

Sunday, 24th December 1944

I spent the afternoon packing, collecting more clearances and collecting my gear from the locker room. [At about] 8.30pm I went to the Mess, as it is invitation evening for officers.

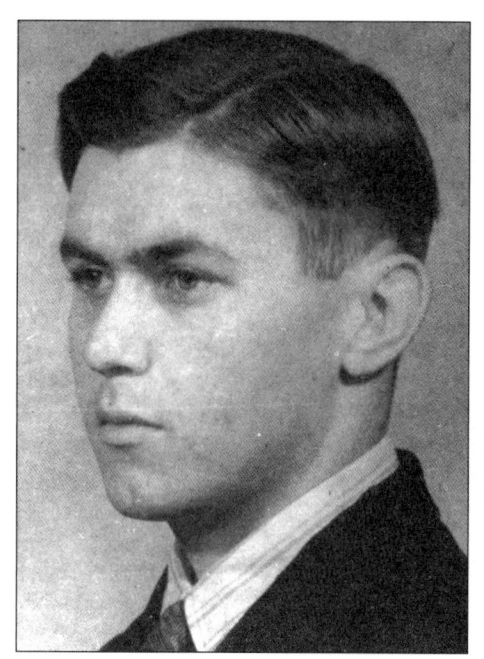

Left: One photograph Reg Heffron, fortunately, never had to show to anyone. Members of aircrew carried small, officially issued, photographs of themselves, which were used on fake documentation, in the event of them being shot down and assisted by Resistance workers. *Courtesy of Reg Heffron*
Right: Bill Vincent, flight engineer on Reg Heffron's crew, photographed with his young daughter Ann. *Courtesy of Ann Hill*

Reg started his day by waking up at twelve noon and then getting up to go to lunch in the Mess. He returned to his room after lunch to get a fire going, a task he had undertaken on numerous occasions, and one he got much practice at whilst at O.T.U., which now seemed a lifetime away.

Reg's second visit to the Mess, during the evening, left him feeling somewhat ill at ease. By the time they closed the bar, the place was an utter shambles, with all the furniture piled up in the middle of the floor, which was awash with beer, and nobody being able to stand without support of some kind. Whilst some might think this was a riotous occasion, and good fun, the scenario before him left Reg thinking it was the most disgusting display of drunkenness he had ever witnessed anywhere.

Monday, 25th December 1944

We woke at 11.00am to find we were in for a white Christmas. There was no snow, but heavy frost was thick on the ground and the trees pure white and [it] remained so all day.

It is not known whether the catering staff in the Sergeants' Mess were involved in the previous night's drunken revelry, but Reg was not impressed with the offerings which were presented as Christmas Dinner.

A return visit to the Mess in the evening, following an afternoon visit to the cinema, did little to restore the antipodean's confidence, with Reg writing in his diary:

… tea at the Mess was worse than dinner, not even up to the very ordinary standard …

With the stench of beer and cigarettes in his nostrils, and the scene being set for a replay of the previous night's performance, Reg set out for a quieter atmosphere, taking Roger and 'Tubby' with him.

On returning to their room later that same night, Reg and Roger got things ready for their trip to London the following morning, when they were scheduled to visit Tom Brown, their crew's former bomb aimer, who was on leave at his home in London.

Tuesday, 26th December 1944
'Tubby' came and woke us up at 7.20am and, after some delay [we] went to breakfast. [We] then set about making the car go.

The severe frost recorded the previous day was not only still evident, but was accompanied by freezing fog. The trio's troubles started when the car's radiator froze and the petrol pump refused to work due to a flat battery. Another battery, found sitting in a nearby parked wreck, was commandeered. The next problem was caused by the oil being so thick the starter could not turn it over in the engine. This situation was overcome by borrowing the coal truck and towing the car behind it; a tactic which finally got the engine started.

All this activity meant that time was ticking away and it was 2.30pm before they finally got going. Leaving the camp, Reg, Roger and 'Tubby' set out, via Mildenhall village, to join the A11 trunk road at Barton Mills.

The journey turned out to be a very prolonged and eventful one, due to the persisting temperature and very dense fog. Every ten minutes they would have to stop in order to scrape the ice off the car windscreen. In the end, tired of this enforced activity and to

A Quanset (Nissen) hut, used by No.622 Squadron, on the far side of RAF Mildenhall airfield, photographed in a heavy frost during the winter of 1944. *Author's Collection*

overcome the problem, Reg drove with his head sticking out of the open window in the driver's door.

Having reached Littleburg, between Cambridge and Saffron Walden, a distance of approximately 30 miles from RAF Mildenhall, the intrepid travellers decided to give up and seek accommodation for the night.

It was whilst the trio were sitting by the fire taking tea in the Queen's Head pub, that they noticed the fog had lifted so, in true explorer fashion, they decided to continue their journey. All went well until about half-a-mile down the road when the radiator froze and the engine started to boil, forcing them to beg, borrow or steal some cardboard with which to protect the radiator against the harsh, cold air draught, by inserting the cardboard around the radiator grill. The plan worked and neither the car, nor its engine, gave cause for further concern. The weather, however, did continue to be a problem when, having reached Epping, just northeast of London, the fog returned with a vengeance. The car crawled along at a snail's pace, with twenty-one miles of the remaining twenty-seven miles of the journey being driven in second gear, whilst the final six miles were driven in first gear.

The trio arrived at Tom's house in Charlton, on the south side of the River Thames, at 3.00am in the morning. They had taken nine hours to cover a distance that could normally be completed in three and a half hours. They had passed five crashes on route but, thankfully, had not been involved in any of them.

Needless to say, the occupants of Tom's house were asleep in bed and oblivious of the battering on the front door and windows, and the hammering on the cast iron rainwater pipes. However, the neighbours were not, and many other doors and windows down the street were flung open before a bleary-eyed Tom, dressed in his night clothes, opened his own front door.

Even at this early hour, the Brown's made their guests welcome and whilst Tom chatted to his three friends, Daphne prepared some soup, made a pot of tea and laid out a selection of cakes. Finally, around half-past-five in the morning, Tom and Daphne returned to their bed, whilst Reg, Roger and 'Tubby' slept on the floor of the lounge.

Revenge it is said is a wonderful thing, and Tom got his later that morning, at 8.45am to be precise, by pounding heavily on the keys of the piano situated in the lounge, a few feet away from the weary travelers.

Wednesday, 27th December 1944

After a good breakfast, we got the car going again, said goodbye and set off through London to *'Tubby's'* home at Henley-on-Thames.

The journey across London took the trio through Queen's Park, Victoria, Hyde Park Corner, Chiswick and out on to the A4 trunk road, westbound, towards Maidenhead. Having reached Maidenhead, Reg turned north towards Henley-on-Thames.

'Tubby's' wife had reserved a table for lunch at the Catherine Wheel Hotel, so their arrival at the Hiscock household at 1.00pm was aptly timed. Following a three-course meal, washed down with ale, they all returned to the Hiscock house for an afternoon of talking by the fire.

Having had only a few hours respite from all the driving, Reg and Roger said goodbye to Mrs Hiscock and, along with 'Tubby,' set off on the return journey back to RAF Mildenhall. From Henley, Reg retraced the route back as far as Chiswick, then turned north onto the North Circular Road around the top of London, via Edmonton and Woodford and back onto the A11.

The visibility was much better than the previous day, which enabled them to make good progress. Having reached Epping Forest, Roger climbed into the driving seat and drove the rest of the way. Feeling in need of refreshment they stopped at Bishop Stortford for supper, before continuing their journey. They finally reached the camp at midnight and, having dropped 'Tubby' off at his billet, they returned to their quarters, where they found all the taps frozen and the bathroom floor covered with ice! Having got a fire going, which helped thaw out the room, Reg and Roger finally tumbled into their respective beds at 1.10am.

The newspapers reported that weather conditions between 24th and 26th December 1944, and daytime temperatures, were the coldest recorded since 1872. An army of plumbers, employed by various local authorities to work on bombed out houses, were expected to be drafted in to assist with thawing out frozen pipework, and to repair the many burst pipes reported.

Thursday, 28th December 1944
Slept in until lunch time, then [we] spent the afternoon packing up our gear in preparation for the evacuation of our billet. After tea in the Mess, more packing.

The rest of the evening was spent in 'Tubby's' room, where they played a few games of cards and talked until midnight. Shortly after they had got back to their own room, around 12.30am, Paul Taylor arrived and started cooking beans on their fire. Unfortunately the next morning, Reg paid the penalty for eating at such a late hour before going to bed. He woke up with a terrible pain in his stomach and a horrible taste of beans in his mouth and it wasn't long before he succumbed to being sick. It was a good job that Reg was no longer on active service, as he returned to his bed and stayed there all day; leaving Roger to get things ready for their trip to Sheffield.

Saturday, 30th December 1944
I woke at 8.00am feeling much better than yesterday, and went down to our own room after breakfast. Roger and I set to [cleaning] up the last signs of our occupation of the place, something we had not done for some months now. All was ready at 10.30am and we fell upon the Morris and did our best to make it go, but there was still a heavy frost (the temperature has been below freezing point for nine days now) and the engine oil was like cement.

After lunch a thaw set in and, with the help of a few extra pairs of hands to push the car, the engine fired up. The time was now around 1.30pm, much later than they had intended to set-off but, with the engine ticking over nicely, Reg and Roger climbed into the Morris and drove off camp.

Their route took them through the English countryside, via Fordham, Soham, St. Ives and Huntingdon, where they joined the main A1 Trunk Road towards Stamford. Having passed through Grantham they continued on to Newark, where darkness, and no doubt tiredness, finally forced them to stop for some refreshment. However, the intrepid travelers, feeling suitably revived, decided to press on through Ossington, Ollerton, Barlborough and finally Sheffield, where they pitched up at 10.15pm. Roger booked a couple of rooms at the Albany Hotel, whilst Reg parked the car at a nearby garage.

The following day, Reg decided he would go and visit his relations William and Martha, at Meadow Lodge, near, Dearham, Cumbria. Unfortunately, due to the irregularity of the railway timetable, Reg was forced to slightly alter his traveling arrangements.

Monday, 1st January 1945
At 12.30am I set off for the railway station, with Roger helping with my bags and [being] guided by a [friendly] local policeman. We (minus the bobby) had tea and cakes at the station, then Roger went back to the hotel.

During his stay with William and Martha, Reg was hoping to visit other relatives in and around the Carlisle area, but his train, due at 1.30am, was running late. When it did finally arrive, an hour later, Reg struggled on board with his luggage, found a seat and went straight off to sleep. Imagine his consternation when he woke up nearly four hours later, just as the train was about to leave Carlisle station. He only just managed to catch the connecting train to Dearham.

During his stay in Cumbria, Reg did manage to catch up with distant family, with whom much chatting was done. He also went to the cattle sales in Cockermouth, visited the theater, took in some of the countryside and did some shopping. He spent at least one evening wrapping and packing a number of items purchased during one of his shopping trips, ready to send to the folks back home in Australia.

Friday, 5th January 1945
Had to begin the return [trip] to Mildenhall today. Catching the 11.00am [train] from Maryport to Carlisle. [visited] the post office where I sent my parcels off, then walked to the station just in time to catch the train.

Having changed trains at Carlisle, where he had an hours wait, Reg finally reached Sheffield at 5.00pm. He had previously arranged to meet Roger at the Albany Hotel in the City center, where Reg found the latter sitting moodily on his bed. No explanation was recorded for Roger's moodiness, but he soon cheered up when the two friends went to the cinema later that evening, followed by a few drinks in the lounge at the Grand Hotel.

After breakfast the following morning, Reg and Roger loaded their luggage into the car and drove south. Their route back to RAF Mildenhall took them through Mansfield, Chesterfield, where they saw the famous wooden, lead-covered, crooked, 13th century spire of St. Mary's and All Saints Church, Stamford, Huntingdon, and then across country to Mildenhall.

The journey back had not gone smoothly, especially the last twenty miles. It was a bit treacherous, with thick ice covering the road, forcing Roger to drive with the utmost care. The ice crackled and crunched under the tires loudly enough to drown out the sound of the engine, which, in this case was not inconsiderable. Finally, at 5.45pm that evening, with a sigh of relief, Reg and Roger arrived safely at the main gate at RAF Mildenhall. The experience had reminded them both of earlier journeys, made in similar circumstances, during previous English winters.

Sunday, 7th January 1945
Slept in until 10.00am then spent the morning doing odds and ends.

After lunch Reg, Roger and the rest of the crew were called together and taken out to their aircraft's dispersal site for an 'End of Tour' photographic session. This ritual, bestowed upon crews who had successfully completed a tour of operations, entailed having a number of photographs taken in and around their aircraft. Standing in line abreast, Reg and the crew were photographed under the nose of the bomber and grouped around the tail turret. This was to be the last occasion during which the crew of E-Easy would be photographed together.

Another practice with tour-expired airmen was to break up their respective crews, which is exactly what happened with Reg's crew. Two days after the photographic session, Max Bourne and Arthur Bourne were posted away, whilst Reg and Roger received notification they were being posted to RAF Woolfox Lodge, near Stamford, to do a week's refresher course commencing the following Thursday.

Thursday, 11th January 1945
[After breakfast] I went to collect the petrol coupons for our trip to Woolfox Lodge and [then] the trouble started.

The Adjutant adamantly refused to sign the necessary form allowing the issue of petrol coupons and, after a bit of strife, made out some rail warrants. The latter were handed to Reg with orders, under threat of detention, for him and Roger to be off the base by midday.

Their journey to Lincolnshire, by RAF transport to Shippea Hill station and then a train via Peterborough to Stamford, was long, arduous and cold. On arrival at Stamford, they telephoned the base and requested transport for the final leg of the journey to the camp. An RAF vehicle duly arrived and took them back to Woolfox Lodge, where Reg and Roger reported in at the guardhouse shortly after 7.00pm.

Had it not been for the transport driver, Reg and Roger would have been sunk, for they found to their dismay that the camp was dispersed over a very large area. With the snow beginning to melt, trekking miles in ankle deep slush did not appeal to either of them.

The course Reg and Roger were attending was supposed to have began at 9.30am on the morning of Saturday, 13th January, but the whole situation fell into chaos with nobody knowing what they were supposed to be doing, including the instructors! For their part, Reg and Roger seemed to have reverted to the training days when Reg spent the best part of his time lighting fires; the only difference being that now the fires remained alight and

A formal 'End of Tour' photograph of 'The Easy Boys,' taken at RAF Mildenhall on 7th January 1945. From left to right, Roger Humphrys, R/G, RAAF; Paul Taylor, W/Op, RAAF; Max Bourne, Pilot, RAAF; Arthur Bourne, Nav, RAF; Bill Vincent, F/E, RAF; Tom Brown, B/A, RAF; Reg Heffron, MUG, RAAF. *Courtesy of Reg Heffron*

An informal 'End of Tour' photograph of three of 'The Easy Boys.' Posing by the rear turret are, left to right, Bill Vincent, F/E, RAF; Max Bourne, Pilot, RAAF; Roger Humphrys, R/G, RAAF. *Courtesy of the Late Max Bourne*

glowing. Each day of the week-long course seemed to be a repeat of the previous day, with short lectures interspersed with trips into Stamford, lunch, fire lighting and the evening spent in a pub.

Saturday, 20th January 1945
Slept in until 12.00, then dressed and dropped in on '*Tubby*' before lunch at 1.30pm.

Having returned to RAF Mildenhall during the evening of Friday, 19th January, Reg was in no rush to go anywhere on the Saturday morning. However, after lunch, he ambled down to the Disciplinary Office to find that he and Roger were shortly to be posted to Brackla, near Nairn, in the north of Scotland!

With thoughts of Scotland running through their minds, Reg and Roger discussed the practicalities of taking the car with them, and came to the conclusion it would not be practicable. They therefore agreed, and arranged, to have the car transferred into 'Tubby's' name. The latter's thoughts on being presented with the gift of a car were not recorded.

Over the coming days, Reg made frequent enquiries about the supposed posting to Scotland, but no news was forthcoming. Daily routine was becoming a bore and consisted mainly of sleeping, eating, visiting the cinema or sitting around roaring fires chatting with Roger and 'Tubby.' The only excitement Reg and Roger got during this period of uncertainty was undertaking frequent raids on the coal dump. Such was the rush of adrenaline that on the night of 30th January, they not only took the usual two buckets with them to fill, but also a sack!

It is not known whether their nocturnal activities were discovered but, five days after the above-mentioned foray, the pair found they were headed in a different direction to the one they expected.

The Move to Church Broughton

Sunday, 4th February 1945
Went off to lunch with Roger at 1.00pm then made our way to the orderly room.

Upon their arrival at the orderly room, Reg and Roger both found themselves in for a big surprise. Their proposed posting to Scotland had been rescinded and replaced with a posting to No.27 Operational Training Unit, at RAF Lichfield! This change in orders necessitated the issue of a few more clearance forms that, needless to say, required further signatures. After spending the afternoon chasing around, calm was restored and Reg and Roger returned to their room to get a fire going.

Tuesday, 6th February 1945
Our last day at Mildenhall.

Reg and Roger's last day at RAF Mildenhall was very quiet with little to do. As a result of this, they did not bother getting out of bed until midday, when they got up, washed and dressed and went to the Mess for lunch.

During the afternoon Reg finished off getting the necessary clearance forms signed, before calling in on Tom Brown.

Back in his room, during the early part of the evening, Reg finished packing his belongings, with the exception of the overnight items he would need and clothes for the next day.

Wednesday, 7th February 1945
We were awakened at 5.45am by the S.P.'s, dressed in a hurry, put away the last of our gear and went to breakfast.

At 7.15am, the camp at RAF Mildenhall disappeared from view as an RAF Motor Transport Vehicle raced down the country lanes of Suffolk towards Shippea Hill railway station. Amongst those on board the vehicle were Reg and Roger, who were to catch the 8.33am train to Rugby. Having left Shippea Hill, the train traveled west via March, Peterborough and Market Harborough to Rugby, where it arrived at 12.10pm.

Whilst waiting the two-and-a-half-hours for a connection to Lichfield, Reg and Roger used the time to have some lunch at the Salvation Army canteen on the station concourse.

When the connecting train arrived, they boarded it and rode the short distance to Lichfield, where they then had a further wait for transport to the new camp.

Eventually, they arrived at RAF Lichfield, situated three miles northeast of the city. To the locals, the base was known as Fradley, due to the village of the same name on the northeast perimeter of the airfield. The airfield, as mentioned above, was home to No.27 Operational Training Unit and was part of No.93 Group, Bomber Command. It was encompassed by water on two sides, with the Coventry Canal flowing along its northeast boundary and another canal bordering its northwest boundary. The airfield, which commanded by Group Captain H.I. Dabinett, was declared operational in 1940. Being built during the RAF expansion programme, it had been constructed with permanent accommodation, three concrete runways of varying length, in the usual 'A' configuration and hardstandings for 25 bomber aircraft. Although primarily an operational training station, many operational sorties were to be flown from the base during its wartime career.

The duo's first port of call was at the guardroom, where all chits, clearance forms and passes were checked. Having satisfied the duty officer, Reg and Roger were allowed onto the camp in order to find their billet. It was whilst they were visiting the blanket store that Reg purchased (of all things) a bicycle!

Thursday, 8th February 1945
We weren't very enthusiastic about the instructional jobs offered us by the G.L. and [we] said so.

Having voiced their opinions about the proposed instructional jobs, the gunnery leader suggested two dead-end jobs at the satellite airfield at Church Broughton, approximately 18 miles north of Lichfield. After some deliberation about their future prospects, Reg and Roger decided to accept the latter offer.

RAF Church Broughton, an airfield that boasted three concrete runways, was opened in 1942. It came under the same group control as its parent airfield and was also used for operational training. It was situated nine miles west of Derby, between the villages of Broughton and Foxton, with the nearest railway station being Tutbury, two miles away.

Following their interview, and after partaking of lunch, Reg and Roger obtained the four necessary clearances, repacked their kit and jumped into another RAF vehicle which took them to RAF Church Broughton.

On arrival at the satellite airfield, they dumped their kit, drew bedding from the store, had tea at the Mess and then, and only then, got down to the job in hand; they undertook a series of circuits and bumps on an instructional basis.

These first flights took Reg over an enormous crater, which had been made a few months earlier when the underground bomb dump near Burton-on-Trent blew up. It was tremendous in size and in Reg's words "could take a couple of dozen houses with a single brick sticking out over the edge."

The bombs were stored in the disused gypsum mines located under the Stonepit Hills, which the Air Ministry had acquired in 1937. Being ninety feet below ground level, the mines were considered ideal for the storage of bombs, plus there was sufficient space to accommodate up to 10,000 tons of high-explosive bombs. Furthermore, there was room for expansion!

The blast, recorded as the world's largest non-nuclear explosion, occurred just before 11.10am on Monday, 27th November 1944, at No.21 Maintenance Unit, RAF Fauld. Sixty-eight people are known to have been killed in the explosion, with hundreds more being injured. An unknown number of animals, grazing in the surrounding fields, were also killed. The resulting crater, the size of which absolutely amazed Reg, was recorded as being eighty metres across and thirty metres deep. Many buildings were destroyed in the incident and debris of all kinds, including bombs, was thrown high into the air. Doors and windows of properties in Coventry, approximately thirty miles away, were reported to have been shaken and blown open.

An RAF Court of Inquiry headed by Air Vice-Marshal A. Lees CB, CBE, DSO, which was convened rather hastily, ruled that in their opinion, the cause of the explosion was due to RAF armourers "chipping out composition explosives from a live 1,000lb high explosive bomb using a hammer and chisel."

During the clear up operation, many of the 250lb HE bombs, small anti-personnel bombs and small-arms ammunition, which had not detonated and had to be recovered, were moved to the emergency stores at either RAF Church Broughton or RAF Tattenhill.

Tuesday, 13th February 1945
Up at 08.00am and just made breakfast, only to turn up my nose at the sight of the bacon and beans [swimming] in grease, so I had some toast instead. [I] then roused the others and we walked to work. [We] began the day by talking round our fire.

Reg's day had not got off to a good start and, according to the entry in his diary it did not get much better. Having aroused Roger from his slumbers, the pair walked to work, got a fire going and stood around it chatting with other colleagues. Reg and his colleagues were still talking when the Station Padre dropped in, which coincidentally coincided with the official time for a NAAFI break.

It was not until around 11.00am that Reg and Roger started stripping down guns in order to clean them. This, according to Reg's scribbling, being at the gunnery leader's insistence. At lunchtime, they left the job unfinished in order to go and get some food which, allowing for 'hunting' it down and eating it, appears to have been a two hour break!

Having finished their lunchtime task, and having reassembled the guns, both Reg and Roger were required to undertake flying duties. Feeling somewhat weary and despondent they completed the monotony of doing circuits and bumps at 6.10pm, dumped their gear and went off to the Mess in search of a late tea. The rest of the evening was spent in the (relative) comfort of the Mess reading. Well, they were warned; the gunnery leader at Lichfield had said that the jobs at Church Broughton were both 'dead end' jobs.

The monotony continued the next morning, having shown up for work, all Reg could find to do was supervise cleaning of the guns. The afternoon was spent watching, in Reg's words, "A very dry film," which all the instructors had been ordered to see, although he (Reg) gave no clue as to the content of the film.

Thursday, 15th February 1945
Up at 9.00am, missed breakfast then off to work calling in at the S.S.Q. on the way.

Whether Reg had passed a derogatory comment about the film he was forced to watch the previous afternoon is not recorded but, on his way to work the following morning, he stopped off at the Station Sick Quarters to have a festering lip attended to. The entry in his diary continued, "I arrived at the section with half a yard of sticking plaster holding my face together."

Reg's misery was compounded by the news that Roger had been posted back to Lichfield and was leaving the next day. All Reg could do was to hope that he might be posted soon as well.

Without Roger around for company, Reg felt even more bored than usual. The daily routine of finding work to do in the armory, attending unnecessary boring lectures, which were of no interest to him, and having to supervise the occasional 'circuit and bump' exercise, continued over the next few weeks. An example of the latter, Reg recorded in his diary.

Sunday, 25th February 1945
Detailed to fly at 1.30pm and after hanging around until 2.15pm, got off on circuits and bumps at 3.00pm. The weather was a bit grim, very windy with cloud down to 800,' so we decided one circuit was enough and tucked the Wellington away in its corner at 3.30pm.

However, the high note on this particular afternoon was the fact that Reg got back to the N.A.F.F.I. in time for tea and cakes. Life was beginning to look a bit more cheery in more ways than one.

Monday, 26th February 1945
Back to the hut to prepare for an early start in the morning, hoping to be at Mildenhall to see '*Tubby*' by nightfall on an unofficial 48 [hour pass].

Having been woken up at 6.00am, Reg had breakfast and then made his way, by various means of transport including foot, bus, train and truck, to arrive at RAF Mildenhall around 4.15pm.

Following tea and cakes in the mess, Reg set off in the hope of tracking down a few of his old acquaintances. First was 'Jonesy' in the Disciplinary Office, then on to the 'Ops' room to see Charlie Wilson who was unfortunately away on leave and then to the briefing room to see Tom Brown. Having had a good chat with Tom and catching up on all the news and gossip, Reg had to wait for three and a half hours before 'Tubby,' who had also been away on leave, returned.

Reg and 'Tubby' talked into the night and, finally, Reg bedded down in 'Tubby's' billet, where he slept until 6.45am the next morning. After eating a hasty breakfast, Reg said goodbye to his friend and retraced his steps, using the same forms of transport, back to Church Broughton.

After his unofficial trip to RAF Mildenhall, life for Reg returned quickly back to the dreary day-to-day routine at Church Broughton. That is, until he received news that he was being posted to Sutton-on-Hull, northeast of Kingston-Upon-Hull, where, to Reg's amusement, he was to attend an aircraft recognition course.

The journey to Sutton-on-Hull, although tedious, went without a hitch, even though Reg had had to catch at least two trains and two buses. He arrived at the camp late in the afternoon on Wednesday, 7th March and, after the arrival formalities, he found himself a bed, changed his clothes, had some tea and then made his way to the village cinema. The next morning things were not so lax.

Thursday, 8th March 1945
Up at 7.00, a quick wash and off to breakfast, then much meticulous arranging of bedding to meet with the Orderly Officer's approval, and after a pretence at a parade, began the morning's lectures. Nothing but aircraft.

The following day, lectures began at 8.15am when everyone had to take a turn at talking about a particular type of Japanese aircraft. Given that nobody attending the course knew anything about the subject, the whole thing ended in chaos shortly after midday, just in time for lunch. The course resumed an hour later, with the afternoon session giving and receiving further lectures!

For a whole week the course took the same form, early breakfast, lectures, lunch, lectures, tea and cakes, revision and finally supper, before bed. On the final day of the course, lectures started at 8.00am and continued through to just before lunch, when aircraft spotting tests were carried out. The written tests were undertaken during the afternoon. With the exams completed, the members of the course were given a 'pep talk' before being dismissed.

The following morning, Reg set off bright and early (albeit in a very heavy fog) to catch the 7.25 train from Sutton station for the start of his return journey to Church Broughton. Although he did not record how he managed it, the final leg of the journey to the camp was made in a Bentley car! Things seemed to be going Reg's way for the moment.

Thursday, 15th March 1945
Went up to the section where everyone reeled back gasping at my unexpected return. However, the situation was soon reversed when I was told I had been posted back to Lichfield, and [that I] have to be on the 9.30am shuttle in the morning.

Reg did not need to record how he was feeling as a return to Lichfield was something he had hoped for, for quite a while. He spent the rest of the day obtaining clearances, saying "goodbye" to everyone at the section and finally packing, although he did spend the evening with his friend George, who was on night duty in the Signals Section. They spent the time sitting by the fire, chatting and listening to the wireless.

Friday, 16th March 1945
Turned my blankets in to the store and then went to the Adjutant's Office to finalise the clearances. I then put all my goods and chattels aboard the 9.30 shuttle to Lichfield. We set off at 10.00am after numerous delays.

Reg may well have been eager to set off, but as the journey to Lichfield only took an hour, he still managed to get to the camp by 11.00am. Having reported to the main gate, his first task was to find himself a bed, which he did and quickly demonstrated it was his by depositing all his equipment and worldly goods on and around it.

The second task, that of finding Roger, took care of itself when Reg met his friend as they both made their respective ways to the mess for lunch. The afternoon was spent checking the 'Daily Orders,' drawing the necessary items from the stores and getting the 'gen' on how the camp had changed during his absence.

Reg very quickly settled in to life back at Lichfield, although according to the entries in his diary, there still didn't seem to be a lot to do. Occasionally, life threw up a little surprise as one entry showed. After having flown with a novice crew, the entry read:

"Did some very violent corkscrews, and an extremely novel take-off (for a Wellington bomber anyway)"!

Three days after his return to RAF Lichfield, Reg discovered that he was to be granted eight days leave. He made the decision to go to Devon and visit cousin Nellie Dawson again, but before he could go anywhere, Reg had the usual task of obtaining all the necessary clearances and signatures.

11

Applying for a Commission

Tuesday, 20th March 1945
I have decided to go to Broadway to visit Nellie Howitt before going on to Devon.

Reg left the camp at Lichfield just after lunch and made his way to Birmingham, where he spent the night. He took in a stage show at the Theater Royal in New Street, before having supper and making the decision to break his journey to spend a few days with his cousin, Nellie Howitt, in the Cotswold village of Broadway.

The following morning Reg made his way to the bus station, where he joined the queue for the bus to Evesham. Standing waiting, he thought about the old Morris car he used to have and wished he had it now. The thought stayed with him as the bus trundled along, taking one-and-a-half-hours to complete its trip. Unfortunately for Reg, the journey was not yet over, as he had to get another bus to take him the final few miles to his destination.

Having first found himself some accommodation in Broadway, Reg made his way to Nellie's cottage, where she was waiting for him at the front door. His elderly cousin, an evacuee from the London blitz, had prepared lunch and the two of them were soon sitting down enjoying their meal and talking 'nineteen to the dozen.'

After lunch, it being a nice sunny day and quite mild in temperature, the two of them took a stroll and headed towards a hill overlooking the valley in which Broadway is situated. There, they continued to chat away whilst taking in the glorious scenery, before ambling back through the village where they took refreshment in a local teashop.

Thursday, 22nd March 1945
[After breakfast] I went round to see Nellie and helped her with the daily shopping. I then set off for Broadway station to enquire about tomorrow's trains to Devon. On the way back, I was stopped by a Brother from the local Roman Catholic School.

The 'man of the cloth' who stopped Reg insisted that the Australian serviceman should go and see the local schoolmistress. Apparently, she made a habit of stopping all 'Aussies' to enquire if they knew her cousin who had gone to Australia way back in 19-something-or-other. Even at this late stage of the war, Reg found this type of enquiry quite common and somewhat annoying. After nearly half- an-hour, during which time he flatly refused to lecture the children on Australia, Reg managed to get away. Back at Nellie's cottage, Reg took solace by tackling an outsize stack of sausages and mash, followed by half a steamed

Applying for a Commission

The village of Broadway, as seen by Reg Heffron, viewed from the top of the Broadway Tower. *Author's Collection*

The Broadway Tower situated on a hill overlooking the village of Broadway, Worcestershire. On a clear day thirteen counties can be seen from the roof of this 215-year-old structure. *Author's Collection*

The 12th century church dedicated to St. Eadburgha, near the village of Broadway. *Author's Collection*

pudding and two cups of coffee. Nellie sat on the opposite side of the kitchen table listening to Reg's morning events, as he ploughed his way through the feast set before him.

During the afternoon, Reg took himself off to Broadway Tower which, in his words was:

"… an ancient piece of architecture, with traditional battlements and round towers."

The structure, which stood 1,024 feet above sea level, on top of Broadway Hill, was built by Lady Coventry in 1797. In 1945, it was occupied by Mr. E.W. Hollington, a local farmer, who lived there with his wife and three children, George, Francis and Cynthia. Apart from being a farmer, Mr. Hollington was also a member of the Royal Observer Corps, who used the flat roof of the tower as a lookout post. The ROC's task was to plot incoming enemy aircraft and report their locations to the RAF Section Operations Rooms.

Having made contact with Mr. E.W. Hollington, Reg was permitted to clamber up the spiral staircase to the rooftop from where, armed with Mr. Hollington's binoculars, he was able to see thirteen different English Counties. Reg stood, catching his breath as he surveyed the wondrous views before him, including the village of Broadway in the valley below. Looking at the structure on which he was standing, his gaze went down to the row upon row of initials and graffiti, some dated, carved into the stonework in front of him, etched into the surface by generations of visitors before him. Reg resisted the temptation to add his own name.

Reg took one last look at the vista before descending the staircase back down to the family kitchen, where the Mrs. Hollington had prepared a glass of lemonade for him. After a lengthy chat, during which time Reg estimated they covered at least ten different topics of conversation, the Australian said his goodbyes. Feeling happy and content, he set off back to the village, walking down the hillside, across the fields, climbing stiles and opening and closing numerous gates. He eventually reached Nellie's cottage at 4.30pm and, although it may have been nearly teatime, Reg's sightseeing day was not yet over.

After partaking of tea and scones in the local teashop, Reg and Nellie walked through the oldest part of the village, where the mellow, honey-colored stonework of the 16th century buildings gave off a warm glow in the late afternoon sun. Proceeding on, towards Snowshill, they came to the 12th century church dedicated to 'St. Eadburgha.' Eadburgha was the grandaughter of Alfred the Great who, on being offered the gift of some jewels or a Bible, chose the latter. She then dedicated her life to the service of God.

In the church, Reg and Nellie admired the stonework pillars, which imply that the nave was built around the year 1200, and the early Norman period font. Their eyes also gazed upwards to the many old carvings, and plaques, some of which dated back to the 17th century. One surprising item which Reg and Nellie may have noticed was the coat of arms for King Charles I which, although dating back to 1641, had survived the English Civil War!

On leaving the church, Reg and Nellie retraced their steps along the country lane, back to the cottage. Their route took them past The Lygon Arms, a 16th century coaching inn, which is one of the oldest hotels in England. Both King Charles I and Oliver Cromwell, the Lord Protector of England, are both known to have used The Lygon Arms as a resting

The four-gable frontage, which forms the main feature of the Lygon Arms Hotel, has dominated the main street in Broadway since 1620, when John Trevis and his wife, who designed it, carved their names in the stonework over the main entrance. *Author's Collection*

place. The former is said to have met his supporters there, whilst the latter spent an evening there before the Battle of Worcester in 1651. The building was first mentioned during the late 15th/early 16th century, when it was known as The White Hart. Over the years it went through a number of name changes until finally, it acquired the name The Lygon Arms. Rumour has it that General Edward Lygon's elderly butler took over the inn around 1840 and renamed it as a sign of affection for his old master. General Lygon was renowned for having fought at the Battle of Waterloo.

Back in his accommodation, Reg thought about his day. Although he may not have thought about the current war, which was almost at an end in Europe, it is possible past conflicts may well have come into one of his conversations, given that he was staying in an area steeped in the history of the English Civil War. Whatever thoughts drifted through his mind as he nodded off to sleep, the day had certainly been a lesson in English history.

Friday, 23rd March 1945
I am off to Devon today to see Nellie Dawson.

After breakfast, Reg made his way down to Nellie Howitt's cottage in order to say goodbye to her before continuing on to the railway station. He faced a nightmare of a journey, which started with him catching the 10.14am train to Bristol and, after two changes of train and a wait of forty-five minutes, culminated with him reaching Braunton station at 5.45pm. He disembarked from the train amidst a crowd of yelling children, who swept him down the platform, with his feet hardly touching the ground. Only when he reached the street outside the station, was he master of his own movements again.

Unfortunately, Reg had still not completed his journey and set off on foot, without being jostled by kids, towards Saunton Sands. He had covered about half the distance when a kind-hearted motorist stopped and offered him a lift.

Nellie Dawson was waiting for Reg, who soon found himself confronted by a plate of poached eggs on toast, which he quickly devoured. This was followed by Devonshire 'cutrounds,' which were washed down with several cups of tea. A 'cutround' is a semi-sweet roll, split open and served with a jam and clotted cream filling.

The next few days consisted of Reg being introduced to Nellie's friends and neighbours, which induced a lot of talking, aided and abetted by the consumption of numerous cakes, buns and cups of tea. Exercise consisted of walks along the cliff tops, taking in the scenery or strolls along the beach. Everything was peaceful and serene in the Devonshire countryside. The only mention of the war in Reg's diary, was when he wrote, "We had news today of the crossing of the Rhine at Wesel and Xanten." However, Reg was soon to have a rude awakening.

Sunday, 25th March 1945
I am leaving tomorrow morning to spend the last day of this leave at Shoreham in Kent.

The following morning, Reg took a last stroll along the beach with Nellie, before catching the bus that would take him to the railway station. He almost missed the bus, so his farewell to Nellie was rather a hurried one.

The journey to London was a tedious one which involved catching the 10.45am train from Braunton to Victoria, two underground trains to get from main line station to main line station once he had reached London, and three trains to get from Charing Cross to Shoreham. The latter part of the trip necessitated two changes, one at Orpington and one at Sevenoaks. However, on his arrival at the house, Mr. and Mrs. White were waiting for Reg (who had obviously been to the house on a previous occasion), and welcomed him with a light meal.

Monday, 26th March 1945
Everything has changed since my last visit. Everyone seems a nervous wreck, the house has been badly blasted by a flying bomb and '*Bimy*' is away in Devon recuperating from shock.

Reg kept his observations to himself, but did spend the evening chatting and playing shove-halfpenny with Mr. and Mrs. White. During that time a number of flying bombs exploded at varying distances from the house, shaking the foundations and rattling the windows. Reg recorded that some of the V.1's exploded almost simultaneously.

Tuesday, 27th March 1945
I was awakened during the early hours of the morning by a loud crash, and shortly afterwards a flying bomb roared overhead at very low altitude, kicking up a terrific din, which seemed to greatly accentuate the silence that followed when the engine cut out.

Those who had to endure the V1 'Flying Bombs' soon realized that it was fine whilst the menace was flying overhead and you could hear the buzz of its jet motor. The time to worry, and take cover, was when the engine stopped and an eerie silence followed. This meant the device had run out of fuel and was earthbound. Given that V1s flew at a relatively low altitude the resulting explosion followed very quickly, usually about eleven seconds later.

The 'Doodlebug' that Reg heard fell to earth about half-a-mile away with a tremendous crash, rattling all the doors and windows. The vibration, which followed the explosion, brought down more plaster that added to the damage already sustained by Mr. and Mrs. White's house. No wonder, as Reg had noticed, "Everybody was on edge." Once he was up and about, and after he had had his breakfast, he went out into the garden to check for further damage.

That same afternoon, Reg packed his gear, said his "goodbyes" and headed for the station. It was not the flying bombs that had dictated that he should leave Mr. and Mrs. White's home, but the simple fact he had to return to RAF Lichfield. He had, however, had another lesson in what, in later years, would become English history.

Once back at camp, the routine for the next week or so hardly changed, with variable weather conditions and very little to do. A limited number of flying exercises were undertaken but, in the main, Reg spent much of his time chatting, writing letters or catching up with outstanding, or long overdue, jobs.

Thursday, 5th April 1945
Flew all afternoon, taking two details up, and did a test flight as well.

One assumes that the flights with which Reg was involved went without incident, as he made no mention of scary moments; unlike an episode which occurred later in the day and was mentioned in his diary. The situation arose when a novice pilot, flying a Wellington bomber, executed a very ropey take-off. In trying to correct the problem, the aircraft veered to one side, ran off the runway, careered along the grass for a distance of approximately 200 yards and then bounced into the air. The lack of any further entry indicates that Reg did not stick around to watch the landing!

Three days later there was another incident on the airfield that did not receive a mention in Reg's diary, but there were mitigating circumstances for this omission.

Monday, 9th April 1945
Woke up feeling a bit off, so didn't have any breakfast. Went to work but there was no flying owing to heavy fog. I was sick several times and went off to my room with my stomach gurgling like a mountain brook. I sat there alternately holding my stomach and dashing outside. I decided to go to the Station Sick Quarters and duly saw the Medical Officer.

Reg's temperature rose to 102 degrees so, without further ado, he was bundled into bed where he slept fitfully until 7.30am the next morning. Whilst Reg was having his own little drama, there was a more worrying drama unfolding out on the airfield.

Vickers Wellington bomber, serial ME881, piloted by Flying Officer S. Bourke, RAAF, was on a training flight and carrying a crew of eight, many of whom were air gunners on an air firing exercise. On return to the airfield, just prior to landing, the port engine failed and furthermore, the crew could not get the starboard undercarriage to lock in the down position. The aircraft eventually finished up as a pile of wreckage, on the overshoot area of the airfield. No major injuries were reported although the event could have been recorded as 'One sick airman, one sick aeroplane.'

Although Reg was feeling better the next morning he was kept in bed all day, and was eventually discharged from the Station Sick Quarters just after lunch the following day.

Sunday, 15th April 1945
Took one detail up during the morning but finished in time for lunch. Flying again during the afternoon, and had to stay up an extra half-hour while a 'pranged' [Hawker] Typhoon was removed from the runway.

Reg's third flight of the day, a night flying exercise, didn't happen, but still managed to create a situation. Two aircraft, one of which Reg was crewing, both developed faults whilst taxiing across the airfield. Both aircraft were immediately declared unserviceable, but not before a faulty engine on one of the bombers had smothered one end of the airfield in thick smoke during run-up on the said engine. A Hawker Hurricane fighter, flying overhead RAF Lichfield at the time, called up control and reported a fire. Consequently, the fire and crash tenders were alerted, galvanized into action and raced across the airfield to the scene of the incident. Fortunately, by the time they arrived everything was back to normal, as the aircrews involved had got the situation under control, had packed up and departed.

Wednesday, 18th April 1945
Called in at the Orderly Room to collect the necessary forms for a commission. I have decided under pressure to give it a go.

It will be remembered that during his recent period of leave, Reg had had numerous conversations with both relatives and friends and likewise, on his return to Lichfield, with flying duties curtailed due to inclement weather, Reg had further ample opportunities for chatting whilst passing the time. Reg did not however, record in his diary who had been putting him under pressure to apply for a commission, but whoever it was, their recommendation had been heeded.

Having acquired the necessary documentation and after writing a letter home, Reg spent the rest of the evening reading through the paperwork and filling it in as required. The process took him longer than he had expected – just like all form filling!

Thursday, 19th April 1945
No flying during the morning owing to fog, so took the opportunity to hand over my papers to the G.L., who promised to send them on the C.I.

Although by late morning the fog had cleared, no flying still seemed to be the order of the day, certainly as far as Reg and Roger were concerned. After he had handed his application papers to the Gunnery Leader, and had received a promise they would be forwarded to the Chief Instructor forthwith, Reg took Roger for a leisurely row on a nearby local lake.

Drifting around in the sunshine, Reg was later prompted to write, "[We] lazed away an hour in a most enjoyable fashion, before we went to lunch."

It was to be the following Monday before Reg recorded enjoying himself again, albeit on the occasion, in an entirely different manner.

Monday, 23rd April 1945
Dashed off to work just in time to collect an air firing detail. Took off at 10.30am and went out over the Irish Sea and got rid of 1,000 rounds.

The air gunners under training who flew on this exercise with Reg as their instructor, having completed their allotted sessions, were then treated to a display of aerial marksmanship. Reg could not resist the temptation of getting behind the guns and firing off a number of rounds at the target drogue, which he duly shot down into the sea. Not content with this exhibition, he then decided to open fire at the lashing cable and shot that off too. Then, with an air of nonchalance, on landing he wrote, 'Had lunch at 1.00pm and then wandered back to work.'

Weather during the rest of April was variable. On the good days, Reg was able to notch up a great deal of time in the air, which also included night-flying. However, other days were a complete washout, not only from the wind and rain, but also with the occasional snowstorm. As Reg wrote in his diary towards the end of the month, "Oh to be in England, now that April's here."

On the last day of April, Reg was called in for interview by the Wing Commander, regarding the former's application for a commission. The applicant listened to his senior officer who, in Reg's opinion, was quite nice about it all. The interview, which had not lasted more than five minutes, concluded with the Wing Commander telling Reg that he (Reg) would be required to see the Group Captain the following day. Unfortunately, for whatever reason, this second interview did not take place.

Roger went on leave on 2nd May, so was not around to see what was about to happen in the room he shared with Reg. However, as Roger had agreed to meet up with the latter in Devon the following week, Reg would no doubt tell him about the mayhem then.

Thursday, 3rd May 1945
There was very little to do all day so we sat around the fire yarning until lunchtime, and then repeated the process in the afternoon, with a break for NAFFI tea at 3.30pm. Went to tea at 5.00pm and then returned to my room to find that Messrs Dabbit & Splash, painters, had been there all day.

Messrs. Dabbit & Splash greeted Reg with a cheery, "Been doing it out." It seemed to Reg as though they have been 'doing it in.' Green, white and buff coloured paint was splattered with reckless abandon over the blankets, kitbags, windows, curtains and beds. The sight of the once highly polished lino flooring covered with paint was almost too much for Reg, but Messrs. Dabbit & Splash just kept dabbing away at anything that didn't move. Around 9.00pm, with them not being able to find anything that hadn't already been painted, Dabbit & Splash began collecting their goods and chattels.

"Well," said Mr. Dabbit, "That's that."

"Hope you didn't mind," chimed in Mr. Splash.

"Oh no," replied Reg, "only too glad to have the place looking despicable again."

With that, Dabbit & Splash disappeared into the night rattling tins and smelling of paint, whilst leaving Reg in a state of disbelief. Getting busy with a broom and hot water, Reg spent the next two hours cleaning up, scraping paint off the blankets and curtains and generally trying to get the room back to how he had left it that morning.

To add to Reg's chagrin, he woke up the next morning to find his face and mouth swollen and a re-occurrence of the festering lip problem. Needless to say, having got dressed, he went straight off to the Station Sick Quarters. Unfortunately for Reg, the Medical Officer had taken himself off to listen to the midday news. Well, there was a lot going on. Hitler was dead, the German forces in Italy had surrendered and the war in Europe had only four days left to run. However, none of this was relevant to Reg at this moment in time. When he finally did see the M.O., the latter prescribed Boracic and ointment for Reg's sadly distorted face.

Saturday, 5th May 1945

Visibility was very bad today so no flying. I went to collect my leave pass and then went off to lunch. I took the afternoon off and got things sorted out for tomorrow.

Reg woke up earlier than he normally did, so took the opportunity of getting to the Station Sick Quarters for further treatment to his face, before a queue started. Having completed this task he set off for work, but was informed that all flying had been canceled due to poor visibility. This news came as a bonus to Reg, who had been granted seven days' leave.

Reg wanted an early start the next day as he was going back down to Devon to see Nellie Dawson again, so he got everything ready in the now spick and span room. He and Roger always kept the room in a neat, tidy and orderly manner in case a snap officer's inspection was called.

Sunday, 6th May 1945

Dressed up in my Sunday best then went down to the mess for some breakfast. Finished packing. Cleaned and tidied up the room then set off on foot towards Lichfield.

Fortunately, Reg had not gone too far when he managed to get a lift to Trent Valley station. From there he was offered another lift into Lichfield where the driver of a milk truck took over and ferried him into Birmingham. Finally, a motorist stopped and offered him a lift to New Street station. Reg may well have thought his luck was in and that this was going to be an easy journey, but how wrong he was to be. First, he had a five-hour wait for the train to Bristol, which eventually arrived thirty minutes later than specified. When it did arrive, it was full and he had to stand for the entire journey. The final insult came when, having reached Bristol, he found there was no onward connection to Braunton. With no other choice, Reg found a Y.M.C.A. center, where he secured a bed for the night.

Applying for a Commission

Monday, 7th May 1945
Went down to breakfast [then] wandered off to the station at Temple Meads and caught the 8.50am to Exeter arriving there at 11am.

Finding he had a forty-minute wait for the train, Reg hailed a taxi and raced across the city to St.John's Road, where he visited his auntie Maud's cousin, Mrs. Hooper. They had time for a very quick cup of coffee and an equally quick chat, before Reg had to jump back in the taxi and race through the badly blitzed city to catch his train.

Arriving at Braunton station just after lunchtime, Reg found a taxi waiting for him. This luxury had been pre-arranged by Nellie, to whom Reg had to do some fast-talking in self-defence, owing to his delayed arrival. Nellie's feigned annoyance quickly disappeared and they sat down to enjoy the lunch Nellie had previously prepared.

The rest of the afternoon and early evening were taken up with a long walk across the Downs to Croyde, where thatched cottages shelter behind the sand dunes, and then on to Putsborough Manor. They returned via Croyde Bay, crossing the beach to Downend Point, then up onto the cliff tops and took the coastal path to Saunton Sands.

Shortly after they had had tea at Nellie's home, the taxi driver who was supposed to be collecting Roger from the station telephoned to inform Reg and Nellie that their friend was not on the train. Without further ado, they made their way to the station to meet the next train but unfortunately, there was no sign of Roger on that one either! To their consternation, Reg and Nellie set off around the town checking out all 'Aussie' airmen, but with no result. Somewhat concerned, Reg and Nellie returned home wondering what could have happened to Roger. The news they heard on the radio later that evening may have given a clue as to what had happened to Roger. Maybe he was caught up in some kind of celebration.

12

Victory in Europe

Whilst Reg waited to see if Roger was going to turn up, he wrote some letters and then read the newspapers. The evening wore on with still no sign of Roger and as the time approached midnight, Reg switched on the radio in time to hear the BBC news. In the reserved tones of a BBC announcer, the newsreader informed the listeners that Victory in Europe had been achieved, following the surrender of all German forces on 7th May. Monday, 8th May was declared VE Day.

Tuesday, 8th May 1945
Spent the whole day waiting about the house for Roger to turn up, but did he? Not he. By tea time both Nellie and I were having visions of cars bearing down on helpless pedestrians, train smashes and other such dreadful possibilities.

Although the declaration of the cessation of hostilities in Europe had been formally announced, there was no further mention of it in Reg's diary, other than the fact he had heard it on the BBC midnight news broadcast. At this important time in everybody else's life, when celebrating was high on the agenda, Reg's first and only thought was for the safety and well being of his friend.

In desperation, Reg sent a telegram to Roger's last leave address. He also notified the Bath police, who duly ascertained that Roger had indeed left for Braunton the previous morning. As the mystery deepened, the anguish and concern grew. With nothing more to be done, at this stage and hour, Reg went off to bed at 1.00am.

Although Reg and Roger did not celebrate VE Day together, a couple of sketches were drawn showing how it would have been if they had been together. One of the sketches is rubber stamped with the date '8th May 1945.'

Wednesday, 9th May 1945
I rang the RAF at Lichfield to enquire if they had any news of the missing gent. They had. He was seen in Lichfield the previous evening.

Relieved that his friend was alright, but equally annoyed that Roger had not turned up in Devon as previously agreed, Reg felt that his friend had a lot of explaining to do.

In an effort to put the stress of the last day or so behind them, Reg and Nellie decided to visit some friends at Ilfracombe. Ilfracombe, the largest seaside town on the North Devon coast is built around a harbor that is overlooked by a chapel dedicated to St. Nicholas, the

Victory in Europe

A photograph of a sketch celebrating VE Day, depicting Bill Vincent, in an inebriated condition, sitting in a make-shift cart reading a newspaper, whilst being hauled around town, by an equally inebriated Roger Humphrys. The caption reads, *"Drive on, to the next Club."* Courtesy of Ann Hill

A second sketch, implying the excesses of the previous day, depicts Bill Vincent and Roger Humphrys, asleep in bed, oblivious to the mess they left on the floor the previous night, whilst serpents float around their unconscious minds. The caption reads, *"Brewers' Asthma."* Courtesy of Ann Hill

patron saint of sailors. For over 650 years a light has shone out from the top of Lantern Hill, as this rock promontory is known, guiding seafarers to the shore and safety of the harbor. The site, which was first mentioned in a register compiled by Bishop Stafford in 1416, has been used as a chapel, a lighthouse/beacon (around the 16th century) and family home.

Reg and Nellie went by train from Braunton, which was bedecked with flags and red, white and blue bunting. Everywhere they looked people were chatting to each other excitedly and wearing huge smiles or grins on their faces. Having endured the relative calm of the short train journey, the reality of the situation came back to Reg and Nellie when they reached their destination. On arrival in Ilfracombe they found the town bedecked in like manner to Braunton, with a children's party in full swing in St. Brannock Park. Having arrived safely at the home of Mr. and Mrs. Baser, their friends, the afternoon was spent taking tea and chatting, with a number of topics of conversation on the agenda. Whilst supping and talking they watched the 'Victory' celebrations going on outside in the street.

The following day proved to be a lazy one for both Reg and Nellie. After a late breakfast, followed a couple of hours later by lunch, they went to Barnstaple and took in a couple of films. On leaving the cinema, they took a stroll across the long, narrow, sixteen-arched bridge, which dated back to the 13th century, which enabled them to visit some friends of Nellie's who lived on the other side of the River Taw.

Friday, 11th May 1945
After lunch I did a spot of gardening, and then later we wandered down to the beach and collected a variety of shells, spending a couple of hours in the sunshine in the process. [Went home] had tea at 6.30pm, and a visit from Jill Dunn, who was out when we visited the farm near Barnstaple yesterday.

Later that same evening, after Nellie's friend Jill had gone home, Reg and Nellie decided to go back down to the beach and give a sand yacht an outing. Unfortunately, due to the lack of any wind, their efforts in hauling the contraption down to the beach went unrewarded. They had little choice other than to retrace their steps across the sand and head for home. Dragging the sand yacht back across the beach seemed a much harder effort on the return trip that is until a loud explosion startled them and caused them to vacate the beach area with amazing mobility.

The entry in Reg's diary for the that afternoon implied that the shells he had been collecting were of the marine variety, but at 11.00pm that night all hell broke loose in the sand dunes when bullets started to fly through the air in all directions, flares rocketed up into the sky and further explosions shook the very foundations of the house! By midnight all was quiet again. It must be assumed that Reg never discovered the reason for the impromptu 'fireworks display,' as it was not mentioned again. Whatever the cause, it was a fitting memory with which to end his period of leave.

Saturday, 12th May 1945
Nellie saw me off on the 8.38am train to London. Had a weary trip via Exeter, Salisbury, and Wimbledon to London, arriving in Waterloo at 3.50pm. Took a taxi to the *'Boomer'* and dumped my kit.

A view looking across Ilfracombe harbor shows Lantern Hill to the top right of the picture.
Courtesy of Robb F. W. Jones

On leaving the Boomerang Club, Reg walked the short distance to Kodak House in Kingsway to sort out some business. He later returned to Australia House, where he had something to eat and indulged himself with an English ice cream, mounted on a waffle and smothered with raspberry flavouring.

Reg observed that although London was happy, with flags and bunting in abundance, there were no other signs of VE day, except for dozens of ex-prisoners of war roaming the streets, all with happy grins on their faces. He also noticed that many of them were Australian Forces. Maybe he should have been in town five days earlier, when masses and masses of people thronged the streets, surged into Downing Street to catch a glimpse of the Prime Minister, Winston Churchill, or stood in the swaying sea of humanity outside Buckingham Palace waiting for the Royal Family to appear. Those same people, who kissed total strangers, danced in conga lines around Trafalgar Square, Piccadilly Circus and other notable landmarks, or simply sat on top of bus shelters watching the celebrations unfold, were now all either back at work or sleeping off the effects of their celebrations.

Although Reg got a taxi to take him to Euston station, where he arrived in time to catch the 5.10pm train to Rugby, the train arrived late at the latter causing Reg to miss his connection to Lichfield. This in turn led to a chain of events that eventually saw Reg reporting back from leave at 1.15am the following morning!

Sunday, 13th May 1945

Slept in until 11.00am. Roger came in with a sheepish grin on his face. His explanation of his doings was decidedly weak, but just strong enough to hold water.

Reg stood ready to hear Roger's tale of woe as to why the latter did not show up at Braunton as agreed, but was not really ready for the explanation Roger gave.

It transpired that Roger had proposed to a young lady by the name of Barbara Ryan, and had planned to get married in a month's time, but was all in a whirl because, in the intervening period, he had been given advanced notification that he was to be sent home to Australia. In an effort to get things sorted out, Roger had been desperately chasing around trying to get his repatriation date canceled or at the very least, put back.

Later that same day (after lunch), Reg received a telephone call advising him that he was required to attend interviews relating to his application for a commission, with the Air Officer Commanding, at Group Headquarters, RAF Abingdon.

The following day, Reg wandered down to the Station Headquarters, where he enquired about his visit to Group H.Q. and to obtain a rail warrant. The warrant having been issued, Reg set off at lunchtime and headed for Birmingham. Finding he had a couple of hours to spare, he went off to the newsreel theater in New Street and caught up with what was going on in the world; who knows, the knowledge gained could prove useful at the interview. Continuing his journey later in the day, he travelled via Leamington Spa and Warwick to Oxford, from where he caught a bus to the town of Abingdon. This left Reg having to walk the last couple of miles to the RAF Station.

Having arrived at the base, and having found himself somewhere to sleep, he was annoyed to find that he could not get anything to eat. Nobody claimed responsibility for the provision of late meals. It took Reg approximately one-hour and a two-mile tramp around the camp, before he was finally rewarded with something to eat and drink.

Tuesday, 15th May 1945
Went to the H.Q. building to have the interviews with the old boy at 9.00am. By 11.00am everyone had been grilled [questioned], (10 of us in all).

The assembled, prospective, officers, having been individually interviewed, were brought together in a group in front of the A.O.C. and given a fatherly talk on the new responsibilities that they were shortly to assume, and that was it. So it was that, at midday, Reg set off back to Lichfield.

Needless to say, the journey back to camp was going to be a long one, so, having reached Oxford, Reg left his baggage at the station and went off in search of a café, where lunch was taken. This was followed by passing an hour or so in a cinema, until it was time to catch the train.

Wednesday, 16th May 1945
Did a couple of [gun] harmonisations during the morning and another after lunch. At 11.00am the Adj wanted to see Roger and me.

The reason that Reg and Roger were called in to the Adjutant's office was so the latter could talk to them about doing a second tour. Roger had managed to get his repatriation date put back, or as Reg put it in his diary "Roger has gotten himself off the boat list." Given that Victory in Europe had been achieved, this chat with the Adjutant could have only related to the fact that the pair might face being posted to the Far East.

The Royal Air Force was, during this period, mustering a large force within Bomber Command, which was to become known as the 'Tiger Force,' in order to take the bombing offensive to Japan. However, the dropping of the two atomic bombs in early August, by the Americans, brought hostilities in the Far East to a speedy conclusion.

Reg made no mention of the 'Tiger Force,' Japan or the Far East in his diary, but did conclude the above entry with the comment that, "Within a few minutes we were signed up."

Although Reg had 'signed up' for a second tour, there seemed little for him to do. During the following week or so, Reg seemed to idle around the camp due to a lack of work, unserviceable aircraft or inclement weather which preventing flying in any form.

This state of affairs continued until the 28th May, when Reg took to writing a specification and 'potted' history of the Lancaster Mk.III in his diary! The following day a little excitement was recorded in both Reg's day and his diary.

29th May 1945

[I] did some flying before lunch finishing at 12.30. I dropped my precious propelling pencil during the trip.

Unfortunately, bending down to retrieve the pencil was not an option for Reg as, much to his annoyance, it disappeared down between the double-skin of the fuselage at the side of the bomb bay. On landing, Reg must have mentioned his plight to a member of the groundcrew, because an hour so later he was reunited with his pencil. It transpired that one of the 'erks' had obligingly hacked away at the fabric of the aircraft, with a knife, in order to retrieve the implement.

Taking greater care of the precious pencil, Reg undertook two more flying details during the afternoon, and a further five night-fighter affiliation exercises that night. He finally fell into his bed at 2.30am the following morning.

31st May 1945

Went down to visit the Adjutant, who informed me that the 2nd tour was off.

Apart from receiving the news that he (Reg) would not be required to undertake a second tour of operational duty, the Adjutant also informed him that his name had been added to the repatriation list and that he would be on a boat heading home anytime after 15th June. Reg did not record his feelings or make any other comment about the latter.

The rest of Reg's day consisted of further training flights and various air exercises, including night flying again. Although he arrived at the flight office at 10:00 o'clock that evening, another ninety minutes were to pass before he got airborne. The pilot was instructed to use the short runway and, much to Reg's consternation, the aircraft just cleared the perimeter fence.

Having completed the second detail, the next pilot was order to circle over the airfield whilst, due to a variation in the wind direction and speed, the landing runway changed. This task kept the aircraft and crew over the airfield for a further twenty minutes.

On landing, Reg waited for the arrival of the third crew he was to fly with that night, but they did not show up. Their allotted flight was therefore canceled, so Reg went off to the mess for some well earned bacon and eggs.

1st June 1945
No flying this morning [so] everyone was busy filling in their log books. Flying this afternoon and did two trips, the second being a most remarkable affair.

The training flight referred to by Reg occurred late in the afternoon. The pilot, an unnamed trainee, set off from the airfield without noting his compass heading. As a result of this error, come the end of the detail, the pilot was lost and did not know which way to turn, literally. A call to air traffic control resulted in the trainee pilot being given a course bearing that, hopefully, would enable him to locate the airfield. This having been achieved, the pilot then made the worst landing that Reg had ever experienced. The aircraft bounced heavily three times in succession, with a solid bone shaking thump on each occasion and the pilot practically losing control of his machine. The entire incident was witnessed by those on duty in the control tower who, after the aircraft had finally come to rest on the ground, directed the pilot to a particular dispersal area where the Wellington bomber could be inspected. However, while parking the aircraft, the pilot ran off the concrete and onto very wet, soft, ground. Within two minutes, having desperately tried to move the aircraft out of the mire, he managed to bog the undercarriage, down to its axle, in the mud. Reg's only comment about this incident was, 'A nice afternoon's work'!

Monday, 4th June 1945
I took the opportunity to get a 48 hour pass and tack a day on each end of it, with the intention of going to Barnstaple to see Jill Dunn. [I] wangled it o.k.

Reg did not waste any time and set off on the first leg of the long, arduous journey after lunch. It was 8.30pm before he reached Temple Meads railway station, Bristol, from where he sent a couple of telegrams, before acquiring a bed in the nearby YMCA.

Up bright and early the next morning, he caught a train to Exeter, where he changed to catch another train to take him on to Braunton. From Braunton, he then caught a third train to take him to Barnstaple, where Jill was waiting for him.

Jill accompanied Reg to Nellie Dawson's home, where they had lunch with Nellie and where Reg was going to stay during his period of leave.

During the afternoon, Reg and Jill went for a walk to Downend Point, a picturesque area on the coast also known as Croyde Point. Off the beaten track in 1945, it has in later years become known as a surfer's paradise.

In the evening, after taking tea in the town, Reg and Jill went to the cinema in Barnstaple, where they saw a film entitled 'The Keys to the Kingdom.' The movie, starring Gregory Peck as a Catholic priest, was one of his earliest films, and also the first motion picture for which he won an Oscar nomination. Vincent Price, another well-known actor, starred alongside Gregory Peck. Given the horror movie roles that Vincent Price portrayed later in his career, as somebody once said, "You cannot imagine Vincent Price as a Catholic priest."

Following supper with Jill at a restaurant in the town, Reg returned to Braunton aboard the 'Drunk's Special.' Having walked a couple of miles in the rain from Braunton station, Reg was pleased when Nellie stopped by the side of the road in a car she had borrowed from a friend, in which to come and meet him. Their evening concluded, back at Nellie's home, with equally large helpings of hot tea, buns and chatter.

Wednesday, 6th June 1945
Nellie and I went to Barnstaple and from there to Clovelly. I have seen nothing to equal it for untarnished old age.

The extremely steep, narrow, winding stepped cobbled street and ancient houses perched in all sorts of impossible positions on the cliffs absolutely amazed Reg. It was, he noticed, unspoiled by any innovations such as road signs, streetlights, regulations and any form of wheel traffic. Lying in a narrow valley between steep cliffs, Clovelly was, and is, one of Britain's treasures.

Nellie and Reg made their way down to the harbor, where they had a good look around and Reg took a number of photographs. Then, when they were ready to leave, came the long haul back up the hill, over the same cobbles that donkeys and mules, equipped with panniers, once trekked when delivering heavy loads to and from the harbor.

Reg woke up late the following morning and, after an egg and bacon breakfast, proceeded to blow the cobwebs off the sand yacht, for another attempt at riding it on the beach. On this occasion, unlike his last leave at Braunton, both Nellie and Reg got in some 'sailing' time, without the hindrance of shells and exploding ammunition. In fact, according to Reg's diary, they had "an hour's sailing (and pushing) up and down the beach."

During the early evening Reg caught the bus to Barnstaple, where he met Jill and accompanied her back to Nellie's home, where it had previously been arranged she would spend the night. After a supper prepared by Nellie, they went for a walk to Croyde Bay. It turned out to be a very late night, and Reg had to be up early the next morning.

Friday, 8th June 1945
Back to Lichfield today.

The friend who had lent Nellie the car a few days earlier, drove Nellie, Jill and Reg to Barnstaple. Once there, having relaxed and chatted over coffee and buns, Nellie went shopping whilst Jill went with Reg to the station to see him off.

Having made the trip so many times, Reg knew what was ahead of him with regard to the journey, so no surprises there. However, there was a major surprise awaiting Reg when he finally got back to camp. Having already passed through Lichfield, on his arrival back to the RAF Station, Reg found a note from Roger asking Reg to retrace his steps to the town, where Roger would meet him. The purpose of this assignation was "to meet tomorrow's bride"!

Back in Lichfield, Reg met Roger in the street, the latter resplendent in a new uniform, complete with Pilot Officer rank tapes. Together they visited the home of the bride to be (no conversations recorded in Reg's diary), before the groom and his best man went to the Goat's Head Public House, supposedly, to see how arrangements for the reception were going. Nothing was recorded, but it must be assumed that Reg and Roger felt duty bound to ensure that the beer and other drinks were suitable for the guests' consumption.

13

Two Marriages, Two Commissions and Masses of Leave

Saturday, 9th June 1945
Got dressed for the big event and biked into town. Everyone was panicking about the Goat's Head putting the final touches to the tables and Roger had to be kicked out.

It is a known fact that it is a bride's prerogative to arrive late at her wedding but, initially, on this occasion, it looked like it was to be the groom who would be rushing up the aisle after the taxi arrived late to collect the groom and his best man.

On arrival at the Holy Cross Roman Catholic Church in Lichfield, Roger and Reg sat in the front pew, where the priest, the Reverend Father Nearey, took it upon himself to avail Roger of a few whispered hints and facts.

The ceremony began when the bride, Miss Barbara Patricia Ryan, arrived at the church. Attired in rose patterned lace over net and taffeta, and carrying a bouquet of red carnations, the bride walked sedately up the aisle on the arm of her father, Mr. G. Ryan. The bride's two sisters, Peggy and Kathleen, together with a friend, Gladys Cartmale, were in close attendance as bridesmaids.

Everything went well during the ceremony, except that Roger had a struggle getting the wedding ring on his new bride's finger, and the muffled whispering which ensued between the priest and the groom, caused a little discreet eyebrow-raising in the pews.

After the formalities the guests repaired to the Goat's Head for the reception, where the celebrations continued until 10.15pm, although one or two people, Reg included, noticed that the bride and groom had sloped off at 9.00pm. In accordance with his duties as best man, Reg, having found the elusive couple back at the house, held them there until Mr. and Mrs. Ryan came to see the newlyweds off in proper fashion. The honeymoon was taken in the Wiltshire city of Bath.

Having fulfilled his duties to everyone's satisfaction, Reg was invited by the bride's father to stay and have a drink, and, as was to be expected, one drink led to another, then another and then another. It was 3.00a.m when Reg finally left the home of Mr. and Mrs. Ryan, feeling just a little the worse for wear, but he was happy and content. He had seen his best friend off in style, and had met some wonderful people during the course of the day.

A week later, on 15th June, a column style entry, relating to the wedding, was published in a local newspaper. The headline read, 'AUSTRALIAN AIR FORCE OFFICER MARRIES A LICHFIELD BRIDE.' Reg still has the cutting.

Roger's commission had come through just in time for him to be married as a commissioned officer, giving the headline a little more status.

Life resumed as normal after the wedding; normal that was for Reg. The next few days were spent as they always seemed to be, flying, chatting, eating, sleeping or waiting for the weather to improve. The one thing that did not seem to improve of late was various pilots' continuing lack of ability to handle a Wellington bomber.

Tuesday, 12th June 1945
Did some flying during the morning, one detail only, finishing at 12.15pm, then off to lunch. Back to work again at 1.30pm and started flying again after 2.00pm. [I] did one detail of two [scheduled] exercises.

It was no wonder that only the first exercise of the afternoon session was carried out as, during the take-off run, the aircraft swung off the runway in a forty-five degree crosswind and actually got airborne off the grass! As the pilot climbed to gain altitude, Reg was thinking that they still had to get down again after the exercise had been completed.

AUSTRALIAN AIR FORCE OFFICER

MARRIES A LICHFIELD BRIDE

A very pretty wedding took place at Holy Cross, Lichfield, on Saturday, between Pilot Officer Roger N. Humphrys, R.A.A.F., son of Mr. and Mrs. F. Humphrys, of 14, Kathleen Street, N. Cottesloe, West Australia, and Miss Barbara Patricia Ryan, daughter of Mr. and Mrs. G. Ryan, of 38, Walsall Road, Lichfield. The service was conducted by the Rev. Father Nearey, R.C., and the bride, who was given away by her father, was attired in rose patterned lace over net and taffeta, carrying a bouquet of red carnations. The bridesmaids were the Misses Peggy Ryan (sister), Gladys Cartmale (friend of bride), and Kathleen Ryan (bride's youngest sister), who was also train bearer, and they wore dresses of gold taffeta and blue taffeta, with accessories to match, each carrying cream roses. Flight Sergt. Reg. Heffron acted as best man, and the organist (Mr. Williams) played appropriate music, including Mendelssohn's Wedding March.

After the ceremony a reception was held at the Goat's Head Hotel, Lichfield. The newly married pair later left for Bath, the bride's travelling costume consisting of powder blue two-piece, with cream travelling coat.

The bride and bridegroom were the recipients of numerous presents, including several gifts of money.

Photograph of the newspaper cutting, from the Lichfield Mercury, reporting the wedding of Roger Humphrys and Barbara Ryan. *Courtesy of Gary Phelps, editor, The Lichfield Mercury newspaper.*

Unfortunately, his concerns proved correct as, on contact with the runway, the aircraft again veered off on to the grass. At seventy miles per hour, the bomber bounced and rattled across the grass, giving all on board a thorough shaking, before coming to a standstill. Another aircraft on which the groundcrew would have to undertake a major inspection before it was allowed back in the air.

Wednesday, 13th June 1945
No flying during the afternoon so, after tea, I went to Lichfield to see Roger's new relations.

Whilst at Mr. and Mrs. Ryan's home, the newly-weds arrived back from their honeymoon, with sheepish grins and shy smiles on their faces. To overcome their embarrassment, it was suggested that everyone should venture down to the Carpenter's Arms for a noggin or two. When the pub closed at 10.00pm everyone, including Reg, went back to the house, and although more sandwiches and drinks were offered around, Reg felt he should leave Roger and his 'new' family to chat amongst themselves. However, every time he tried to take his leave, another sandwich or drink was thrust into his hand until, finally, on his fifth attempt to leave, at 1.15a.m in the morning, Reg managed to achieve his aim.

Thursday, 14th June 1945
No flying today, so I collected some pay and then spent a couple of hours yarning over tea and cakes with '*Blue*' Baxter, the pay clerk. [Later] I got dressed for the big party being held in Lichfield.

According to the entry in Reg's diary, the party was to 'celebrate' the closing of the RAF Station, but it was in fact a farewell party on the disbandment of No.27 Operational Training Unit. RAF Lichfield, as a base, did not close officially until 1958.

Having made his way into town by bicycle, Reg went to the Ryan's house to meet up with Roger and Barbara. Together they walked to the Turk's Head public house, where the party was being held. Around 10.00pm, things started to get a bit hectic, so the trio left and went back to the home of Barbara's parents, where they joined the latter for supper.

Saturday, 16th June 1945
Spent the afternoon organizing some clearance signatures, for we expect to be leaving Lichfield about the 20th.

Having got the most important tasks out of the way during the afternoon, Reg spent the evening with a group of colleagues in one of the local pubs. Again, with a drinking session on the horizon, he elected to cycle there! However, at the end of the evening, he thought he was going to have to walk back to the camp that night, not due to the effects of drink, but due to the effects of a puncture in the rear tire of his bike. Fortunately for him, Reg managed to scrounge a lift in a Jeep heading in the same direction.

Monday, 18th June 1945
After lunch [I] went down to the orderly room to find that my commission had come through.

Before he could do anything else, Reg had a lot of form filling to contend with; a task that took him approximately two hours. Then, on top of that, he had numerous signatures to collect on other documentation. Finally, he had to arrange a travel warrant for the next morning so that he could go to London to collect the necessary kit. The latter being Reg's terminology for new uniforms, hats and the other accessories befitting an officer.

Reg's way of celebrating receiving his commission was to go to the pub with 'Blue' for a few drinks and a few games of darts.

Tuesday, 19th June 1945
Woke up at 4.30am and couldn't go back to sleep again (most unusual) so got up at 7.00am, tidied the room up a bit and [then] went to breakfast.

It is possible that a subconscious excitement woke Reg at such an early hour; it was after all an important day.

Reg turned out of the camp gate and set off to walk the all too familiar route towards Trent Valley railway station but, as often happened, he had not gone far before he was offered a lift. Although the train journey necessitated two changes, at Nuneaton and Leighton Buzzard respectively, he still managed to arrive at London's Euston station around lunchtime. Reg made his way to Australia House in the Aldwych, where he took lunch in the Boomerang Club before visiting Kodak House. At the latter, there was more form filling, along with a few questions and answers, before he was sent around the corner to a depot in Kean Street, where Flying Officer Reg Heffron drew his kit. To his utter surprise, along with the new equipment, etc., Reg was also issued with a hefty trunk to put everything in. From Kean Street it was a race back to Australia House, where Reg had an appointment with a tailor with whom he placed an order for a new uniform.

With the formalities of the occasion out of the way, Reg was able to undertake a bit of shopping, which he did at a more leisurely pace. He even bumped into a couple of old friends, with whom he was able to spend the evening. First they visited the London Pavilion in Piccadilly Circus, where they saw a film entitled, 'The Way to the Stars.' As the title suggests, the storyline of the film revolved around an aviation theme and focused on a group of friends serving with a bomber squadron in the Royal Air Force, during 1940. Amongst the known actors of the day who starred in the film were John Mills and Michael Redgrave (both of whom, in later years, were knighted), Trevor Howard and Stanley Holloway. Later, after the film, they had supper at a Chinese restaurant in Wardour Street, before venturing off to Gloucester Road, South Kensington, in search of accommodation for the night.

Wednesday, 20th June 1945
Set off by the underground to Holborn and had lunch at Australia House.

After lunch, Reg ambled off to the Haymarket, just off Piccadilly Circus, in order to visit Burberry's where he ordered a new cap. This was followed by a visit to a tailor's shop in Villiers Street, alongside Charing Cross station, in Reg's words, "to have some pretty braid sewn on my sleeves 'while-u-wait.'"

Having ventured back to the Boomerang Club, Reg loaded his 'paraphernalia' into a taxi and headed to Euston station to catch the 4.05pm train back to Lichfield. On arrival at the latter, Reg left his trunk at the station and got a lift back to the camp. A secret smile must have crossed his face as he passed through the main gate at RAF Lichfield and received the salutes of the airmen on duty there.

Thursday, 21st June 1945
Began the day's panic to get clearances done for Roger and I, in fact, most of the remaining Aussies are posted to Brighton tomorrow.

With Roger's help, Reg got all the necessary signatures and handed his airman's kit back in to stores, then came the part that nobody liked, a visit to the Medical officer for the necessary jabs and inoculations.

During the late afternoon, Reg packed as much kit as possible into the hefty new trunk that he had been given whilst drawing his officers' kit at the stores in Kean Street, London, a couple of days earlier. At the time he wondered why he was being issued with such a sturdy piece of luggage, now he was finding out and was very glad he had got it.

Later in the day, after tea, came the time for relaxation, so Reg made his way into Lichfield to spend the evening at the Swan pub with Roger and Barbara. Later, after closing time, they made their way back to Barbara's parents' house, where they all had supper together.

It was quite late by the time Reg got back to bed; in fact it was the early hours of the morning.

Friday, 22nd June 1945
Woke at 8.00am and rushed out of bed to finish packing and put my gear in the transport at 8.30am.

An hour after Reg had put his kit on the crew transport bus it pulled out of RAF Lichfield with its human cargo of Australian airmen for the last time. Its destination was Trent Valley railway station, which Reg had come to know so well. Prior to boarding the bus, there had been many handshakes and goodbyes. There were also, according to Reg, some "not so complimentary farewells."

On their arrival at Euston, the group laden with their kit struggled down the platform to the station forecourt, where another crew bus was waiting to take them to Victoria station to catch a train to Brighton. Having reached Victoria, the 'Aussie' airmen had an hour to wait before the train departed. They therefore stacked their gear into a pile on the platform and then all headed off in search of lunch.

Reg and Roger adjourned to a nearby café in Vauxhall Bridge Road, where they tucked into hamburgers, fries and onions and some "horrible coffee." After this somewhat unappetising meal, they slowly ambled back to the station to find all the gear had already been put on board the train. They therefore found a couple of seats, made themselves comfy, and settled down to read until their departure time.

It was a hot, sunny, day, and as the train raced along the track through the pleasant Sussex countryside, the only clouds occasionally obscuring the scenery were those issuing from the funnel of the stream locomotive at the front of the train. Every now and then, when approaching a crossing point or similar hazard, a shrill blast or two was heard from the engine's steam whistle.

At Preston, a large junction, the train began to slow down as it negotiated the multitude of tracks criss-crossing the junction, and thus heralding the approach into Brighton station and the end of the line. The train pulled slowly into the terminus, edged up to the buffers, stopped and let out a great expanse of steam, together with a noise similar to that of a human letting out a great sigh.

Reg and Roger alighted from the train, walked to the Metropole Hotel where they were to be billeted and checked in. They visited their respective rooms, and tested the beds for comfort, before going off in search of a café for tea.

Although it had already been a long day, the duo were not finished yet and, after a meal in a café in West Street, they went to the Imperial Theater to see a show called, 'Bahama Passage.' After the show, they retraced their steps back towards the station for a visit to Tommy Farr's pub for what Reg recorded as "a brief visit"!

It was only after leaving the pub that they decided to wander back to the hotel where, having sorted out their kit from the pile of gear waiting to be claimed, they hauled the trunks etc. up to their rooms on the seventh floor.

Saturday, 23rd June 1945

At 9.30am everyone gathered in the cinema for a few instructions and also to fill in numerous forms. We are to go on ten days' leave this afternoon compulsorily.

With all the formalities completed by mid-afternoon, the Australian contingent started to wander, in dribs and drabs, towards the railway station. This included Roger and Reg who, having only just left Lichfield, decided to go all the way back there. Roger was obviously going home to see Barbara, so Reg decided to accompany his friend.

The duo retraced their route to Victoria station in London then continued their journey via Paddington and Birmingham to Lichfield, where they arrived at 10.30pm that night. Their arrival at the Ryans' house, unannounced, caused quite a stir however, much activity quickly produced supper, bottles of stout (a dark English beer) and a great amount of conversation.

For the first couple of days of his leave, Reg did very little. He went out a few times with Roger, but in the main let the newlyweds get on with their own lives. On Monday, 25th June, Reg decided to visit William and Martha in Dearham, whom he had not seen since the New Year.

Tuesday, 26th June 1945

Called in at the telegraph office on my way to the station. Caught the 11.00 o'clock train from New Street station via Crewe and Penrith to Carlisle, arriving there just in time to catch the 4.15pm to Dearham Bridge.

At least on this occasion, Reg's train journey north was at a more respectable hour than his previous visit to Dearham Bridge last January, when he had to catch the train at 1.30 in the morning.

Having reached Dearham Bridge, Reg left the station and walked through the village to Meadow Lodge, where he found William and Martha busy in the garden. A warm welcome was quickly followed by the British tradition of the offer of a cup of tea. After a lengthy chat, William drove Reg around the area so the latter could catch up with other friends whom he had not seen for quite a while. With so much going on, it was gone midnight before Reg fell into his bed. The following morning, after a leisurely breakfast, Reg said goodbye to Martha prior to William driving him back to the railway station, where he would catch a train, via Lancaster and Preston, to Manchester.

The reason for going to Manchester was to visit Joe and Dorothy Dawson at Irlam, as Reg had not seen them since his visit back in November 1944. On that occasion Reg had dropped Roger off in Sheffield and then driven across the moors to Irlam in gale force winds. On journeys like this one he was about to undertake, involving a number of changes on the transport system, Reg often yearned for his little car, but definitely NOT when he recalled the memories of that November night. Having sent Joe a telegram before boarding the train, advising the latter of his arrival, Reg could now sit back and relax.

On arrival at the Dawson household, Reg found Joe preparing tea. Dorothy came in a short while later when, in Reg's words, "chatter waxed fast and furious until all were silenced by mouthfuls of lettuce and radish." Later in the evening there was no chatter, they had elected to go to the theater, and sat there spellbound enjoying the show.

The next day, Reg moved on in what was fast becoming a round Britain tour, when he said farewell to Joe and Dorothy and headed south to Braunton. Finding he had a two-hour wait at Barnstaple for his connection to Braunton, Reg took the opportunity of replenishing his strength with cups of tea and buns; Reg was never one to go hungry.

Having travelled overnight, Reg finally arrived at Nellie's house around breakfast time, only to find that she was out shopping. The lack of any mention of sending a telegram to Nellie implies that she was possibly not expecting him. However, when she did arrive home later in the morning, Nellie was laden with baskets of strawberries and other good things, so maybe she was expecting Reg after all!

Saturday, 30th June 1945
Slept in until 11.00am then had a hot bath, breakfast and lunch all in quick succession. In the afternoon, Nellie and I went by bus to Croyde Bay then walked to Baggy Point.

Baggy Point is a promontory of land, owned by the National Trust, affording glorious scenic views along the landscape of sandy beaches and towering cliffs. The 'white horses' of the Atlantic surf, breaking over those same beaches adds to the magnificent natural beauty of the area. It was here, for several hours, that Reg and Nellie scrambled up and down the cliffs, clambered over boulders and ventured into a number of caves. They both thought it time to quit when, having entered one cave, as Reg later wrote in his diary, "We were startled to see a luminous eye peering at us from the darkness in the cavern."

As Reg and Nellie started to walk back across the sands, the weather took a turn for the worst when very high winds blew in off the Atlantic Ocean, bringing with them continuous, torrential rain.

By the following morning the rain had stopped, but stiff breezes and strong winds were still evident; just the weather for sand yachting. Following breakfast and lunch, which were taken almost simultaneously, Reg and Nellie took the sand yacht down to the beach, where good use was made of the prevailing winds. Several hours were spent sailing back and forth along the sands, with the final run of the day being made along the high water mark

The waves gently break on the flat sands of Croyde Beach with Baggy Point forming the backdrop. Apart from the modern day lifeguards' vehicle on the beach, this view remains unchanged nearly seventy years after Reg first gazed upon it. *Author's Collection*

collecting flotsam; and gathering up some really hefty planks and boxes in the process. Reg did not record what, if anything was in the boxes.

The price of the afternoon's entertainment was paid in energy, when they had to haul the sand yacht, and their booty, back up the hill to the house.

Monday, 2nd July 1945
Up at 7.00am with a cup of tea. Then, [after breakfast,] Nellie drove me to the station to catch the train to Exeter.

Reg was heading back to Lichfield to meet up with Roger, although the route via Exeter, Bristol, West Bromwich and Lichfield actually took him the best part of the day. The good thing was though, having arrived at his destination, he could spend the evening relaxing, chatting and playing cards with Roger, Barbara and the Ryans.

Tuesday, 3rd July 1945
Slept in until 9.30am then had a quick wash and flew down to breakfast before the taxi arrived to take Roger and me to the station.

With their ten-day period of leave over, Reg and Roger had to make their way back to Brighton, which they did by way of London. Having arrived at Euston station at 1.00pm, they took a taxi to the Aldwych, where they had lunch in the Boomerang Club. Feeling replenished, the duo caught another taxi that took them to Victoria station, where they were able to catch the 4.28pm train to Brighton.

On arrival in the south coast resort, Reg and Roger walked along the sea front to the Metropole hotel, where they checked in, dumped their kit in the allotted rooms and then went out on the town. A visit to the Regent Theater, to see American comedian Jack Benny in a show called, 'The Fifth Chair,' was followed by supper taken in a nearby basement café. The evening concluded with a stroll back to the hotel and then bed.

Wednesday, 4th July 1945
[Went] to the unit post office before wandering up into the town to visit the barber. During the afternoon we collected some tropical kit from the stores and marked our trunks for the sea voyage.

With the issue of tropical kit, and the labeling of trunks and personal kit etc., in preparation for the forthcoming sea voyage, it looked as though the Australian airmen really were going home. However, they were all startled when, out of the blue and with no hint of what was to come, the whole contingent was granted a further fifteen days leave.

Somewhat amazed by the turn of events, Reg and Roger continued to sort and pack their kit, presumably on the off chance that the aforementioned leave period could be canceled just as quickly as it had been instigated. Their task took them into mid-evening, at which point they decided it was time to retire to a nearby café for supper. Whilst in the café and after having eaten his meal, Reg telephoned Nellie in Devon to explain the situation and let her know he was intending to visit her again.

Thursday, 5th July 1945
Spent the morning getting organized for leave, and was ready to go after lunch. Caught the train from Brighton to Victoria and then took a taxi to Paddington.

On his arrival at Paddington station, Reg discovered he had a ninety-minute wait before his train departed for the West Country. He used the time to send Nellie a telegram, informing her of his chosen route, and then went to the station café for some refreshment.

At the allotted time, the train guard looked down the length of the platform to ensure all the carriage doors were shut, gave a shrill blast on his whistle and waved the green flag above his head. On receipt of both signals, the engine driver gave a responsive blast on the train whistle, opened the valves, released the brakes and, like a steaming, snorting monster, amidst clouds of smoke, the locomotive edged forward trailing the carriages behind it.

Reg sat in one of the carriages gazing out of the window, watching the buildings that made up that part of West London race past, as the train gathered speed. From west London the train travelled via Reading, Swindon, Bath, Bristol, Weston-super-Mare and Taunton. It was at the latter station that Reg heard an announcement being broadcast over the public address system and was startled when he realized that it was his name being called on the loudspeakers. He left the train and raced to the station office where he was informed that he must change trains in order to reach Barnstaple that same evening. The porters held up both the Plymouth Express and the Barnstaple train while he moved his luggage from one train to the other!

Sitting on the Barnstaple train, Reg mused over the wonderful service provided by the British railway system, something he had not encountered before. How on earth did they know he was on the Plymouth Express, and, how did they know where he was going?

When his train finally pulled into Barnstaple station at 11.10pm, Reg got the answer to both his questions. Nellie was there to meet him and admitted responsibility for having him change trains at Taunton. It transpired that, if Nellie had not contacted the appropriate railway authority, Reg would have been stranded in Exeter!

Friday, 6th July 1945
Went to Barnstaple on the bus with Nellie to do some shopping. [We] spent the whole morning [wandering] about the market and shopping center. During the afternoon I pottered about in the garden fixing this and that, and putting the sand yacht in order.

That evening, Reg found another job to do, which took him some time to sort out. In his diary he wrote, "After supper, I spent a couple of hours fixing the dining room table's rickets." It was not recorded whether the table had wobbly legs, bow legs or was just shaky on its legs!

It was a wonder that Reg was not shaky on his own legs the next morning, as the day dawned bright with a cloudless sky, and got hotter and hotter as the sun climbed higher into the sky. It was weather that Reg was not used to, even though he had experienced British summers before. He even commented on it in his diary.

Although it was hot, there was still work to be done and Reg spent the day repairing the steps at the bottom of Nellie's garden. In the evening, with temperatures still relatively high, he found plenty of other jobs in and around the garden that needed some attention. He finally fell into his bed just before 1.30 the following morning.

Having slept in late, Reg awoke from his slumbers at lunchtime the next day. It was another warm day, one which Reg spent loafing around in the garden and bewailing the lack of wind which would have enabled him to use the sand yacht.

Monday, 9th July 1945
Up at 8.00am and after breakfast began some jobs in the garden. This kept me occupied until 11.00am, when I went with Nellie to Braunton to do some shopping.

During the afternoon, having had lunch on the newly restored dining room table, Reg put in another session in the garden. By now, Reg must have become an accomplished landscaper/gardener, whilst Nellie must have had the neatest, most well laid out garden in Braunton!

His labors for the day being ended, Reg was partaking of supper with Nellie when there was an unexpected knocking on the front door. Upon opening the door, Nellie found Roger and Barbara standing there. The visitors were quickly ushered in, supplied with refreshments and then taken out for a stroll across the sands and up over the rocks and cliffs of the local coastline. It being a beautiful evening, the four friends did not return to the house until almost midnight. In fact, on return to the house, and with it being such a lovely night, Reg decided to make up his bed on the veranda and sleep under the stars.

Although the following morning dawned bright and sunny, there was a breeze in the air, so Reg, ably assisted by Roger, took the opportunity of doing a few more jobs in the garden. During the early afternoon, Reg decided to relieve some more items of furniture of their ills, by spending time mending various household furnishings.

With the breeze building up to a suitable strength, and his chores for the day completed, Reg trundled down to the beach with the sand yacht in tow. He enjoyed a couple of hours sailing back and forth across the wide expanse of sand, with the wind increasing in strength all the time.

Wednesday, 11th July 1945
Up at 7.15am and after breakfast I spent a couple of hours mending 3 prawning nets in readiness for the afternoon.

All thoughts of getting home to Australia seemed to have disappeared as Reg and Roger enjoyed what amounted to an additional, expenses paid holiday, in the United Kingdom. The weather remained good, with brilliant sunshine, continuous blue skies and beautiful sandy beaches. Surely, it was almost like Australia itself.

Reg, Roger and Barbara spent the morning swimming in the cool waters of the Atlantic Ocean, then lazed about on the beach for an hour, sunning themselves, chatting and generally relaxing.

After lunch, which had been taken back at the house, the three of them ventured down to the rock pools at Downend with the nets that Reg had repaired earlier that morning. They spent the whole afternoon catching prawns and, apparently, made quite a good haul, as was borne out by the comment in Reg's diary, "[had] a terrific tea."

Friday, 13th July 1945
After lunch, Roger and I mowed the lawn then decided to take advantage of a good wind with the sand yacht.

Rock pools and the cool waters of the Atlantic Ocean gave Reg and newlyweds Roger and Barbara hours of pleasure on the warm July days of 1945. *Author's Collection*

A view from the hill overlooking Saunton Beach shows the wide expanse of the golden sands where Reg Heffron loved to spend time *"sailing"* on his land yacht. *Author's Collection*

Many people would not dare to venture out of the house on Friday, 13th, but the two intrepid Australian aviators were made of sterner stuff and decided to go and have fun with the sand yacht.

Having got it down onto Saunton beach, Reg and Roger raced the machine back and forth across the sands, sometimes veering round for a change of direction on two wheels. With the sail billowing in the wind, they carried out these manoeuvres for an hour or more until suddenly, and without warning, the back wheels emitted a dreadful groan and fell off. This incident necessitated half carrying and half pushing and pulling the contraption up a very steep hill back to the house. For both Reg and Roger, it proved to be very hot work.

Having parked the wreck in the garden, the lure of a supper of salmon and salad, followed by fresh strawberries and cream, all washed down with real Devon cider, prevented the 'boys' from worrying any further about the sand yacht.

The next morning, Reg was up early and set about trying to repair the damage to the sand yacht. However, this proved easier said than done and, after a couple of hours of thankless toil, he finally gave up. A more drastic approach to the problem was made during the afternoon, when Reg and Roger took the axle off, whilst Nellie borrowed a car from an understanding neighbor. Accompanied by Reg, Nellie then drove to a garage in Braunton, where the offending axle was fixed with the aid of a large spanner and a very hefty hammer! After a race back to Saunton, Reg and Roger had the sand yacht re-assembled and ready for a test run by teatime.

Even though the war in the Far East was still ongoing, there was absolutely no mention of it made in Reg's diary. Ordinary, everyday occurrences filled the diary's pages. For Reg, who was thoroughly enjoying his stay in Devon, the last few days of his leave went all too quickly and he and Roger soon had to retrace the arduous train journey back to Brighton, via London.

It did not take Reg long to find out that nothing had changed during his enforced period of leave from Brighton. There was still no news on a repatriation date, and even worse, there was little to do around the place. It soon became obvious that a further period of leave was forthcoming.

Tuesday, 24th July 1945
Spent most of the morning getting leave passes, then set off to walk to [Brighton] station to catch the train to Victoria [station], London.

On his arrival in London, Reg took a taxi to the Boomerang Club, where he had lunch, before making his way to Waterloo station for the next part of his journey. Where was he headed, but back to Braunton, Devon.

For reasons not recorded, although it could have been for a change of scenery if nothing else, Reg decided to take a new route, which took him from Waterloo, via Andover Junction, Salisbury, Sidmouth Junction to Exeter, where he changed for Barnstaple and Braunton. Needless to say, by the time he reached his destination, it was quite late in the evening.

The following day was spent, as on previous occasions, doing various odd jobs in and around the garden, included making a new gate for the chicken run. However, the next day would hold something of interest, even though it came as a shock to Reg.

Thursday, 26th July 1945
Up at 7.00am with the intention of going to Plymouth with Nellie for the day. It rained all night and still at it when we set off.

The journey to Plymouth was a long one, taking three and a half hours to complete. Given that they arrived at Drake's Circus, in the city center, after midday, Reg and Nellie thought they would have lunch before starting their walking tour.

Setting out in the rain, Reg was to gaze upon some of the worst blitz damage he had ever seen. Several acres of the business and financial areas were completely destroyed, whilst scores of other buildings were completely burned out. Plymouth, the largest city in the West Country, is situated between the mouths of the Tamar and the Plym rivers and being a natural harbor, has been home to the British Royal Navy for many centuries. This latter fact in itself made Plymouth an obvious target for the Luftwaffe on more than one occasion.

Nellie continued the tour, taking Reg to the Barbican from where the Pilgrim Fathers set sail for America, in the Mayflower, in 1620. From there they walked round the Royal Citadel overlooking the Plymouth Sound, to the spot on the Hoe where Sir Francis Drake was (reputedly) playing bowls when the Spanish Armada was sighted. As Nellie related the story, Reg turned to peer through the rain and out over the Hoe, and was amazed to see a modern day armada in the form of a squadron of Short Sunderland flying boats moored in the harbor.

Taking their leave of the battered city, Nellie and Reg went off in search of some refreshment before undertaking the journey back to Braunton.

Friday, 27th July 1945
Went shopping with Nellie in Barnstaple. [We] spent most of the morning in the market and center [and] spent the afternoon preparing for the trip to Manchester tonight.

Two Marriages, Two Commissions and Masses of Leave

Present in the family wedding photograph on 28th July 1945 were (standing left to right) Anthony Boydell, Groom's Brother; Donald Mackinnon, Best Man; Kathleen Sephton, Bridesmaid; Reg Heffron and William Hall. Seated (left to right) Groom's Grandmother; Groom's Father; Groom's Mother; Jock Boydell, Groom; Dorothy Boydell (nee Dawson), Bride; Joe Dawson, Bride's Father; Martha Hall, Joe's Sister. *Courtesy of Reg Heffron*

Having received an invitation to attend the wedding of 'Jock' Boydell and Dorothy Dawson, Joe's daughter, Reg had decided to travel overnight to Manchester in order to attend the celebrations at Irlam. To Reg's consternation, the train was absolutely packed and, in his words, "everyone played sardines in the corridors and generally felt and looked very uncomfortable all night."

It was just after 8.00am the following morning when the train reached its destination. The cramped passengers almost fell out of the carriages on to the platform, when the passenger able to do so, opened a carriage door.

By the time Reg reached Irlam, Joe and Dorothy were just beginning to rise from their slumbers, as were William and Martha, who were staying at the house in order to attend the wedding. Having joined everyone for breakfast, Reg excused himself and went off to catch up on some of the previous night's lost sleep.

At 3.00pm that afternoon, everyone made their way to St. Bartholomew's Church, in Liverpool Road, for the wedding ceremony. The bride and groom, Dorothy and Jock, both arrived on time and there were no hitches. After the register had been signed, the guests all attended the wedding dinner back at the house and then, in the evening, were entertained at the Opera House in Manchester.

Sunday, 29th July 1945
Return to Braunton today.

Having said goodbye to those still at the house, Reg was driven to Manchester station by Joe, where the former caught a train heading for Exeter. Although the train was not as crowded as on the outward journey, Reg still had a scramble to get a seat.

The journey was long and tiring with the last part, between Exeter and Braunton, being the slowest. Finally, after hailing a taxi, Reg arrived at Nellie's house at around midnight.

Over the last seven weeks, apart from anything else Reg may have done or been involved with, he had celebrated two marriages, two commissions and masses of leave.

14

Japan Surrenders

At 8.15am on the morning of 6th August 1945, the United States of America dropped the world's first atomic bomb on Hiroshima in Honshu, Japan. The aircraft carrying the bomb, a Boeing B-29 Superfortress bomber from the 509th Composite Group, United States 20th Army Air Force, piloted by Colonel Paul W. Tibbets, had taken off from Tinian, in the Mariana Islands, at 2.45am that morning.

The weather conditions over the target having been found favorable, the bomb was released from the aircraft at an altitude of 31,000.' It was primed to explode approximately 2,000' above the city, thus extending the area covered by the resulting blast. A total of 4.7 square miles of the city was destroyed, obliterating over 80% of the buildings.

The human cost was estimated to be 71,379 killed or missing and over 68,000 wounded and injured. However, many of the latter would succumb to their injuries in later years.

Three days later, on 9th August, a second atomic bomb was dropped over the city of Nagasaki. Again, a Boeing B-29 Superfortress bomber, from the same unit was used in the attack. On this second occasion, the pilot was Major Charles W. Sweeny, Commander of the 393rd Bombardment Squadron; the 509th's only combat unit.

Due to the fact that the hills surrounding Nagasaki shielded it from the full effects of the bomb blast, only 1.4 square miles of the city was destroyed, whilst the casualty figures were recorded as between 26,000 and 40,000 killed and between 23,500 and 60,000 wounded or injured.

The following day, the Japanese Government sent a message through diplomatic channels, saying it would accept the peace terms issued at Potsdam on 26th July, on condition that the Emperor's prerogatives as a sovereign ruler were not prejudiced.

On the morning of 14th August, at a meeting at the Imperial Palace, the Japanese Government agreed to accept the peace terms presented by the Allied Forces. That same morning, whilst the Japanese Government was deciding its fate, Reg was half a world away in Brighton, safely asleep in his bed.

Tuesday, 14th August 1945
Slept in until 10.00am, then had a leisurely shave and then wandered down to make enquiries, and was requested to take another 14 days' leave.

The news of Japan's surrender had not yet filtered through; certainly not to the general public anyway. Reg, in blissful ignorance, went to make further enquires about his repatriation date, only to be asked to take a further two weeks' leave.

Reg spent the early afternoon preparing for yet another period of leave. He visited the unit post office to collect his mail, and then went off with 'Blue' Baxter, a RAAF pay clerk, for an afternoon's entertainment.

Whilst Reg was in the theater, both the American President and the British Prime Minister were making preparations for the announcement of the Japanese surrender. Reg went to bed at 11.00pm that night had he stayed up one hour longer he would have heard Prime Minister Clement Attlee reading that same announcement.

15th August 1945

Heard the news this morning of Japan's surrender and everyone was acting a bit on the screwy side.

When Reg left the hotel that morning and was on his way to the railway station, he could not believe his eyes. The streets were littered with paper, and in front of the Metropole Hotel there had been a huge bonfire, which had been fuelled mainly by deckchairs and esplanade seating, the latter being ripped from their fixings.

At Brighton station, Reg caught a train to London, where he arrived during the late afternoon, to find the city had gone crazy. The place was full of revelers. Taxis were not to be had and buses were crammed to capacity and could hardly make any headway through the sea of humanity. The streets were packed tight with people wearing paper hats, waving flags and swinging rattles. Hundreds were linking arms and singing and dancing in tightly confined spaces. The few private cars that had ventured out on to the streets could hardly be seen under the number of bodies swarming over the vehicles. Reg saw several cars with twenty or more people hanging on for a free ride.

He gathered up his kit and set out to walk from Victoria, along Buckingham Palace Road and up the Mall to the Boomerang Club in the Strand. A walk that should have taken about thirty minutes, on this occasion took him one-and-a-half-hours. Every building he passed was bedecked with bunting and flags.

Every time he made headway through the crowd, he was swept back the way he had just come, by the force of the current generated by the tide of bodies. Outside Buckingham Palace it proved practically impossible to move, and it took Reg twenty minutes to cover a distance of only 100 yards.

The noise of jubilation filled the air, and in Trafalgar Square the noise was amplified by the crackle of fireworks mingling with the pealing of the bells from St. Martin-in-the-Fields Church. In the Strand, the occasional bus was able to crawl along, sounding its horn to clear a path through the crowd. Reg had to rely on gaps appearing in the mass of people to proceed at anything like a normal walking pace, which only happened as he neared his destination.

Reg felt relieved when he reached the Boomerang Club, not least of all for the reason he could dump his baggage, which he had been clinging to for the last ninety minutes. His next priority was to get some tea which, after his endeavours to reach the club, revived him and slowly brought him back to normality.

Feeling somewhat refreshed, Reg set off to find Nellie, who was in London and whom he had previously arranged to meet at 6.00pm. They were to travel back to Devon together, but on finding that their train did not leave until the early hours of the following morning, they decided to go and see some friends who lived in Richmond.

After a pleasant evening they caught a train from Richmond station back to Waterloo. The views through the carriage windows revealed that the majority of people were still celebrating, as there was scarcely a street without a great bonfire burning in the middle of the road. The scenario in each street was practically the same, great bonfires, surrounded by children and adults alike, rockets whizzing up into the night sky and other fireworks much in evidence, all surrounded by great palls of thick smoke which drifted gently on the night air.

The British Forces sweetheart, singer Vera Lynn, had recorded a song in 1942 entitled, 'When the lights go on again all over the world.' Well, Reg and Nellie saw some of those lights that night. Still having time to waste before catching their train, they walked across Westminster Bridge and saw Big Ben and the Palace of Westminster floodlit, both Whitehall and Parliament Street were a blaze of light and Admiral Lord Nelson on top of his column in Trafalgar Square was also the subject of floodlights. Other London landmarks that received the same attention included the dome and towers of St. Paul's Cathedral, the London County Council building County Hall by the River Thames, and Shell Mex House. Reg recorded that the area was just as busy at midnight as it had been at midday, but noticed there were now signs of weariness and tired feet amongst many in the crowd.

Returning to Waterloo, Reg and Nellie boarded their train, found a couple of seats and settled down for the journey. The motion of the carriage, once the train had pulled out of Waterloo, soon sent the weary pair in to a snooze and then sleep.

The train pulled into Braunton station at 8.00am that morning, leaving Reg and Nellie to get a taxi to the house at Saunton. On arrival at the village, they found evidence of the 'morning after the night before' feeling, from those who had joined in their own 'Victory in Japan' celebrations in the local pub.

Over the next few days, with London and the victory celebrations far from his mind, Reg got on with all manner of odd jobs, some were in the house, but most were out in the garden.

Although Reg received a telegram from the RAF Personnel Depot at Brighton on 21st August, which read, "Prepare to embark," there seemed to be little or no activity on that front from either Reg or the RAF. In fact, Reg spent the next eight days building a substantial hut in Nellie's garden!

On the morning of 29th August, whilst preparing to leave Nellie's house, Reg received another telegram, again, from the RAF Personnel Depot, at Brighton. This one advised him that he had been given a two-day extension to his leave period! Reg wasted no time in getting back into his working clothes and out into the garden.

Reg finally left the house at Saunton after lunch on Friday, 31st August. Although Reg did not fully appreciate it at the time, this would be the last time he walked out through the front door of Nellie's house. It would also be the last occasion on which he used Braunton Railway Station. The rural station, with its signal box and road-crossing gates at the end of the platforms, had become a familiar landmark to him.

Reg endured a miserable overnight journey back to London, with the train being packed to capacity. He finally reached Brighton around 9.30am the following morning. The journey between Waterloo Station and Victoria Station gave him another chance to see London by night with all its lights, which presented a vastly different spectacle from that to which Reg had grown accustomed. He recorded in his diary, "It is an utterly different and so happy and friendly London."

Braunton Station, Devon. Note the signal box and railroad crossing at the far end of the platforms. In post-war years, the railroad was closed down and the station, signal box and level crossing were all demolished to make way for a car park. *Author's Collection*

The information board to the front left of the picture advises the reader that the signal box on Braunton station stood to the top left of the grassed area in this photograph. The railroad-crossing gates were situated where the two pedestrians wait to cross the road at the center right of the image. *Author's Collection*

Saturday, 1st September 1945
Went along to the office to find I was wanted for a ceremonial parade on Wednesday, but nothing [mentioned] about going home.

Although Reg had not recorded any thoughts of frustration in his diary over the lack of being given a repatriation date one cannot help but feel that there were underlying tones of vexation.

Having checked that Roger was back in the hotel, Reg went off in search of his friend. After running up and down stairs, and walking backwards and forwards along numerous corridors, the two finally bumped into each other.

After breakfasting together, and catching up on the news, the pair were required to attend a short parade, possibly a form of rehearsal for the ceremonial parade mentioned by Reg and programmed for the forthcoming Wednesday. The rest of the day was spent at the local stadium watching the greyhound racing, where Roger's luck fluctuated, whilst Reg stood to one side and watched.

Sunday, 2nd September 1945
[Caught] a bus at Pool Valley and spent the afternoon on the Sussex Downs by the Arun river. Also saw Arundel Castle perched on the hillside.

Although not recorded in Reg's diary, probably because at that time he would not have known, Sunday, 2nd September 1945 was a very important day in world history. At 1.30am Greenwich Mean Time, or 10.30am Tokyo time, the 1939-45 war officially ended, when the unconditional surrender of Japan was signed. The ceremony took place on board the American battleship, 'USS Missouri,' which was anchored in Tokyo Bay.

At 9.00am (Tokyo time) Japan's Foreign Minister Mamoru Shigemitsu, representing the Emperor, accompanied by General Yoshijiro Umezu, who was representing the Japanese General Headquarters, together with a retinue of aides, boarded the battleship. Those representing the Allies, General of the Army Douglas MacArthur, Supreme Commander for the Allied Powers, supported by Lieutenant-General Jonathan Wainwright, United States Army, and Lieutenant-General Arthur E. Percival, were already on board 'USS Missouri.' Lieutenant-General Percival was a very experienced and respected officer in the British Army, who had served during the First World War. For his courage and fortitude, he was awarded the CB, OBE, DSO and Bar, MC, CdG (France) and two Mentions-in-Despatches. Both Wainwright and Percival, who had experienced the humiliation of having to surrender to Japanese forces earlier in the war, now stood behind General MacArthur at this historical time.

At the appointed hour, both General MacArthur and Foreign Minister Umezu affixed their respective signatures to the Japanese Instrument of Surrender. Following a rendition of the tune 'The Star Spangled Banner,' World War II was officially over.

In the aftermath of the war, when war crime trials were held, no evidence of war crimes was found against General Yoshijiro Umezu, but he was sentenced to life imprisonment for conspiring to wage aggressive war against both China and the Western Powers.

In contrast to the power and emotion of the events taking place that day in Japan, Reg and Roger were walking across the Sussex Downs, admiring the beautiful stretches of countryside around them. Much of the land across which they were walking formed part of the 11,000-acre estate owned by the Duke of Norfolk, Earl Marshal of England.

The castle, which was originally built just after the Norman Conquest, stands high above the town, which Reg and Roger ventured into in search of refreshment before heading back to Brighton.

Wednesday, 5th September 1945
Nothing much to do until 11.30am when we had a parade in Sunday best and marched to Hove, behind an RAF Band.

The parade was in tribute to Admiral of the Fleet, Sir Andrew Browne Cunningham, 1st Viscount Cunningham of Hyndhope, KT, GCM, OM, DSO, who had been granted the Freedom of Hove. Admiral Cunningham, known as 'ABC' to his friends because of his initials, was a distinguished member of the Royal Navy, who served in both the First and Second World Wars.

Enthusiastic crowds lined the route, clapping and cheering as the Royal Air Force band, playing suitable marches, led the parade along the seafront. As they passed the saluting base, with flags flying, Sir Andrew acknowledged the 'Colours' in accordance with military tradition.

The parade over, the rest of the day reverted back to normal, with Reg and Roger going off in search of refreshment.

Thursday, 6th September 1945
Went down to the flight office to see what was happening. Roger's name was on the draft [list] but mine wasn't.

On being advised that his name was on the list for repatriation, Roger decided to rush off on a last visit to Lichfield and left that afternoon. Reg on the other hand, frustration now coming to the fore, returned to the flight office to make further enquiries, but ended up making a nuisance of himself and generally causing a disturbance. The result of this outburst was to have his name appended to the draft. Having succeeded in his task, Reg returned to his room, where he spent the afternoon packing away the gear he knew he could manage without or didn't need. The evening, after tea, was spent in the Castle Inn, with 'Blue' Baxter, the RAAF pay clerk.

The next couple of days were spent, usually accompanied by 'Blue,' on shopping expeditions for civilian clothing, but two days and many miles later, tramping around every shop in Brighton resulted only in Reg purchasing two pairs of shoes, a sports jacket and a shirt. He gave up in disgust and opted to go with 'Blue' to the cinema.

During this same period of time, whilst Reg was on his way to breakfast, he ran into Max Bourne, his former skipper on No.622 Squadron. The pair had not seen each other since they left the squadron at the beginning of the year and got so engrossed in conversation that neither of them noticed the door to the dining area being locked at the end of the breakfast session.

Sunday, 9th September 1945
After lunch went with '*Blue*' and '*Curly*' [Max Bourne], by bus from Pool Valley to Beachy Head. Had half-hour's walk from the road to the cliffs.

By the time the trio got to the top of Beachy Head, they found the visibility not very good, but on the up side, they had passed through some lovely countryside on the way. Apart from the scenery, there was also an abundance of ripening blackberries to sustain Reg and the others as they walked. After an hour relaxing on the cliff top, they made their way down to Eastbourne, where they took tea before catching a bus back to Brighton and its numerous pubs.

Whilst Reg had been munching his way through the English countryside with Max and 'Blue' Baxter, Roger and Barbara had been traveling down from Lichfield. Due to the fact the three ramblers had succumbed to the call of a public house, where they spent the evening drinking, Reg was unaware that Roger and his wife were in Brighton. He did however meet up with them the following morning, when they all had breakfast together. Later in the day, following a Pay Parade in the station cinema, Reg and Roger met up again with Barbara and they all spent the evening at the movies.

For Reg, the next three days were spent finalizing various details, preparing kit, writing letters, shopping and wining and dining in the many pubs and cafés where Reg and Roger had become known. The excuse given for visiting these latter establishments being so they could say their farewells to proprietors and friends.

Finally, after all the delays, Reg and Roger were going home.

15

The Voyage Home

Friday, 14th September 1945
Met *'Blue'* [Baxter] at 10.00am, and later we met Roger and Barbara and had a farewell lunch with them at the Imperial Café. *'Blue'* is going on leave to Lichfield and taking Barbara back.

Reg and Roger traveled from Brighton back to London with both 'Blue' and Barbara, saying their farewells to the latter at Euston station. With mixed emotions, Reg and Roger boarded a bus that took them down Kingsway to Australia House, which enable the homebound 'Aussies' to make a last visit to the Boomerang Club. Having taken tea at the club, they made their way along Fleet Street for a last visit to the Codger's Club. By the time they left the Codger's Club, it was drizzling with rain, which added to the emotion of the day.

Reg's spirits didn't improve any when having boarded the train at Victoria for the return trip to Brighton, he found there were no seats available and that he and Roger would have to stand. This inconvenience lasted all the way to Brighton, thus ending Reg's last leave visit to London.

Expecting to leave on the first leg of the return trip to Australia on Sunday, Reg spent Saturday, 15th September, getting ready for his imminent departure; fixing up details of pay, packing and attending to other such details. He found time to phone Nellie Dawson before going out in the evening with Roger and Max Bourne, to a couple of local 'watering holes' for final farewell drinks.

Sunday, 16th September 1945
Roger and I carted our baggage down ready to be taken away. Had lunch at 12.30, then finished packing the [personal] cases, and by 3.00pm were ready to leave.

Unfortunately, the boys still had twelve hours to waste as they were not scheduled to depart until 3.00am the following morning.

The afternoon was spent in Reg's room until, after tea, Reg, Roger and Max wandered into town where they visited the same 'watering holes' for further final farewell drinks. The middle part of the evening was spent taking supper at a café on the seafront, before adjourning to the Grand Hotel in preparation for departure. Given that there was still a considerable amount of time to go before setting off, the three of them settled down to wait, drinking copious amounts of tea to wash down the vast number of biscuits they ate.

Monday, 17th September 1945
3.00am arrived at last and so did the trucks for our cases and the buses for us. We loaded the gear and [ourselves] into the respective conveyances and, after a roll-call, set off for Brighton station. The first leg of the journey home had begun.

The convoy of trucks and buses having reached the railway station, the chaos and bustle of trying to locate one's own kit amongst the hundreds of bags and cases being disgorged from the back of the trucks began. Having reclaimed their respective items of kit, Reg and Roger filed down the platform and piled into one of the carriages of the allotted train.

At 5.00am a whistle blew, the engine belched a great head of stream from its funnel, the driver on the footplate released the brake lever and the locomotive shunted forward. Slowly the train gathered speed, heading north via Haywoods Heath, Willesden Junction (north-west of London), Rugby and Crewe to Liverpool. On arrival at the latter, a convoy of RAF trucks was lined up ready to take the airmen to the dock, where the 'S.S. Stratheden' was embarking numerous 'Aussies.'

The 'S.S. Stratheden,' which was commanded by Captain S. W. S. Dawson, was one of five ships in the 'Strath' class. It was built by Vickers-Armstrong at Barrow-in-Furness and was launched on 10th June 1937. The four sister ships were named, 'S.S. Strathaird,' 'S.S. Strathnaver,' 'S.S. Strathmore' and 'S.S. Strathallen.'

The 'Stratheden,' which measured just over 664' in length and 82' across the beam, was a single funnel, two masted vessel weighing 23,732 gross tons. Built for cruising with the P&O Line, the ship had accommodation for 530 First Class passengers and 450 tourist class passengers although, on the trip Reg was about to embark, it was later recorded that this figure, as with most troopships, was greatly exceeded.

Having been requisitioned by the Ministry of Shipping on 19th March 1940 for service as a troop transport, 'S.S. Stratheden' was used to ferry servicemen to various locations around the world. The ship was to be finally released from service in July 1946 and returned to the role of a cruise liner with P&O Lines on 29th May 1947. Twenty-two years later, during 1969, 'S.S. Stratheden,' sailed to Spezia in Italy, where she was broken up and scrapped.

On this particular voyage, apart from the crew, the ship would be carrying 3,667 servicemen comprising 2,184 Navy personnel, 1,254 officers and airmen of the Royal Australian Air Force, 153 members of the New Zealand Army and two A.I.F. men.

Reg and Roger stood on the quayside, along with the rest of their contingent, answering to a final roll call, before receiving boarding instructions and boarding the ship. At thirty-minutes-past-midday, Reg ascended the gangway up to the ship, bearing the weight of a kitbag on his shoulder and a case in his hand. Having located their respective cabins and got settled in, Reg and Roger set about getting some lunch before having to attend lifeboat drill exercises.

At 6.15pm, the fore and aft hawsers were cast off and the ship, assisted by tugboats, began to manoeuvre away from its mooring basin and out into the River Mersey. Under the guidance of a pilot on the bridge, the ship slowly negotiated its way along the river to the estuary, where the pilot handed command of the ship back to the captain, and disembarked onto a waiting harbor vessel.

'S.S. Stratheden,' the cruise liner on which Reg returned to his native Australia.
Author's Collection – Original Source Unknown

As the ship sailed out into the estuary, Reg recorded seeing two half submerged wrecks, but did not say if they were casualties of war. On a lighter note, he also recorded seeing the Blackpool Tower away in the distance to the north. An hour or so later, Reg took a last look at the lights of England twinkling up and down the coast between Liverpool and Blackpool; a sight which he had not been seen during the previous five years.

Tuesday, 18th September 1945
Politely awakened by the cabin orderly at 7.00am it being essential to get up in order to get hot water for shaving etc., as it is turned off at 7.30am until the following morning.

Breakfast was a very dignified affair, with Reg and Roger attending the second sitting. The menu consisted of porridge and snags, supplemented by quantities of bread and jam. Reg did not record whether it was due to the sea air but did state that, "everyone seemed to have horses' appetites."

Roger spent the first morning at sea in the ship's lounge, where he read, talked and played cards until lunchtime. The afternoon was a repeat performance of the morning's activities until teatime and then dinner. Unfortunately for some, Reg and Roger not included, the medium swell and slight pitching and rolling of the ship started to have an effect on the stomachs of those who had gorged themselves earlier in the day.

Wednesday, 19th September 1945
Up at 7.30am and just caught the last of the hot water. Went to breakfast then spent the morning about the deck, reading and walking.

At midday, having left the Bay of Biscay, the mountains of Spain came into view, and a while later the ship sailed past Cape Finisterre, the headland on the west coast of Spain. By this time, the 'S.S. Stratheden' was in Atlantic waters and heading south. The fact that marine crafts of all shapes and sizes were in these same waters induced Reg to record,

"After lunch there were sixteen ships in sight at once between us and the coast, but these disappeared one by one as we continued on with the Portuguese coast just visible on the port beam."

That night Reg and Roger spent some time on deck admiring a really perfect evening. An almost full moon was shining on the sea from a cloudless sky, with a cool breeze evident, which put a flawless end to a very calm and sunny day. One wonders whether Roger secretly wished that it was Barbara on that deck with him instead of Reg!

Thursday, 20th September 1945
Up at 7.30am and off to a lousy breakfast at 8.15am, after which I put in the morning up on the boat deck reading and talking. Passed quite close to Cape St.Vincent then lost sight of land during the afternoon until the Moroccan coast came into view ahead of us.

During the early evening, the ship steered onto an easterly heading, into the Gulf of Cadiz, and sailed almost parallel with the Spanish south coast in order to pass through the Straits of Gibraltar, passing Cape Trafalgar on the way. Fifteen minutes later the Moroccan city of Tangier appeared a couple of miles off the starboard beam and, from his viewing point on the deck, Reg was able to distinguish the old quarter, situated on high ground above the port area, standing out quite clearly. He also noticed that seemingly, without exception, all the buildings were painted white.

As the 'S.S. Stratheden' entered the Strait, still some fifteen miles or more from Gibraltar, an electrical storm blew in ahead of them and completely blotted out the view of the famous rock, which everyone on board was on deck to see. However, on the starboard side of the ship, a very tall cliff, whose almost perpendicular face was so high as to be hidden in the clouds, was clearly seen along that part of the North African coast. The Atlas Mountains, well inland behind Tangier, were also visible until the storm engulfed the ship.

As the full force of the storm hit, the 'S.S. Stratheden' was tossed and pitched about on the rolling swell. Some of the smaller vessels which were sailing near the liner, fared much worse, and Reg actually saw one or two of them pitching to an angle of thirty degrees on each new wave. By this time, nearly 9.00pm, it was quite dark except for the lightning, which was quite frequent and of a peculiar dark blue color.

Although it was not really a time to think about food, as Reg lay in his bunk down in his cabin, he thought about the number of complaints that had been made about the meals they were being served. As a result of the complaints Reg, and a number of other officers, had been informed earlier in the day, that they would shortly start taking their meals in the 1st Class dining saloon.

Friday, 21st September 1945
All day at sea again with a strong wind blowing and rather poor visibility. [I] spent most of the day reading, and feeling the lack of good meals.

Around dusk the lights of Algiers came into view on the starboard side of the ship, but could not be seen too clearly. However, by a strange contrast, the Atlas Mountain Range, which was now somewhat closer to the coast than it had been at Tangiers, was clearly visible behind the town and remained so until darkness fell.

Saturday, 22nd September 1945
Up again at 7.30am and after breakfast went up on deck to enjoy the sunshine.

Fortunately, for all the non-sailors on the ship, the storm had blown itself out and the day dawned sunny and with blue skies. As a result, visibility was also restored and Reg noted that the North African coast was in view practically all day; most of it extremely mountainous and barren.

Around lunchtime, the 'S.S. Stratheden' sailed through the Canal de la Galita, a strip of sea dividing the island of Galita and the Tunisian coastline and, from the deck of the ship, the island looked very small and precipitous. A short while later, the vessel steamed past the Fratelli rocks and Bezerta before entering the Gulf of Tunisia, where a number of other small islands were sighted, amongst them Biana, Zambara and Zambaretta. All earned the same description from Reg that he had given to the island of Galita.

The warm sunny day, which everyone on board had taken advantage of, gave way to dusk. With the darkening sky came a cloudless but windy evening, accompanied by a full moon, the reflection of which danced across the rippling water.

Around 9.30pm, the liner sailed past the island of Pantellaria, which slipped quietly by on the port side of the ship. Even though it was now dark, Reg saw the island as mountainous and treeless and, as the wind was now increasing in intensity, he went below to his cabin where he recorded the fact in his diary.

Sunday, 23rd September 1945
Much commotion in the cabin woke me at 6.30. We were lying off the entrance to the harbor of Valetta and moving very slowly in between two breakwaters.

From the deck of the ship, Reg noted that Malta was not as mountainous as some of the other islands they had recently passed, although it was by no means flat. It also appeared to Reg to be very barren and dry, with the few trees he could see in the streets of Valetta, looking very parched.

Nobody was allowed to go ashore, as this was to be only a brief stop, but Reg was still able to see the large amount of bomb damage inflicted on the island during the numerous and ferocious air raids by the German Luftwaffe.

Valetta was unlike any other city Reg had seen. The steeply sloping streets were extremely narrow and ran back from the high rock walls of the harbor. They were bordered by three and four storey buildings, built without exception, of white, or near white, stone, on which the sun shone, from a cloudless sky, with great strength. The glare of the sun bouncing off the white stone, made it difficult and painful on the eyes to view the scene for long. Reg therefore turned his gazed to the locals in their strange little boats, begging or diving into the water to retrieve the coins thrown to them.

The 'Stratheden' was anchored in the middle of the harbor, where she was being tended by a number of lighters who were replenishing the liner with supplies for the next leg of the journey. Also in the harbor, Reg noticed four sunken wrecks and a number of naval vessels, including an aircraft carrier. He also noted that the harbor was not of an exceptional size, but was well sheltered from the elements.

Reg and Roger stayed on deck all morning, watching the hive of activity going on around them, until just after mid-day when the ship weighed anchor and slowly slipped out of the harbor and resumed course into the Mediterranean Sea.

Half-an-hour later, the island of Malta had disappeared from view, but, as the ship headed east towards Port Said, the south coast of the island of Sicily became visible, for a period of time, away to the north.

Life on deck began to settle down, and the day passed without further excitement. Reg and Roger decided to do the same and spent the rest of the afternoon taking full advantage of the sunshine. However, it was not a case of idling away the time on sun loungers, for, after their evening meal, Reg and Roger spent an hour exercising by walking back and forth along the deck, before retiring to their respective beds.

The following morning they awoke to another day of cloudless skies, brilliant sunshine and a calm flat sea. After a leisurely breakfast with no islands to look at, there was little to do other than laze about on sun loungers again. By teatime, with their lips parched by the sun and their throats dry, Reg and Roger went down to the 1st Class lounge where they slaked their thirst. In fact, they enjoyed their drinks so much that they visited the lounge again later in that evening to repeat the exercise. Life certainly seemed very easy for at least two of the 'Easy Boys.'

Tuesday, 25th September 1945
Our clocks [and watches] were advanced another hour at 3.30am. After breakfast we again went up on to the boat deck to sit in the sunshine, which is now becoming a bit fierce. The morning and early afternoon passed drowsily, the heat of the lunch hour being relieved by a visit to the lounge for some iced drinks.

Around 3.00pm that afternoon, a rush to the ship's rails was made by all on deck, followed by much pointing of fingers and shading of eyes. This flurry of action announced that land had been sighted for the first time in two days.

The cause of the excitement was the Egyptian coast, looking flat as a pancake, and just as hot. The most prominent features being the chimneys and towers of Port Said, visible at a surprising distance. As the ship proceeded towards the Suez Canal entrance, the blue of the Mediterranean Sea faded to a dirty green as the water grew shallower.

The 'S.S. Stratheden' slowly edged its way inside the two-and-a-half-mile long breakwater, which also serves to keep the silt of the River Nile from the canal. As the ship inched towards the port area, 'natives' popped up by the dozen in boats, seemingly from nowhere, and a great yelling contest began between them and the RAAF. Reg and his contemporaries had previously been warned of the wiles of the locals and their manner of trading, and consequently the latter became the recipients of large quantities of rubbish and a number of buckets of water, most of which were well aimed and thrown with great enthusiasm.

From what Reg could see of Port Said from the ship, was enough to douse any hopes or wishes to go ashore, for it looked extremely hot and dry, and very uninviting. It appeared to be made up of docks, railway sidings, oil tanks and coal dumps. The cramped 'native' quarter could be seen only from a distance, which was close enough for Reg. In the dock area itself, there were numerous ships, including a burned out liner and a sunken wreck that had broken in two.

Moving at a snail's pace, the 'Stratheden' nosed into port and tied up in the canal about two miles from the sea. Within a matter of minutes, a floating gangway was connected to the ship from the quayside, as were a number of pipelines through which fuel and oil were pumped from tanks on the dock.

Having been warned about the wiles of the locals trying to sell their wares, many a laugh was raised at the antics of these people as they dodged about in their flimsy boats trying to avoid not only the attendant barges servicing the liner, but also the police who had arrived in a motor launch.

As the day wore on, and the mayhem died down, Reg and Roger decided to take their evening exercise around the deck but, on this occasion, they gave up very quickly and retreated below deck due to a pall of smoke drifting in the air.

Wednesday, 26th September 1945
Woke up to find Port Said fading into the heat haze behind us as we moved slowly down the canal through perfectly flat desert country which carried no vegetation at all and whose white surface reflected the sun's glare with terrific intensity.

Occasionally Reg noted an item of interest like a military camp or a control station. Such was the scenery or lack of it, that he was prompted to write, "it was nearly 11.00am before we saw a tree." However, things began to look up when the ground became more undulating and the occasional olive grove lined with miserable looking trees, came into view. Once in a while a train would rattle by on the tracks running along the canal banks, blowing swirls of hot sandy dust into the air as they passed by.

Around noon, the ship entered the first of the Bitter Lakes, passing Ismailia on the starboard side. Here there were more trees and even small areas of grass, but even so, Reg did not find this aspect pleasing. Perhaps the mid-day sun was finally taking its toll on him.

As the ship entered the canal again, the tall twin towered memorial to the defence of the canal came into view. Set back a few hundred metres from the canal bank, the French designed memorial, for which 4,700 tons of granite was used in its construction, stands 50 metres high and is 240 metres long. It was erected to commemorate the defence of the Canal Zone from threat of the Turkish Army in World War I.

After the memorial, the landscape returned to the vista of sand, sand and more sand, with only an occasional tree to break the monotony that Reg was feeling. Arriving at the second lake Reg bucked up as there was something else for him to look at. The second lake proved to be larger than the first one and steaming across it the 'Stratheden' passed several ships heading north. Reg was also surprised to see two battleships, of unknown nationality, riding at anchor.

After sailing across the lake for an hour, the liner re-entered the canal, and with it came the view Reg was now getting so bored with, shimmering desert on either side as far as the eye could see. Whilst navigating this latest section of the canal, an incident occurred which could have caused a major problem. The ship had passed several batches of locals repairing the banks without mishap to themselves, however, this was about to change. Panic ensued amongst one group of labourers when the wash caused by the ship's screw struck the barge from which they were working. The barge, which contained all their gear and equipment, broke free of its mooring rope and drifted out into the middle of the canal. The last Reg saw of this episode was the group of workers, shouting and yelling, waving their arms in the air, whilst their barge floated some short distance away.

The next stop for the 'S.S. Stratheden' was Suez, which was reached during the early evening that same day. The liner dropped anchor a mile or so from the docks and awaited the arrival of one or two official launches. The choppy sea obviously kept the hordes of 'natives' and their flimsy boats away.

Reg recorded that, although still hot and dry, Suez was more attractive than Port Said, having a range of hills on one side of the harbor, while the port area had trees and cultivated grass growing in street plots; the port area being connected to the town on the mainland by a long causeway. Yet again, unfortunately for the RAAF contingent, they were still not allowed off the ship, so Reg spent the evening watching the lights of the town twinkling and glittering on the warm night breeze, before retiring to a hot and humid cabin.

Thursday, 27th September 1945
Still in Suez harbor during the morning and the sea being much calmer, we were besieged by boat loads of yelling locals trying to sell their wares, mostly leather handbags and wallets at about three times their value, and doing a good trade in spite of the warnings we had received.

Although nobody on the ship had been allowed to go ashore the previous night, an additional contingent of troops was taken on board during the mid-morning period. The latter had probably had an opportunity to purchase over-priced souvenirs from the shore based bazaar traders, and therefore had no need of the wares being offered for sale by the 'boat people.' However, this did not prevent the latter from making frantic, last minute effort sales as the 'S.S. Stratheden' cast off and slowly edged her way out of the harbor and into the Gulf of Suez.

With the bare, shimmering desert on either side, and here and there a range of brown peaks which looked as though they had never known rain, breaking the line of the horizon, the ship headed towards the Red Sea. Once out in the open sea, the sea breezes made the temperature a little cooler, but not enough to make it comfortable for those on board the ship. The humidity was becoming more unbearable each day, as the vessel sailed closer to the equator.

For a while, Reg and Roger escaped the sun by taking lunch in the 1st Class dining room, where the meal was served in proper style, over the left shoulder, by waiters dressed completely in white. Everything was perfect and Reg had not enjoyed such a meal for years. In a mood of total satisfaction, Reg spent the rest of the afternoon reclining in the shade, under one of the large deck awnings.

Friday, 28th September 1945
We had a [life] boat drill and after that played cards over iced drinks in the lounge until lunch time.

Reg spent the afternoon, in the shade, on the boat deck, reading. Occasionally he looked up from his book and glanced at the coast of Ethiopia on the starboard side. Anything more than a slight movement of the head provoked a bout of perspiration, as the temperature was rising higher. Even below deck, Reg had found the heat stifling, as the forced draught of the so-called ventilation system seemed to do little to relieve the situation.

The following day was no better, and in view of a recently imposed restriction on water for washing clothes, Reg felt that any appreciable form of activity, which produced volumes of perspiration, was not a good idea. The only time Reg moved was when he went to lunch, but he returned to his 'perch' in the shade immediately after. During the mid-afternoon, Reg went below again, on this occasion feeling he was in need of a bath and a snooze.

Although land had not been visible all day, by mid-evening a lighthouse came into view on the port side. The warning services of the lighthouse were not needed as the sea had been calm all day, but unfortunately, along with the calm sea, there had been no breeze, which in turn made conditions below deck at night very uncomfortable. Reg took solace in a few iced drinks and another bath before turning in.

Sunday, 30th September 1945
Had a restless night due to the stifling heat and rose at 6.00am. [I] went up on deck for air to find land quite close on our starboard [side].

The Red Sea became the Strait of Bab El Mandab as the 'S.S. Stratheden' sailed towards the Gulf of Aden, passing two ships and an Arab Dhow in the Strait. The Arabian coast could be faintly seen through the haze, but the hills of Somaliland were clearly visible. An hour later, when Reg returned to the boat deck after enjoying breakfast, the scene had changed as both coastlines were almost out of sight.

Accompanied by a gentle breeze, and thin wispy clouds in the sky, the ship sailed on, passing the port of Aden which was out of sight. The breeze, which lasted all day, made conditions much more pleasant and bearable, although Reg still took refuge from the sun during the afternoon, and even managed a snooze or two. Apart from a few flying fish, a couple of porpoises and nothing but water within the field of vision, there was little else to look at.

At the end of another day at sea, and an hour before midnight, the ship crossed a time line, where all on board were instructed to put their respective watches forward twenty-minutes. This ritual was to be repeated every night for the next week or so.

The following day, Monday, 1st October, Reg spent virtually the whole day lazing in the sun with Roger, reading a book and supping iced drinks. Reg did, however, record that for the first time since the 'S.S. Stratheden' had left Gibraltar, the ship encountered a strong wind and a noticeable swell, which made the vessel roll. Later in the evening, when Reg was taking his constitutional walk around the deck before turning in for the night, he found the wind had picked-up in strength and the sea had become rougher, making it difficult to walk in a straight line.

Tuesday, 2nd October 1945
Up at 7.15am and had the usual wash and shave before going to breakfast. Then up on the deck and lazed about reading until the time came to think about lunch.

The book, which was grabbing Reg's undivided attention, was about the life of the British Statesman, Benjamin Disraeli, the grandson of a Venetian Jew. Born in 1804, Disraeli converted to the Christian Faith in 1817. Twenty years later he entered Parliament and from 1842 led the Young England group of Conservatives. He held the position of Chancellor of the Exchequer three times and succeeded Lord Derby as Prime Minister in 1868. He was later created the 1st Earl of Beaconsfield. Benjamin Disraeli died in 1881.

Breaking away from the tome he found rather interesting, Reg took time out only for lunch, before venturing below deck to his bunk, accompanied by his book and a bag of sweets. That same evening was spent in the confines of his cabin alone, except for the book and whatever remained in the sweet bag.

Although no further mention was made of the sweet bag, Reg spent the following day in similar vein, first lounging on the boat deck in the shade and later, in the afternoon, on his bunk with the same book. Iced drinks were taken before lunch, followed by a short snooze afterwards.

Thursday, 4th October 1945
During the first course [of breakfast] I was busy shovelling in corn flakes when a tooth broke with a crack that seemed to split my head open. In my surprise the piece of tooth went down with the corn flakes.

Having got up early and ventured down to the First Class diner for a leisurely breakfast before the masses arrived, things didn't quite work out as Reg had intended.

Cereals, especially when soaked in milk usually became soft or soggy, therefore not requiring a lot of effort in the chewing department. Upon this evidence, it can only be concluded that having scoffed a bag full of sweets a day or two before had not been one of Reg's better ideas, especially if they were boiled sweets and he had been crunching them between his teeth instead of sucking them. However, a tooth had shattered and the broken piece of tooth had been swallowed along with the breakfast cereal. Shortly after this, Reg became aware that his teacup seemed to be revolving around the empty cereal bowl with ever increasing speed. Suddenly, and to Reg's horror, the revolving teacup and bowl spun into the form of a large red dragon, rearing up ready to pounce on him. In a state of confused fear, Reg lost his balance and fell into a deep pit.

Reg awoke out of this nightmare in a lather of sweat to find the Medical Officer, with a brace of waiters and a couple of helpful diners, crowding around him. After a drink of water and a few minutes rest, he was escorted to the ship's sick-quarters for medical examination, accompanied by an amazingly large number of bodyguards, but no dragon. By the time he was transferred to the ship's hospital, Reg protested that he felt fine again but, unfortunately for him, everybody steadfastly refused to believe him and he was ordered to remain in bed for the whole day.

That evening, Reg was up to receiving three visitors, one of whom was Roger, who arrived all smiles and took great delight in seeing Reg at the mercy of the M.O. However, it was Reg who was secretly amused when Roger was 'kicked out' by a medical orderly who had come to put the lights out at 10.00pm.

At 4.00am the following morning, the ship crossed the equator into the southern hemisphere. Reg noted in his diary, "There was no noticeable bump."

Friday, 5th October 1945
Up at 6.00am and had a wash and a shave long before anyone began to stir. I was comfortably back in [my] bed before breakfast arrived.

The doctor commenced his morning round of the patients and finally got to Reg. The former checked the condition of the latter and found Reg to be back in full health, apart from the broken tooth. Having washed and dressed, Reg wandered off, back to his cabin, waving a fond farewell to the nursing staff over his shoulder as he went.

Later in the morning, Reg went to visit the dentist about his tooth, but felt he got no satisfaction and as a result decided to let it be. His displeasure over the dental foray did not however stop Reg from attending lunch in the 1st Class dining room, shortly after 12.30pm.

Having spent the afternoon on his bunk, still reading the biography of Disraeli, Reg later went with Roger to the lounge for a drink before dinner. Having successfully negotiated the meal without seeing either spinning cups and plates or red dragons, Reg took his first walk around the boat deck in two days. To his surprise, Reg found it very windy, even though the ship had been gently rolling a little all day, but not enough to cause discomfort. He did find it a bit odd to see people walking in all sorts of curves getting from one place to another. Those same people probably thought the same about Reg the night before. Whilst on deck, Reg also noticed the sky was pitch-black, but no mention was made about seeing stars; in any context.

The following day the weather was much cooler and the sun hardly put in an appearance all day. The only excitement concerning the elements was the very strong wind encountered on the high sea and that the ship passed through a number of rain squalls, the first rain they had endured for weeks. Although the weather was out of character, Reg's daily routine was not, and the usual activities of reading, writing, drinking and eating, carried on as normal. It was after having taken part in the latter ritual of having lunch, that Reg became the victim of circumstance. Prior to going into the 1st Class lounge for his meal, he had visited the orderly room to arrange details appertaining to leave pay. However, whilst enjoying his food, an unrecorded situation arose which led to Reg being informed, as he left the 1st Class accommodation that in future he was to return to the rating's mess, commonly referred to as 'Belsen,' for the rest of the trip.

Sunday, 7th October 1945

Went to breakfast in 'Belsen' then went up on deck in the sunshine until a rain squall spoilt things.

When the rain started everybody on the boat deck scattered and made for the decks below, including Reg. He passed the rest of the morning playing whist until just after 1.00pm, when he ventured, somewhat reluctantly, to the rating's mess for lunch.

When the sun reappeared in the early afternoon Reg returned to the boat deck for a quiet read, but unfortunately, so did everybody else on board. However, the weather was playing jokes and by mid-afternoon more clouds billowed up, so Reg gave up in despair. He returned to the solitude and quiet of his bunk, where he snoozed until the early evening.

Monday, 8th October 1945

Had a wash and a shave and sat on my bunk reading until breakfast at 8.15am.

Reg's thoughts on his first meal of the day were recorded in his diary. He did not enjoy his breakfast and left most it, as did everyone else. He did not remain in the mess for longer

A photograph reputedly showing *'HMS Swordfish,'* the British 'S' Class submarine which Reg Heffron thought he saw in the Indian Ocean during October 1945. However, *'HMS Swordfish'* was recorded lost in the English Channel in November 1940. *Author's Collection - Original Source Unknown*

than necessary and eagerly made his way up to the boat deck for both the fresh air and the sunshine.

The highlight of the morning was seeing and passing another ship, the first since passing Aden eight days earlier. Reg recorded in his diary the name of the vessel as the Royal Navy ship 'HMS Swordfish,' a British 'S' Class submarine. However, it must be assumed that Reg actually saw one of the sister submarines in the same class, as research indicates that 'HMS Swordfish' was lost four years earlier, on 16th November 1940, after being struck by a mine in the English Channel.

As with his breakfast, Reg left most of his lunch. It was nothing to do with the fact that a slight swell on the Indian Ocean was causing the ship to roll, it was just that he and many others, found the food unpalatable. Reg found teatime totally frustrating when it took him forty-five-minutes to acquire a slice of bread and jam, and dinner was just recorded as, "a plate of hash"!

It is not known whether official complaints had been made about the quality of the food being served in the rating's mess but the following morning, Reg found a great improvement. In fact, not only did he enjoy the meal placed in front of him, but also made up for those meals he had been unable to eat.

With the intention of taking some exercise, Reg made his way up to the boat deck, but the sunshine was quickly overtaken by very cloudy weather, accompanied by strong winds. The strength of the wind made it slightly chilly on deck, so Reg spent most of the day down in his cabin, reading more of the Disraeli book, writing, snoozing and playing cards. It was the latter pastime that Reg indulged in when Roger turned up after dinner that evening for a few hands of whist.

Wednesday, 10th October 1945
[After] breakfast [I] made up my bed and then went up on deck for a bit. It was [still] very windy and after being buffeted about for an hour or so, returned to my bunk and finished packing my gear ready for disembarkation at Freemantle tomorrow.

The drop in temperature had caused the majority of the men to discard their shorts, which had been the general dress since passing Gibraltar, for warmer clothes. Only a few die-hard types remained in shorts. Reg did not record what he elected to wear.

The sea was rougher then it had ever been, but everybody seemed to have become accustomed to the rolling and pitching of the ship, as no one seemed affected by its movement.

The news on the ship was that the 'S.S. Stratheden' was to dock in Freemantle the following day, where some of the returning servicemen would disembark and travel by train from Perth to Adelaide, whilst others would stay on board the ship and sail on to Sydney. Whatever the orders were, by 9.30pm that evening, Reg had sorted out his packing, taken an early bath and retired to bed. He was both ready and eagerly anticipating setting foot on Australian soil once more.

16

Back in Australia

Thursday, 16th October 1945
Up at 6.30am, had a wash then went on deck for half-an-hour before breakfast and after that sat in the sunshine.

After eating another very satisfactory breakfast, Reg returned to the boat deck, where he sat quietly in the sunshine. Suddenly, the peace was shattered by much excited chatter and pointing of fingers.

At 10.00am, on the morning of Thursday, 16th October 1945, Rollnest Island off the Western Australian coast, came into view of those assembled on the deck of 'S.S. Stratheden.' Forty-five-minutes later, the island, which is low-lying and not very large in area, could be plainly seen off the starboard side, as the ship made its way towards the Australian mainland. Having made a couple of last minute changes in course, which put Fremantle on the port side of the ship, the vessel sailed slowly on past Cottesloe where Roger's parents settled having emigrated from New Zealand, and where Reg's former pilot, Max Bourne, was born, and Mosman Park, where Max grew up.

A burst of warm sunshine made the Australian servicemen feel welcome on their return to their homeland, but their cheers diminished when, just reaching the harbor, the ship's engines were cut and the vessel slowly came to a standstill. It was to remain stationary, outside the harbor entrance, for half-an-hour, before gently edging its way through the breakwaters and into the port area.

As the returning servicemen looked down from the ship's decks, all that was visible to them was a sea of human heads. The quayside was crowded with mums, dads, brothers, sisters, aunts and uncles, all of whom had come to welcome their lads home. A crescendo of noise, made up of music being played by the Royal Australian Air Force band, cheering, singing, screaming and screeching rose up from the crowded mass of humanity, all frantically waving flags, banners, handkerchiefs and any other suitable item, which would attract attention.

Then, amid all the excitement and gaiety came a general panic, especially in the orderly room to which Reg and Roger were attached. It seemed that all plans and orders had been changed at the last minute and the ship was to sail on to Melbourne, where Reg's contingent were to disembark, instead of going to Sydney as first informed.

Apart from the above oversight, through a rearrangement of the berthing plans, the 'Stratheden' had proceeded into the harbor ahead of the pre-programmed schedule, thus creating a problem. However, once the ship was safely moored, the Officer Commanding

Western Area, Group Captain D.E.L. Wilson, went aboard the vessel to formally welcome the 103 Western Australian airmen, who were disembarking at Fremantle, home.

Having previously given Reg instructions on how to find the home of Roger's parents, Roger was allowed to go ashore He was required to report to the Personnel Depot Receiving Center at Subiaco, at 3.00pm that afternoon, before going home to be greeted by his ecstatic parents.

Order on the ship was restored when it was announced that everyone had leave until mid-night, and that three special trains would be leaving the wharf for Perth at fifteen minute intervals. Also, a number of Royal Australia Air Force trucks would also be available for the same purpose. Reg left the ship and managed to jump onto one of the vehicles for the very bumpy, half-hour ride into Perth.

Reg's impression of the city was not particularly good, as he commented on the streets being dirty, and although there were some fine buildings, there were far more shabby ones. What did amaze Reg, and many other returning servicemen, was to see the shop windows full of apples, oranges, bananas, pineapples and many other such fruits which had not been seen in England, by many, for four or five years. Such was the temptation that the majority of those perusing these tasty delights entered the shops and bought as much as they could carry.

Reg was more controlled, and purchased just one banana, which he ate whilst still standing in the store. However, he had thoughts on a much more succulent prize, a large steak, with eggs and a pile of fries, which he managed to acquire in a nearby café.

A slow amble around the shops, looking at items for sale that Reg had not seen for a number of years, led him towards the antiquated railway station, where grass grew between the platforms and the railway tracks and waved gently to and fro on the evening breeze.

Eventually Reg arrived at North Cottesloe where Roger's parents lived and, following the instructions he had been given, managed to find his way to the house. Reg was cordially received by Roger's family who were busy plying the latter with questions, minutely examining photographs and eating the chocolates that Roger had taken home with him. Reg spent a couple of hours at the house being entertained by Roger and his family, but all too soon the evening came to an end and, on taking his leave, Reg was accompanied back to the railway station by Roger and his two brothers. Having said his farewells, Reg boarded a train that would take him back to Fremantle station, which was only a stone's throw from the quayside. Back on board the 'S.S. Stratheden' Reg first took a hot bath, before climbing into bed around mid-night; thus ending his first day back in Australia.

The ship sailed on to Melbourne with the remaining contingent of seventyfive South Australian airmen. Once there, and with the formalities completed, Reg disembarked and returned to Adelaide, where he was reunited with his family, whom he had not seen for two years.

In those same two years, like all young men thrust into the military, Reg had learned many things, from how to overcome the frustrations of lighting a fire in a damp and soggy Britain (and keeping it alight), to being part of a highly proficient crew on a bomber aircraft. During that time, there was laughter and sadness, good days and bad days, but Reg was proud to have been part of it all. He is equally proud of the title Ann Hill bestowed upon him and the rest of the crew – **'THE 'EASY' BOYS.'**

• • •

Flying Officer Reg Heffron was discharged from the RAAF on 3rd December 1945, having served with the Royal Australian Air Force/Royal Air Force for approximately two and a half years. In 1946, he returned to his former employment as an upholsterer in the family coach building company and remained there until the business closed in 1961. Later, Reg took a job with the Marion Council in Adelaide's southern suburbs, where he drove a grass mowing tractor unit around the local parks. He remained in this job until his retirement in 1982 at the age of sixty.

During 1953, having first built a house, which he named *"Ashmead,"* Reg married Phyllis Sandarcock, with whom he had two daughters, Debbie and Wendy. Both daughters married and eventually presented Reg and Phyllis with five grandchildren. Reg and Phyllis still live in the house he built for them.

"Ashmead" was the name that Nellie Dawson used for her home in Saunton Sands and, having sought Nellie's permission, Reg used the name for his house as a reminder of all the happy times he spent in Devon.

Back in Australia

FROM THE REG HEFFRON FAMILY ALBUM

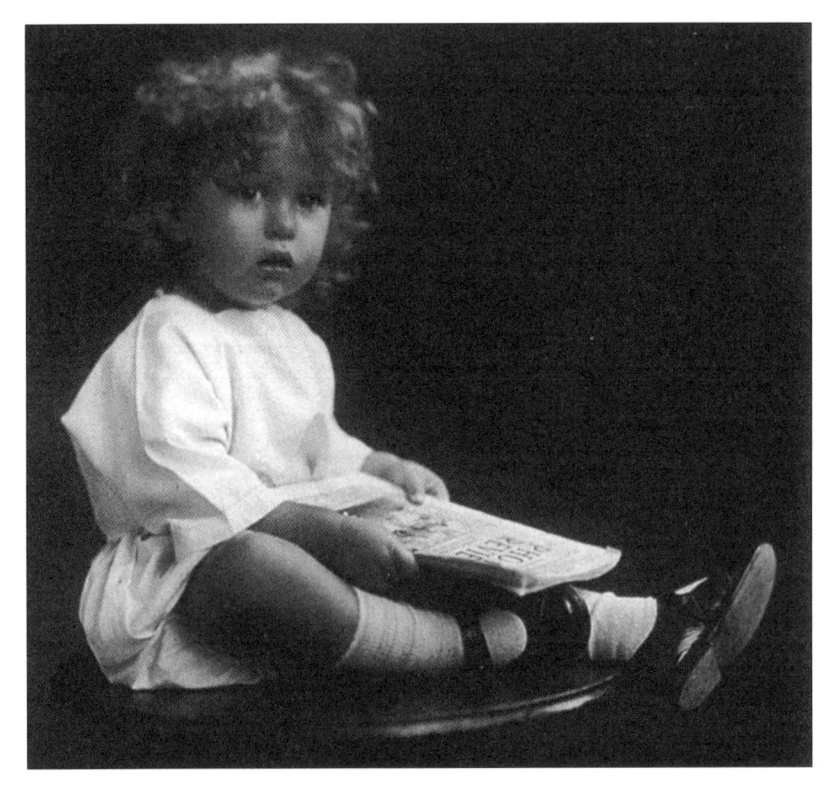

Reg Heffron was one-year-and-nine-months-old when this photograph was taken during February 1924. *Courtesy of Reg Heffron*

The *"Easy" Boys*

Reg Heffron with his wife Phyll (center) and his mother Edith photographed in 1975. *Courtesy of Reg Heffron*

Reg and Phyll Heffron with Beatrice Geb-hardt, The latter being their neighbor of fifty years. The photograph was taken on the occasion of Beatrice's 92nd birthday, on 4th April 1987. *Courtesy of Reg Heffron*

Max Bourne (left) photographed at his home on the occasion of a visit from California, by Ruth and Roger Humphrys, during 1999. *Courtesy of the Late Max Bourne*

Max Bourne (left) photographed with Reg Heffron at the latter's home, on 10th March 2006. *Courtesy of Reg Heffron*

The "Easy" Boys

THE PERMANENT TRIBUTE

Part of a piston head from a Rolls-Royce Merlin engine adapted to form an astray is surmounted with the model of an Avro Lancaster bomber, coded GI-E, of No.622 squadron. *Courtesy of Ann Hill*

Above: A framed photograph of *'The Easy Boys,'* rests in its permanent position on an occasional side table, together with the Lancaster ashtray in the lounge of Ann Hill's home. *Courtesy of Ann Hill*

Below: Ann Hill, daughter of Bill Vincent, one of *'The Easy Boys'* with her permanent tribute to the crew of Avro Lancaster bomb, E-Easy, of No.622 Squadron, Royal Air Force. *Courtesy of Ann Hill*

Appendices

Appendix 1

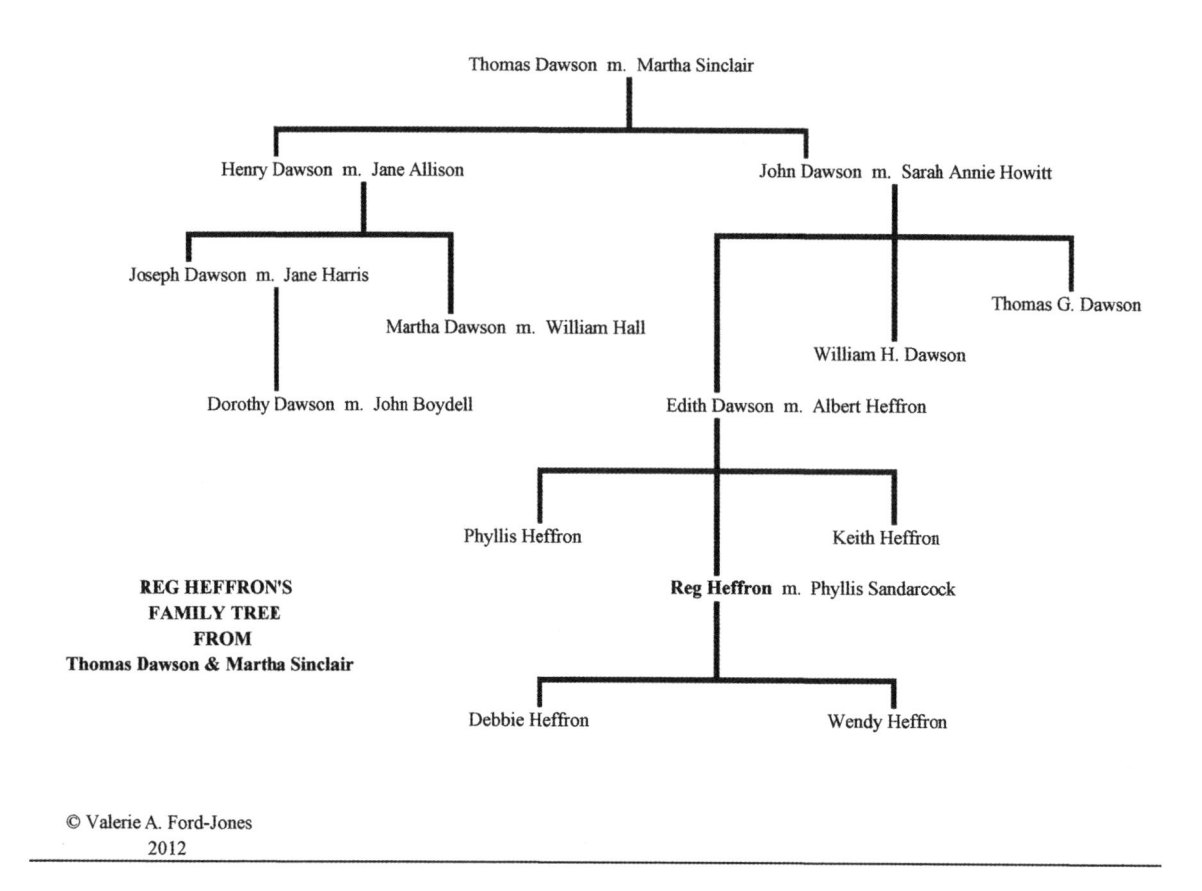

```
                    Thomas Dawson  m.  Martha Sinclair
            ┌──────────────────────┴──────────────────────┐
   Henry Dawson  m.  Jane Allison              John Dawson  m.  Sarah Annie Howitt
   ┌───────────┴───────────┐                   ┌───────────┬───────────┐
Joseph Dawson m. Jane Harris                                        Thomas G. Dawson
                     Martha Dawson m. William Hall
                                                William H. Dawson
   Dorothy Dawson m. John Boydell      Edith Dawson m. Albert Heffron
                                       ┌───────────┴───────────┐
                                   Phyllis Heffron         Keith Heffron
                                           Reg Heffron m. Phyllis Sandarcock
                                       ┌───────────┴───────────┐
                                   Debbie Heffron          Wendy Heffron
```

REG HEFFRON'S FAMILY TREE FROM Thomas Dawson & Martha Sinclair

© Valerie A. Ford-Jones
2012

Reg Heffron's Family Tree *Courtesy of Valerie A. Ford-Jones*

Appendix 2

Operational Sorties Undertaken by Flying Officer Reg Heffron, Air Gunner, Royal Australian Air Force.

Sortie No.	Date	Target
01	08/08/44	Petrol and oil dump at Doullens, France.
02	09/08/44	Flying-bomb storage sites, Fort-d'Englos, France
03	11/08/44	Railway yards, Lens, France
04	12/08/44	Opel car factory, Russelsheim, Germany
05	14/08/44	German troop concentrations, Falaise, France
06	16/08/44	Stettin, Germany
07	18/08/44	Bremen, Germany
08	29/08/44	Stettin, Germany
09	31/08/44	V-2 rocket storage sites, near Abbeville, France
10	05/09/44	German troop concentrations, Le Havre, France
11	06/09/44	German troop concentrations, Le Havre, France
12	10/09/44	German troop concentrations, Le Havre, France
13	11/09/44	Oil plant at Kamen, Germany
14	17/09/44	German positions in and around Boulogne, France
15	20/09/44	German positions in and around Calais, France
16	23/09/44	Railway yards and docks, at Neuss, Germany
17	25/0944	German defensive positions at Calais, France
18	26/09/44	Gun battery positions at Cap Griz Nez, France
19	14/10/44	Dock facilities at Duisburg, Germany
		Posted to Sheffield Disiplinary Camp for three weeks
20	11/11/44	Oil and chemical works at Castrop Rauxel, Germany
21	15/11/44	Oil storage depot, Dortmund, Germany
22	16/11/44	German lines near Heinsberg, Germany
23	20/11/44	Synthetic oil plant at Homberg, Germany
24	28/11/44	Railway yards at Neuss, Germany
25	30/11/44	Factories at Bottrop, Germany
26	04/12/44	Marshalling yards at Oberhausen, Germany
27	05/12/44	The Schwammenauel Dam, Germany
28	06/12/44	Leuna Synthetic oil plant at Merseberg, Germany
29	11/12/44	Railway yards at Osterfeld, Germany
30	19/12/44	Mine-Laying in the Baltic Sea

Appendix 3

Aircraft Flown on by Flying Officer Reg Heffron

Serial	Mk	Code	Unit	Flight
Vickers Wellington Bombers				
X3880	III	-	26 O.T.U.	Training
BK130	III	WG-H	26 O.T.U.	Training
BK457	III	-	26 O.T.U.	Training
BK498	III	-	26 O.T.U.	Training
DF674	III	-	26 O.T.U.	Training
Short S.29 Stirling Bombers				
R9254	I	-R	1653 HCU	Training
W7561	I	-	1653 HCU	Training
BK564	III	-	1653 HCU	Training
BK811	III	-	1653 HCU	Training
EF152	III	-	1653 HCU	Training
LJ445	III	-E	1653 HCU	Training
Avro Lancaster bombers				
L7532	I	A5-P	3 LFS	Conversion Flight
R5674	I	A5-	3LFS	Conversion Flight
DV242	III	A5-	3 LFS	Conversion Flight
HK615	I	GI-Z	622 Sdn	Operational
HK651	I	GI-B	622 Sdn	Exercise
LL803	I	GI-G	622 Sdn	Operational
LM291	III	GI-F	622 Sdn	Exercise
LM577	III	GI-E	622 Sdn	Operational
PD223	I	GI-G	622 Sdn	Operational
PD228	I	GI-A	622 Sdn	Operational
PD229	I	GI-K	622 Sdn	Operational
PD336	I	GI-E	622 Sdn	Operational

Bibliography

Bourne, Arthur, *Private Diaries, Notes and Log book,* (England, Unpublished 1944/45)

Bourne, Arthur 'Max,' *Private Diaries, Papers and Logbook,* (Australia, Unpublished 1944/45)

Commonwealth War Graves Commission. *Commonwealth War Grave Registers,* (Berkshire, England, Various Dates)

Ford-Jones, Martyn R., *Private Collection of Documents, Photographs and Ephemera,* (Wiltshire, England, Unpublished Various dates.)

Ford-Jones, Martyn R. & Valerie A. Ford-Jones, *Oxford's Own – Men & Machine of 15/XV Squadron RFC/RAF,* (Atglen, PA: Schiffer Publishing Ltd., 2000).

Heffron, Reg, *Private Diaries and Logbook* (South Australia, Unpublished 1944/45)

Middlebrook, Martin & Chris Everitt, *Bomber Command War Diaries,* (Middlesex, England, Viking. 1985)

National Archive, *No.622 Squadron, Form 540, Air 27.* (London, England, 1944/45).

Payne, L.G.S. Air Commodore, *Air Dates* (London, England, William Heinemann Ltd. 1957)

RAF Museum, *RAF Loss Cards 1939-1945,* (Hendon, London, Various Dates)

Reed, John, *After the Battle No.18, 21 Maintenance Unit, RAF Faulds* (London, England, Battle of Britain Prints International Ltd, 1977)

Richards, Denis, *RAF Bomber Command in the Second World War – The Hardest Victory,* (England, Penguin Books. 2001)

Various Editors, *World War II* (England, Orbis Publishing Ltd, 1974)

Vincent, Bill, *Private Papers and Logbook,* (London, England, Unpublished 1944/45)

Willis, Steve & Hollis, Barry, *Military Airfields,* (Enthusiasts Publications, Buckinghamshire, England. 1989)

Wrath, Michael, *Wings Over Wing* (Bedfordshire, England, The Book Castle. 2001)

Index

Personnel
Baxter, "Blue", 174, 187, 191, 192, 193
Brown, Daphne, 8, 101
Block, Sgt Noel, 35, 36
Buckingham, W/C G.K., 7
Coombes, F/S Keith "Erk", 66, 67, 77, 81, 89, 99, 109, 112, 121, 122
Cox, DFC, F/L John, 8, 9, 135, 136, 137, 138
Cunningham, Kt, GCM, OM, DSO, Admiral Sir Andrew Browne, 191
Davis, F/O Vincent, 127, 128
Dawson, Dorothy, 37, 122, 178, 185
Dawson, Joe, 36, 37, 38, 44, 80, 122, 178, 185
Dawson, Harry, 45
Dawson, Nellie, 153, 157, 158, 162, 170, 193, 208
Edwards, RAF, A/Comm Hughie I., 13
Gibson, W/C G.H.N., 6
Goode, F/L H.M., 6
Hall, Martha, 31, 45, 144, 177, 178, 185
Hall, William, 45, 144, 177, 178, 185
Hill, Ann, 4, 8, 11, 207, 210
Hiscock, 'Tubby', 87, 106, 107, 114, 125, 131, 133, 134, 135, 139, 141, 142, 143, 147, 151
Howitt, Nellie, 80, 154, 157
Barbara Humphrys nee Ryan, 26, 168, 172, 173, 174, 176, 177, 179, 181, 182, 192, 193, 196
MacArthur, General Douglas, 190
Mackenzie, F/O D., 127, 128, 130, 132
Martin, S/L John, 6
Middleton, F/L H., 113, 125
Ostler, F/O Robert, 128
Percival, CB, OBE, DSO, MC CdG (France) Lt.Gen Arthur E., 190
Sanders, F/L Frederick, 117, 118
Shigemitsu, Mamoru, 190
Simmons, W/C Henry, 35, 36
Skilbeck, P/O Robert, 127
Swales, W/C Ian, 7, 9, 63, 64, 65, 69, 108
Umezu, Gen Yoshijiro, 190
Wainwright, Lt.Gen Jonathon, 190
Watkins, W/C William, 117, 118
Williamson, F/L George, 66, 89, 95, 109, 110, 112, 121, 122, 123
Wilson, RAAF, Gp.Capt D.E.L., 207
Wilson, Sgt Patrick, 15, 127

Buildings, Clubs & Establishments
Australia House, London, 44, 51, 55, 100, 167, 175, 193
Boomerang Club, London, 44, 52, 55, 100, 167, 175, 179, 184, 187, 193
Broadway Tower, 9, 155, 156
Codger's Club, London, 51, 55, 100, 193
Kodak House, London, 44, 100, 101, 167, 175
Lygon Arms, Broadway, 9, 156, 157
Morley's Café, Mildenhall, 90, 97, 98, 99, 102, 114, 125, 139
Rosemary's Café, Beck Row, 126
Royal Australian Air Force Stores, 52
Tilley's Café, Mildenhall, 105